THE WORKS OF SRI CHINMOY

PLAYS

VOLUME I

THE WORKS OF SRI CHINMOY

PLAYS

VOLUME I

★

MY RAMA IS MY ALL

THE SINGER OF THE ETERNAL BEYOND

SIDDHARTHA BECOMES THE BUDDHA

THE SON

LORD GAURANGA: LOVE INCARNATE

DRINK, DRINK MY MOTHER'S NECTAR

THE DESCENT OF THE BLUE

MATSYENDRANATH AND GORAKSHANATH:
TWO SPIRITUAL LIONS

LYON · OXFORD

GANAPATI PRESS

LXXXVIII

© 2018 THE SRI CHINMOY CENTRE

ISBN 978-1-911319-01-6

See appendix for notice regarding this edition.

FIRST EDITION WENT TO PRESS ON 13 APRIL 2018

PLAYS

VOLUME I

PART I

MY RAMA IS MY ALL

WHY SHOULD I BE RESPONSIBLE?

SRI CHINMOY

RA I. DRAMATIS PERSONÆ

NARADA (A SAGE)
RATNAKAR (A ROBBER AND MURDERER)
FATHER OF RATNAKAR
MOTHER OF RATNAKAR
WIFE OF RATNAKAR
SON OF RATNAKAR

MY RAMA IS MY ALL

RA 2. SCENE I

(A forest. The sage Narada is walking through, singing the praises of Lord Vishnu. The notorious robber and murderer, Ratnakar, suddenly attacks him.)

NARADA   Ratnakar, what are you doing? Don't you see that I am singing to the Lord Vishnu? I am invoking him. I am chanting his name.

RATNAKAR   Vishnu? Who is Vishnu? There is only one person on earth and that is I, Ratnakar. I have killed hundreds of people, and I have cut off one thumb from each person. When I have one thousand thumbs, I shall make a garland of them and wear it around my neck. Nobody can save you from me.

NARADA   No? Don't you know that I have spiritual power, occult power? I can easily free myself from you. So don't threaten me.

RATNAKAR   Ha! Spiritual power, occult power! I shall kill you right now! *(He is about to stab Narada with his dagger.)*

NARADA   Wait a minute! What do you want? Do you want money?

RATNAKAR   Yes.

NARADA   How much do you want?

RATNAKAR   Whatever you have.

NARADA   I can give you whatever I have, and again, with my occult power I can give you double what I have. Look, I have a hundred-rupee coin. Can you see?

RATNAKAR   Yes.

NARADA   Now search me. Search all my garments. There is no money.

(Ratnakar searches him thoroughly.)

NARADA   Now just close your eyes.

(Ratnakar closes his eyes. From nowhere Narada takes another hundred rupees.)

NARADA   Look, Ratnakar, what I can give you.
RATNAKAR   *(amazed)* Where did this money come from? I searched you thoroughly.
NARADA   Ratnakar, Ratnakar, no matter what amount you want I will be able to give it to you, and I *will* give you. But before that I want to ask you something.
RATNAKAR   What?
NARADA   You know that what you are doing is absolutely wrong. You are acting like an animal, killing people and taking away their money. Now don't you think that you will be held responsible for all this in your life after death? Don't you know that you will be condemned to hell and punished severely? Why do you do this kind of thing? You alone, you and nobody else, will suffer for all these horrible deeds.
RATNAKAR   What do you mean, I alone? I do it because I still have a sense of responsibility. I have two old parents; I have a wife, a beautiful wife, and a beautiful son, I have to think of all of them. I am responsible for my parents, for they are invalids. I am responsible for my wife, who is helpless without me. And my son is only a little boy, so I have to think of him. It is for all of them that I do it.
NARADA   And do you think that they will also take responsibility for you when you get punishment in your after-life? When you die, you will be the one to be punished for this karma in the other world, Ratnakar.

RATNAKAR If I am punished I am sure they will share my karma with me, since I am doing all this for them. I have no other way to make money. This is the only way I can support my family.

NARADA All right, this may be the only way, but I tell you, these people will never take responsibility for you.

RATNAKAR Why not? They should! It is only fair, if I am doing it for them. Today, if anything happens to me, my parents will perish. My wife and son will probably die, too. I am sure they will all be willing to share my punishment in the after-life since it is I who am maintaining them in this life.

NARADA All right, Ratnakar. Let us see. You feel that your parents, your wife and your son will take responsibility for your undivine actions because you are feeding them, you are clothing them, you are taking care of them by doing all this. Go home and ask them. If they agree, then I shall give you any amount of money you want, and double the amount. I tell you, Ratnakar, they have a claim on your earnings but have nothing to do with your sins. This hard fact will give you a rude shock and then you will take to holy living. I want you to go home and see. I will wait here.

RATNAKAR You are a holy man. You won't break your promise?

NARADA I won't break my promise. I am doing this out of my compassion for you. I can easily leave this place with my occult force — as easily as I brought the money I showed you. Right now I can use my occult power and chase you away from here with my light.

RATNAKAR Oh yes? Show me, show me!

(Narada opens his third eye, and immediately Ratnakar starts trembling.)

RATNAKAR   Stop, stop! The volcanic fire from your third eye is burning me to ashes. I am going. I am going to see my family and I will bring you the news. They will take responsibility for me.

NARADA   Go and see.

MY RAMA IS MY ALL

RA 3. SCENE 2

(Ratnakar's home.)

RATNAKAR   *(to his parents)* Mother, Father, I have been working hard for you.

FATHER   Yes, my son, you are working very hard and we are pleased with you.

RATNAKAR   They say that killing people is bad, robbing is bad. I have been killing, robbing, doing many, many things, only to support you and the rest of my family. Now, O Father, O Mother, tell me. I am your dearest son. Will you not take responsibility for my actions when I die, when I am punished by the law of karma in the other world?

BOTH PARENTS   Son, why should we accept the responsibility? When you were a young boy we brought you up, we fed you. We looked after you and we did not ask you to take responsibility for our actions. At that time it was our duty. Now you are grown up, mature, and now it is your duty to feed us, to take responsibility for us.

(Ratnakar is taken aback. He goes to his wife.)

RATNAKAR   Now, darling, will you not accept responsibility for me? You say that I am dearer to you than your life. I have done so many wrong things. Every day I harass people, I torture people, I kill people and take their money. What for? Only to feed you and to feed my family. I am sure you will take some of the responsibilities in my next life, in the other world, when I am punished. I am sure you will also share the burden.

WIFE Me? Why should I be held responsible? I am your wife, but it is your responsibility. Did you ever hear of a wife going out to make money for her husband? It is the duty of the husband to make money and feed the wife. Are you a fool? I thought you had some sense. People will laugh at you if you ever say that I have to take the responsibility for supporting myself. It is your duty to support me. So why should I be held responsible when it is your duty?

(Sadly Ratnakar goes to his son.)

RATNAKAR My child, will you not take responsibility for what I am doing? I am torturing people, strangling people and killing people. What for? Only to support you, your mother and my parents.

SON Father, I am only a child. I do not know how to work. I am unable to support myself. You take care of me. For that I am grateful. But how can I be responsible for what you are doing? I am not doing a thing; I am helpless. When I grow up I will be responsible for you — to feed you and support you. I will take care of my grandparents and my mother. But now, Father, I cannot be responsible for you. It is you who have to take responsibility.

RATNAKAR *(giving a smart slap to his son)* You ungrateful creature! *(He kicks his wife.)* You ungrateful creature! *(He strikes his parents.)* You ungrateful parents! I have nothing on earth to hold on to.

MY RAMA IS MY ALL

RA 4. SCENE 3

(In the forest again. Ratnakar has returned to Narada.)

NARADA So, you have come here to take your money? Take as much as you want. Why are you so sad? Tell me, what is the news? What is your news?

RATNAKAR My news is that I have given up my family. I will not be responsible for them since they do not feel responsible for me. They are a bunch of ungrateful creatures: my son, my wife, my parents. I do not want them. I do not need them. Right here, tell me what I should do. I will listen to you.

NARADA My only advice to you is this: repeat only one name — Rama, Rama, Rama. He will forgive you. He will give you salvation. And it is you who will immortalise him on earth. He will take human incarnation and you will write his biography. Long, long before he is born, before he comes into this earthly existence, you will write his biography. You will tell about his immortal life, his life of dedication, his life of glory, his life of fulfilment. All this you will write down in his biography, From now on repeat his name: Rama, Rama, Rama. Just repeat it and let me hear.

RATNAKAR Mara, Mara, Mara.

NARADA Can't you say his name?

RATNAKAR I can't.

NARADA Rama, Rama. See what you have done? You cannot repeat his sacred name because you have done thousands of terrible things. Thousands of times you have acted like an animal. You are so impure, you are so mercilessly caught by the hostile forces that you have become like a real *asura*. Now you cannot even repeat Rama's name. You can only say

Mara, which is "Rama" said the other way around. All right, then, say Mara. Repeat Mara and in a few years' time you will be able to say Rama properly. Rama is the heart. Even if you cannot properly pronounce his name, he won't mind. With a soulful heart if you pray every day, repeating the name Mara, Rama will come to your rescue. He will forgive you, he will liberate you. It is to you that he will give the glory of immortalising him here on earth. You will write his biography, you will reveal him and manifest him. You will be the harbinger of his coming. When he comes down into the world and operates on the physical plane, you will see that the biography which you have written about him will immortalise you. He has chosen you to immortalise him, Ratnakar. And the day you start writing his biography, Lord Rama will enter into you and change your name. When you start writing his biography your new name will be Valmiki the Sage. Valmiki will be your real name. "When the power of love replaces the love of power, man will have a new name: God." With your love of power you wanted to destroy the world, but with your power of love you will liberate the world. You will be a messenger of truth, a messenger of fulfilment.

(Narada blesses Ratnakar and departs.)

DASHARATHA PROMISES AND RAMA EXECUTES

SRI CHINMOY

RA 5. DRAMATIS PERSONÆ

MANTHARA (MAIDSERVANT OF QUEEN KAIKEYI)
QUEEN KAIKEYI, QUEEN KAUSALYA, QUEEN SUMITRA (WIVES OF KING DASHARATHA)
RAMA (SON OF KAUSALYA AND DASHARATHA)
KING DASHARATHA (KING OF AYODHYA)
LAKSHMANA (FIRST SON OF SUMITRA AND DASHARATHA)
SITA (WIFE OF RAMA)
BHARATA (SON OF KAIKEYI AND DASHARATHA)
SHATRUGHNA (SECOND SON OF SUMITRA AND DASHARATHA)
VASHISHTHA (A SAGE)
OFFICERS IN BHARATA'S ARMY

MY RAMA IS MY ALL

RA 6. SCENE I

(Queen Kaikeyi and her maidservant Manthara.)

MANTHARA   O Queen, do you know? Do you know what will happen tomorrow?

KAIKEYI   No, I do not know. Please tell me.

MANTHARA   Tomorrow Rama is going to be the *yubaraj*. He is going to become the crown prince.

KAIKEYI   Oh! How delighted I am to hear that! You are the first person to give me that happy news. Take this necklace from me. *(She hands the necklace to her maidservant.)*

MANTHARA   *(throws away the necklace)* O Queen I never thought that you were such a fool. I thought that God had given you some real wisdom. Don't you realise that when Rama becomes the ruler he will be all devotion to his own mother, Kausalya, and not to you? You will have no place here then. Your own son Bharata, will be like a servant. Now he and Rama are like two friends, two brothers. But the day Rama becomes King, Bharata will be nowhere.

KAIKEYI   No, don't say such things. My Bharata and Kausalya's Rama are inseparable brothers. I am so happy that my Rama, who loves me more than he loves his own mother, who serves me more than he serves his own mother, is going to be the ruler of this vast kingdom. O Manthara, the news that you have given me has made my life extremely happy. You don't know how much joy I am getting now. My Rama, my own Rama will become the King.

MANTHARA   O Queen, just wait and see. Kausalya's life of joy and victory will begin tomorrow. Your life of frustration and destruction will begin tomorrow.

KAIKEYI   Manthara, stop! Enough of your evil tongue. I am the Queen. I know what is best for me, best for my life. King Dasharatha has three Queens: Kausalya, Sumitra and I. But you know Dasharatha loves me most. He would not do anything which would eventually make me sad.

MANTHARA   Yes, I know he loves you most. But when Rama becomes the crown prince, instead of your son, your suffering will know no bounds. This is not my curse; it is just a bare fact. Rama will banish your son from the kingdom and he will treat you as you are treating me, your maidservant. Today you are the Queen, the most beloved Queen of Dasharatha; tomorrow you will become a maidservant like me in the service of Rama.

KAIKEYI   My love for my Rama is boundless. He is the embodiment of Truth and Light. In him I see the message of Divine Perfection. To be his maidservant is to be the great instrument of God. I am prepared to be his maidservant or whatever he wants me to be when he becomes the ruler of Ayodhya.

MANTHARA   O Queen, still there is time. Don't act like a fool. You are still the most beloved wife of Dasharatha. Have you forgotten that he once promised you that he would fulfil your desires, no matter what they were? When he was ill, you served him, you nursed him and you cured him. Because of your dedicated service he offered you two divine boons. You told him that when the time came you would ask him. Now the time has come. Do you remember how many times you have been unkind to Kausalya? When she becomes the mother of King Rama, don't you think she will pay you back?

KAIKEYI   That is true. I scolded her and insulted her many times, just because I knew I was the favourite wife of King Dasharatha. But Kausalya's heart is big. She is full of love and compassion. When her son becomes King she will not pay me back in my own coin. She will forgive me. As a matter of fact, she has already forgiven me.

MANTHARA   Wait, just wait. It is only a matter of a few hours until tomorrow, and then your sorrow begins, your suffering begins. The night of excruciating pangs begins for you, O Queen!

KAIKEYI   I am fully prepared. Whatever is going to happen will happen for my own good. My Rama will not do anything wrong to me. Kausalya will never do anything to humiliate me. Both of them are great in heart and soul.

MANTHARA   You must know that it is not for my sake that I am asking you to ask the King for the boons. My only interest in life is your joy. My life on earth is only to please you, only to make you happy. Now here is my humble suggestion. Go to the King and ask him for your two boons. Then, when he agrees to give them, ask first that Rama be exiled for fourteen years. And for the second boon, ask that your son, Bharata, be made the crown prince.

KAIKEYI   *(shocked)* I? I should ask Dasharatha for these boons?

MANTHARA   Yes, Rama has to go into the forest for fourteen years and your son Bharata has to be installed on the throne. Only then will you be happy, I tell you.

KAIKEYI   Shame, shame, unutterable shame on you, Manthara! Your advice is poison, nothing else! Leave this place immediately, before I kick you out!

MANTHARA   *(leaving)* O Queen, tomorrow you will see!

(Exit Manthara. Kaikeyi sits down and rests her chin on her hands. She is thinking.)

KAIKEYI   *(to herself)* Perhaps she is right....

RA 7. SCENE 2

(Dasharatha and Rama are together. Both are happy. Enter Kaikeyi.)

KAIKEYI   Rama, my darling, I have something important to discuss with your father. Will you leave us for a moment? I shall call you back when our discussion is over.
RAMA   Certainly, Mother, certainly.

(Exit Rama. Kaikeyi's expression immediately changes to one of bitter distress.)

DASHARATHA   Kaikeyi, why is it that you are so distressed all of a sudden? Please tell me what is wrong with you. Are you feeling unwell? All the physicians of the world are at my disposal. Has anybody done anything wrong to you? If so, I assure you that he will be put to death. I have never seen you unhappy. Your sorrow is piercing the very depths of my soul.
KAIKEYI   My King, it is easy for you to talk about your love for me, but I know you are not sincere. You try to please me daily with empty flattery and falsehoods. But do you have even an iota of love for me? No, it is all deception.
DASHARATHA   *(shocked)* Kaikeyi! I can't believe my ears! Is this really you? Tell me when I have ever deceived you.
KAIKEYI   You have never deceived me?
DASHARATHA   Never! Never have I deceived you and never will I deceive you. You are my favourite Queen. I am all love, all sacrifice for you.
KAIKEYI   Then prove it.
DASHARATHA   I am at your disposal.

KAIKEYI Send Rama into exile in the forest for fourteen years and make my son Bharata the crown prince tomorrow.

DASHARATHA *(collapses, stunned)* Ohhh. Kaikeyi, to hear this from you! Tomorrow was to have been the happiest day of my life, and today you are giving me such a cruel blow. In one blow you have taken away all my joy, all my happiness, the very life from my heart.

KAIKEYI I have only made a legitimate claim. Don't forget that you made a promise to me once. You granted me two boons. When you were practically dying, I nursed you back to health. You were so pleased with me that you granted me two boons, and I told you that when the time came I would ask for them. Now the time has come. Keep your promise if you are a man of truth. If not, the world will soon have a different opinion of you.

DASHARATHA Kaikeyi, I am more dead than alive. You ruined my kingdom, you have killed me. I shall keep my promise, but do me at least one favour.

KAIKEYI What do you want me to do?

DASHARATHA Very simple. On my behalf you tell Rama that he has to go into the forest. On my behalf you tell your son Bharata that he will be the crown prince tomorrow. That's easy enough. *(He faints.)*

KAIKEYI *(calls aloud)* Rama! Rama!

(Enter Rama.)

RAMA Mother, is anything wrong with you?

KAIKEYI Nothing is wrong, Rama. This very day you have to retire into the forest for fourteen years of exile. My son Bharata will be the King, and not you. Your father has promised.

(Seeing that his father is lying unconscious, Rama runs out and returns with Lakshmana, Kausalya, Sumitra and Sita.)

RAMA   *(to Kaikeyi)* Mother, I shall obey your command. You want me to go into the forest for fourteen years. You want my dearest brother, Bharata, to be the ruler. I am fully prepared to keep my father's promise to you. I am glad it is I who will have the opportunity to prove to the world that my father knows how to keep his promise.

(Lakshmana, Kausalya, Sumitra and Sita burst into tears.)

LAKSHMANA   Impossible! Brother, you cannot go into the forest! You cannot leave us!

SITA   My Lord, you cannot go! The world wants *you*, and not Bharata.

KAUSALYA   Rama, my darling son, don't go!

RAMA   I know, Mother, that you will miss me. I shall also miss you, I shall miss my wife Sita and I shall miss my brother Lakshmana. I shall also miss my brother Bharata and my brother Shatrughna. I shall miss all my family. But Mother, my suffering and your suffering have no meaning in my life. Only the fulfilment of my father's promise has real value for me. The world must know that my father Dasharatha has kept his promise. There is nothing so great as to keep one's promise. I want the world to be proud of my father's promise, my father's sacrifice. Mother, Sita, Lakshmana, Mother Kaikeyi, Mother Sumitra — I am leaving. It is only a matter of fourteen fleeting years. Then I shall be back with you again. Now my joy is in fulfilling my father's promise. Fourteen years from now my joy will be in living with my dear ones.

SITA   Lord, you cannot go without me.

LAKSHMANA   Rama, you cannot go without me.

RAMA   Sita, do you want to go with me into the forest? You will suffer much. How can I bear your suffering? A woman like you, who has been brought up with such care, love, affection and adoration, and all the comforts of wealth, cannot live in the forest. You must not think of going with me,

SITA   My Lord, without you my life has no meaning. To live with you in hell would give me greater joy than to live without you in Heaven. To be with you is to be in the highest plane of Delight. Wherever you are, I must be with you. I cannot remain without you. To be at your feet is my constant and eternal goal.

LAKSHMANA   Brother, to live without you is to live in ignorance, bondage and hell. I am not such a fool. This brother of yours will be your eternally devoted and dedicated slave. You are fulfilling Father's promise. Now you must also fulfil my wish and Sita's wish.

KAUSALYA   Rama, my son, take them with you. I shall remain here to look after your father. I love you more than I love my own life, but your aged father now needs my care. I do not know whether he will recover from this shock or not. But for the remaining days, the remaining hours, I want to serve him.

RAMA   Mother, you are doing absolutely the right thing. Father needs your care. He needs you badly. After fourteen years we three will come back. Mother Kaikeyi, please tell Bharata that I give him all my love, all my joy and all my blessings. Let him rule the kingdom in his own way. I am sure he will rule well. And Mother Kaikeyi, my only request to you, my last request to you, is that you will treat my mother Kausalya well.

SUMITRA   Rama, my son, you are the embodiment of truth, light and forgiveness. My heart breaks into pieces to see you and my Lakshmana leaving. But my other son, Shatrughna, is with Bharata now at his maternal uncle's home. Shatrughna will remain here. He is fond of Bharata, he is all for Bharata as Lakshmana is all for you. I shall stay here and look after your mother. I am also a Queen, but from today she will be my dearest sister. In every way I shall try to make her happy. That is my promise. That is my promise to you, my son Rama.

KAIKEYI Rama, I know that from today the world will hate me. I will be an object of contempt.

RAMA No, Mother, the world will not hate you. But even if the world hates you I will love you. You have given me the opportunity to keep my father's promise, and my mother Kausalya has given me the capacity to keep his promise. Her sacrificing heart-power has given me the capacity to keep my father's promise. Your demanding vital-power has given me the opportunity to fulfil my father's promise. I am equally grateful to you both.

MY RAMA IS MY ALL

RA 8. SCENE 3

(Kaikeyi, Bharata and Shatrughna. Bharata is weeping bitterly.)

BHARATA Shatrughna, brother, go and bring that filthy animal Manthara. Bring that hunchbacked creature here. I shall set it all right. Bring her here.

(Shatrughna goes out and returns dragging Manthara. Bharata violently and ferociously grabs her by the ear, pulls her hair and gives her a violent kick.)

BHARATA You, you are the culprit! You are the one who inspired my mother, who instigated my mother to send Rama into exile for fourteen years. My dearest Rama, the light of my heart!

(Manthara falls to the ground unconscious.)

BHARATA *(turning to Kaikeyi, nearly in tears)* Mother, are you a human being? Have I to call you Mother? You have acted like an animal. Do you think that you have made me happy? I shall treat you ruthlessly. Every day I will make your life miserable! *(Pauses.)* No, no. You are forgiven. Rama's heart of forgiveness, his heart of compassion has forgiven you. He will be sorry if I treat you this way. But I tell you, I am Rama's brother Bharata, and not your son! My mother is Kausalya, and not you, you ingrate, you impostor! I am leaving for the forest. I will bring my brother back. It is he who will rule the kingdom. I am not only his brother, I am his devoted slave. I will not come back unless and until I have brought the brother of my heart and soul, Rama, back to Ayodhya, to his kingdom.

(Exit Bharata.)

MY RAMA IS MY ALL

RA 9. SCENE 4

(Lakshmana, Sita and Rama in the forest of Chitrakut. Rama has started his spiritual life.)

LAKSHMANA   Look! Look, Rama! Brother Bharata's army! Bharata is invading us. Perhaps he thinks that when you go back after fourteen years you may create trouble for him. He wants to prevent any future trouble. Look at that ungrateful creature! Like mother, like son. It is his mother, Kaikeyi, who has sent you here to this life of hardship and humiliation. Now her son is coming to destroy you with his army. What else can you expect from your Bharata? After all, he is the son of Kaikeyi.

RAMA   Lakshmana, my brother, don't be so rash. How do you know that he is coming to kill me? He may be coming to take me back to the kingdom.

LAKSHMANA   *(laughing)* Brother, you are not only the embodiment of truth but also the embodiment of innocence. If he wanted to take you back he would come alone. Why has he to bring his huge army? O Brother, sometimes your innocence amazes me.

(Enter Bharata followed by officers. He prostrates himself before Rama and weeps bitterly.)

BHARATA   Brother, I am here at your feet. This army is yours. Come back! The kingdom awaits your arrival. I have not accepted my mother's foul offering to me. I have not fulfilled her foul wish. We have lost our father. Your physical absence has sent him into the other world.

(Lakshmana, Sita and Rama burst into tears.)

LAKSHMANA Father is no more?

BHARATA No more. He is in the world beyond. My mother Kaikeyi has ruined us all. Only your presence, Brother Rama, can bring happiness back to my life, and to our kingdom.

RAMA Brother Bharata, it is you who have to rule the kingdom. That was Father's wish.

BHARATA No, never! It was the wish of my cruel, brutal mother, Kaikeyi. I won't listen to you, Brother. You must come back with me. I will be your perfect slave. You are the legitimate ruler of Ayodhya, not I. Lord, come back with me, or let me stay with you here to serve you. I shall also lead an ascetic life.

RAMA Beloved Brother Bharata, I have embraced asceticism to obey my father and my mother Kaikeyi.

BHARATA Kaikeyi is inhuman! She is not your mother. She is God's worst mistake; she is man's worst curse. Never will I call her Mother. She has ruined our family. She has done something terribly wrong to you. I do not approve of our father's action.

RAMA Who are you to approve or disapprove of our father? It is my bounden duty to obey him.

BHARATA If it is your bounden duty to listen to our father, then it is my bounden duty to serve you here. I am not going back. I will not go back to the kingdom. *(Speaking to officers and to everyone present.)* My brother Rama shows no pity for me; he gives no consideration to my prayer. I shall lie down and fast unto death.

RAMA Brother Bharata, this is not the way you should behave. You are a King, and you must face the world. You have to face the present situation with your manliness. It is I who am asking you to go back and rule the kingdom. If you wish to serve me, then you can serve me best in this way. The ocean may dry up, the sun may lose all its brilliance, but I will not be false to my father's divine promise. I shall remain in exile for fourteen years.

BHARATA   Nor can I be false to my promise. I am going to stay with you.

RAMA   Then you are disobeying me, your elder brother.

BHARATA   I am not disobeying you. I cannot live without you, that's all. You are my Lord; you are my God. I can't live without my Lord and God.

(Enter Vashistha.)

VASHISTHA   With my occult vision I have come to know what is happening here. O Rama, O Bharata, I can solve your problem.

RAMA AND BHARATA   Please, please, O Sage Vashistha, solve our problem.

VASHISTHA   Bharata, do not sit on Rama's throne. But go and be his agent. You rule on his behalf.

BHARATA   O Sage, that will not satisfy me. If he will allow me to keep his wooden sandals to represent him on the throne, then I shall go back. But I shall not go back to Ayodhya. No, I shall live in the village of Nandini which is on the outskirts of Ayodhya. From there I shall carry out Rama's orders. Brother Rama, every day I shall place your sandals on my head and on my heart before I speak to anyone. It is your sandals that will represent you on the throne and give me my authority. You are the King. I am your deputy. I shall look after your kingdom as your deputy. If you should fail to return to Ayodhya on the first day of the fifteenth year, the appointed day, you will not see your brother Bharata alive. I shall consign this body to flames, while uttering your sacred name.

RAMA *(embraces his brother)* Brother, I assure you of my return. I shall keep my promise. I make one last request to you. Do not torture our mother Kaikeyi. Ignorance has covered her life. Let us both forgive her. Through our forgiveness her inner illumination will take place.

(Rama gives Bharata the wooden sandals from his feet.)

BHARATA *(places the pair of wooden sandals on his heart)* This is the symbol of my loyalty to you, Rama, my brother, my father, my All. *(Embraces Lakshmana and touches the feet of Sita.)* Mother Sita, I shall do everything for you and for my brothers Rama and Lakshmana. As an anxious mother waits for her son's arrival after a long journey, as a dying man cries for a new life, I shall wait for your arrival and cry for your return.

THE GOLDEN DEER

SRI CHINMOY

RA 10. DRAMATIS PERSONÆ

RAMA
SITA (WIFE OF RAMA)
LAKSHMANA (HALF-BROTHER OF RAMA)
MARICHA (THE DEER)
RAVANA (KING OF THE DEMONS)

MY RAMA IS MY ALL

RA II. SCENE I

(Rama, Sita and Lakshmana are in the forest early in the morning. Sita is plucking flowers.)

RAMA   Sita, they say that flowers are beautiful, but I wish to say that you are infinitely more beautiful than any flower. The beauty of all the flowers put together is no match for your beauty.

SITA   Do you really think so, Rama? It is so kind of you to say it.

RAMA   They say that flowers have fragrance, but I wish to say that the fragrance of all the flowers put together cannot equal the fragrance of your heart.

SITA   O Lord, you are seeing me with your eye of unconditional appreciation, and not with the eye of a critic.

RAMA   My life should be at least a life of appreciation for you. Your life is a life of constant sacrifice for me. But my sincerity speaks, Sita. You are infinitely more beautiful, infinitely more fragrant than all the flowers of the world put together.

SITA   If I have a heart of gratitude, then that heart is for you, only for you, my Lord. Oh, look! Look at that beautiful deer! I have never seen such a beautiful deer! Never! It is so strikingly beautiful!

RAMA   Yes, it is extremely beautiful.

SITA   Look how charming it is, nibbling the grass. How soulfully it gambols and frisks. Look! It is multicoloured, and it has lustrous spots. I need this deer, Rama. I want it to be my deer.

RAMA   Is there anything that I will not do to please you, my Sita? I shall bring you the deer.

LAKSHMANA Brother, don't go. That is the demon Maricha playing a trick. He can assume any form, and he has taken the form of this animal. He is deceiving us. That is not a real deer.

SITA I don't believe you, Lakshmana. That is a real deer. I can see its beauty. I can feel the innocence of the animal. Rama, my Lord, chase it and catch it alive. If you can do that I will be so grateful to you.

RAMA Lakshmana, I am off. Look after Sita.

(Rama chases the deer.)

MY RAMA IS MY ALL

RA 12. SCENE 2

(Another part of the forest. Enter the deer, followed by Rama, panting.)

RAMA Ah! One moment the deer is near, and the next moment it is quite far. This moment I am about to catch it, and the next moment it is beyond my reach. This is indeed a mysterious animal. I have been running after it for a long time. Now I am tired, exhausted. Sita wanted me to bring back this deer alive if possible. But I find it is not possible to catch it. Well, I shall shoot the deer with my bow, but I shall not kill it. I shall wound it and then take it home to Sita. She will nurse and cure the animal.

(Rama aims his unfailing arrow at the deer. The deer falls down.)

DEER *(in Rama's voice)* Ah Sita, Ah Lakshmana! Ahhh Sita, Ahhh Lakshmana.

RA 13. SCENE 3

(Sita and Lakshmana, still at the same spot in the forest.)

SITA   Listen, Lakshmana! Your brother is in danger! He is crying, "Ah Sita, Ah Lakshmana." He needs you! Go to him!

LAKSHMANA   Mother Sita, I cannot obey. My brother asked me to look after you. If I leave you alone here he will be extremely displeased with me. I assure you, my brother can never be in danger. There is nobody who can defeat him in fighting. He is all-powerful. I am sure that Maricha is playing a trick on us.

SITA   *(angrily)* Lakshmana, you have come into the forest, and you are making everybody feel that you are my husband's greatest friend, his dearest brother. But you are a rogue, a rogue. Rama is in terrible danger, I feel it. And you don't want to leave me. Why? You have some immoral interest in me. If your brother dies, you are hoping to have me, you brute!

(Lakshmana covers his ears with his hands.)

LAKSHMANA   O Mother, be calm, please. Do not speak such awful words. Nobody in the world is like Rama. His life is quite safe. The voice that we have heard can never be the voice of my brother. It is a trick of that demon Maricha. Rama has posted me to look after you here. How can I disobey him?

SITA   Yes, Maricha is imitating Rama's voice and you are imitating Rama's character, his heart of wisdom and illumination. You rogue! You impostor! You fool! You have all darkness, all filth, all ignorance in your mind and in your heart! Leave me alone! You can't obey me even when your brother is dying? I know, I know what your secret intention is. I tell you, your dark dream will never be fulfilled. Go! You have your wife, Urmila. Why did she not come with us? Then she could have been with her husband. Why are you bothering me? Who has asked you to come here? Before I let you touch me, I shall throw myself into the River Godavari.

LAKSHMANA Mother, I shall have to disobey my brother, then, in order to obey you. I am disobeying my brother to please you. Please be alert. I am marking a ring for you. Please do not go outside the boundary of this ring. This ring is the ring of protection.

SITA Protection? I do not need your protection. You go and protect your brother. He needs your protection. He is dying, and here you are wasting time, delaying, so when you go there you will see that he is no more. Well, no harm. If he is gone I shall join him in the other world. This life of mine is not to be with you. You brute, you unthinkable creature, deceiving the whole world by pretending to be devoted, faithful, unconditionally surrendered to your brother!

(Lakshmana, shedding tears, draws a ring.)

LAKSHMANA Mother, I go.

(Exit Lakshmana.)

RA 14. SCENE 4

(Lakshmana is walking through another part of the forest in search of his brother.)

LAKSHMANA O God, you know my heart. I adore Sita as my own mother. I have never even seen her face. I always keep my eyes on her feet, on the dust of her feet. Such adoration I have for her, such devotion! And she insults me. Is this my fate? The world is full of misunderstanding. Are all women of this type? No, it cannot be. My Urmila was shedding bitter tears when I left the palace with my brother. She wanted me to remain with her, but I came here to please my brother and myself. But who is pleasing her? O Urmila, the world will not know of your inner suffering, your divine sacrifice. But my heart of love will know. My heart of gratitude will know what you are doing in silence, through your tears, with your magnanimous heart. Eternally your Lakshmana will be grateful to you and proud of you. My outer life is not near you but my inner life is with you and for you.

MY RAMA IS MY ALL

RA 15. SCENE 5

(Sita is seated in the circle awaiting her husband's arrival. Enter Ravana, the King of the Demons, in the guise of an ascetic. Sita receives him with reverence. He chants from the holy scriptures.)

SITA   O Saint, my husband is in danger. I have scolded his brother mercilessly, and he has at last gone to help him. He did not want to listen to me. He thought that I would be in danger here. But I am perfectly safe. Now a saint has come to console me. O Saint, tell me what I can do for you.

RAVANA   I am hungry, Mother, I am hungry.

SITA   I shall give you food.

RAVANA   Mother, what is this? This circle?

SITA   Oh, Lakshmana made this circle for me. He said that I must not go outside it. He said that if I go outside this circle I will be in danger.

RAVANA   Mother, you know that you are not in danger here. I am a saint. I have come here just to console you. I feel sure that your husband will come back safe. He is a great hero. Now Lakshmana is with him. Even if he is in danger, he will come back, Mother.

SITA   I shall bring food for you.

(Sita goes outside the circle and immediately Ravana grabs her, puts her on his shoulder and runs. Sita begins to scream.)

SCENE 6

(Another part of the forest. Enter Ravana with Sita. He puts her down.)

SITA You tempted me! You deceived me! You have now paved the way for your destruction! When Rama and Lakshmana come back and don't see me, they will search for me and discover what you have done. Today's crime marks the beginning of your death.

RAVANA Threaten as much as you want to. Do you know that the sun subdues its scorching rays the moment I face it? The rivers suspend their flow the moment I stand in front of them. The forest foliage ceases to wave the moment I glance at it. Before me, your Rama is smaller than a puny insect.

SITA You wretch, you rogue, you brute! What else can I expect from a *rakshasa?* Death is the only punishment you deserve, you braggart, and you will get it very soon. In your destruction the world will have a new life, a life of aspiration and perfection.

MY RAMA IS MY ALL

RA 17. SCENE 7

(In the forest where Rama has wounded the deer. Enter Lakshmana.)

RAMA   Lakshmana, are you here? Who is looking after Sita?
LAKSHMANA   *(falls at the feet of Rama)* Brother, what could I do? She forced me to come here. I told her repeatedly that you were not in danger, that Maricha was imitating your voice, but she would not believe me. She insulted me so badly, she scolded me so badly. You can't imagine the words she used. She literally forced me to come to you. The last thing she said was that she would throw herself into the River Godavari if I did not come to save you, so I came.
RAMA   Lakshmana, you did the right thing.
LAKSHMANA   I have listened to her and not to you, Brother. Now we may not see our dearest Sita again.
RAMA   I also fear the same.
LAKSHMANA   How hard it is to please two masters. I wanted to please you, I wanted to do everything for you. But when she insulted and scolded me and finally alarmed me by saying she would throw herself into the River Godavari, I was helpless. I came. Now let us hurry back to her.

RA 18. SCENE 8

(The spot in the forest where Lakshmana left Sita. Enter Rama and Lakshmana. Sita is gone.)

LAKSHMANA   Brother, I knew it. I knew it.
RAMA   I don't blame you, my dearest Lakshmana. But now we have to find Sita. Life without Sita is meaningless for me.
LAKSHMANA   Rama, life without you is meaningless for me. Now what can we do?
RAMA   Let us search for our Sita. Sita, Sita, no matter where you are, this heart of love is for you, only for you.
LAKSHMANA   Sita, Sita, no matter where you are, Mother Sita, this heart of adoration, Supreme Adoration, is for you.

DASHARATHA'S DREAM IS AT LAST FULFILLED

SRI CHINMOY

RA 19. DRAMATIS PERSONÆ

RAMA
BHARATA, LAKSHMANA (HALF-BROTHERS OF RAMA)
URMILA (WIFE OF LAKSHMANA)
SITA (WIFE OF RAMA)
OTHER MEMBERS OF THE ROYAL FAMILY
A LARGE CROWD OF PEOPLE

MY RAMA IS MY ALL

RA 20. SCENE I

(Rama, Lakshmana and Sita return to Ayodhya after they have been in exile for fourteen years. Bharata receives them with boundless joy and love. There is a long procession as every person in the kingdom comes to receive them. The whole kingdom is in the seventh Heaven of delight.)

BHARATA Rama, you have come back. You have kept your promise. If you had not kept your promise, if you had broken your pledge, you would not have seen me here on earth in the land of the living. *(Touches Rama's feet.)* Here is your kingdom, Brother. Now, as before, I shall be your loving brother and slave. I submit totally to your will.

RAMA Bharata, you have shown your heart's magnanimity and your soul's nobility. You could have easily kept this kingdom for yourself. You were the King, in accordance with Father's wish.

BHARATA *(interrupting)* No, never! Father's wish was that you would be King, not I. You fulfilled Father's promise to my undivine, hostile mother. Her undivine desire compelled you to suffer much. It doomed you to fourteen years of misery, and I suffered as well. Now the darkest night is over; it is all day. The light of joy, the light of progress and achievement has dawned at last. O Rama, you have come to fulfil Father's dream. Father's lofty hopes for you will now be manifested in this kingdom on earth.

(The members of the royal family are all around. Urmila, the wife of Lakshmana, bows down to Rama and Sita, and then to her husband. While touching Lakshmana's feet, she sheds tears.)

LAKSHMANA   Urmila, why do you weep? I have come back to you. Today should be a day of enormous joy.

URMILA   My Lord, I am not weeping tears of sorrow. I am shedding tears of joy. Your body left me, but not your soul. Your soul stayed inside my heart. Now I have your body and soul together with me again.

(Urmila sings.)

Nayane nayane gopane gopane
shayane swapane madhu jagarane
jibaner dole maraner kole
taba prema-lila amar bhubane

(In secrecy supreme I see You.
You live in my eyes,
In my sleep, in my dreams,
In my sweet wakefulness.
In the stupendous mirth of life,
In the abysmal lap of death,
You I behold.
Your love-play is my world.)

URMILA   If you had remained here at the palace you would have done your human duty to me. But your soul wanted you to do your divine duty, which was to serve your dearest brother, Rama. He is all Divinity. He is the incarnation of *dharma*. You left me to be of service to him. You have come back again only to be of service to him. But your presence gives me enormous joy. I shall have you around me. I shall be with you. When it is a matter of serving, the Divine comes first and foremost. You did the right thing. You are doing the right thing. And in your sacrifice my glory looms large. In your feeling of oneness with the divine Rama, my oneness with the divine Rama shines.

RAMA Urmila, your silence when we left for the forest was deeply appreciated and admired by me. You sacrificed your husband in silence. Your life of silent sacrifice has touched the very depths of my heart. Your sacrifice springs from your divine wisdom. Your soul-stirring philosophy is absolutely correct. The Divine comes first, and not the human. I see your life of oneness with your husband, your life of inner wisdom. You are all for the cause of my divine manifestation on earth. Urmila, feel my heart's enormous delight and my soul's transcendental pride.

MY RAMA IS MY ALL

SRI CHINMOY

RA 21. DRAMATIS PERSONÆ

A KING
HANUMAN (A GREAT DEVOTEE OF RAMA)

MY RAMA IS MY ALL

RA 22. SCENE I

(A King and Hanuman.)

KING   Hanuman, I have heard much about your strength and your sacrifice. It was you who discovered Sita in Lanka. It was you who took Rama's message to Sita and Sita's message to Rama. It was you who enabled Rama to conquer and kill Ravana. Without you Rama could not have won the victory.

HANUMAN   O King, I don't want you to utter falsehoods. Rama is God. It was most kind of him to appoint me as his messenger. It was most kind of him to ask me to fight for him. But Rama did not need my help. Rama does not need anybody's help. He could easily have conquered Ravana himself. He can protect himself. He is all power. He can conquer the whole world at his sweet will.

KING   I deeply admire your heart's nobility.

HANUMAN   I shall also deeply admire you when you speak the truth. It is Rama who can do everything. Rama is all-powerful.

KING   Yes, your Rama is all-powerful. He is everything. Are you happy now?

HANUMAN   Yes, I am happy. I am happy. When you say this, I become happy.

KING   I have a gift for you, Hanuman, a most precious gift.

HANUMAN   Thank you.

KING   *(holds out a pendant)* I wish to place it around your neck myself. I am pleased with your strength, proud of your love for Rama and proud of your sacrifice.

HANUMAN   O King, my sacrifice for whom? If you say, "For Rama," I shall not accept your gift. I shall return it immediately. I made no sacrifice for Rama. His very existence on earth is the supreme sacrifice for me and for earth.

KING *(places pendant around Hanuman's neck)* This pendant looks wonderful on you. I am so happy to see you wearing it.

HANUMAN It certainly does. I deeply thank you for this necklace.

(Hanuman starts fondling the locket. Finally he takes the necklace off and starts to break open the locket.)

KING Hanuman, what are you doing? You are a fool! That is such a precious locket! Can't you see the diamonds on it?

HANUMAN But I want to see what is inside it. *(Breaks it open.)* Ah, nothing! *(Throws it away.)*

KING What a fool! What am I going to do with such a fool? You have no sense! Why did you break the locket? Why did you throw it away?

HANUMAN I wanted to see if there was a picture of Rama inside, but there was no picture. I did not see anything of Rama inside the locket. So why do I need it? I only need the things that have Rama in them. Without Rama I do not exist. No matter how expensive, how valuable your locket is to you, it is of no value to me. With Rama, everything is most precious to me. Without Rama, everything is useless to me.

(Hanuman sings.)

MY RAMA IS MY ALL

Tumi shudhu bandhu amar
tumi amar pran
baul haye desh bideshe
gahi jena bhalobese
jiban bhare tomar jaya gan
tumi shudhu bandhu amar
tumiy amar pran

(You are my only Friend,
You are my Life.
Like a divine mendicant, from
 one country to another
May I sing a song of You
With all my love.
May I sing the Song of
 Your Victory all my life.)

HANUMAN   King, since you do not care for Rama, I cannot waste one minute more of my precious time here. Good-bye.

(Exit Hanuman.)

KING   Hanuman's strength is unparalleled, but his blind and stupid faith in Rama is also unparalleled. In God's creation, it seems perfection will never dawn.

FIRE SURRENDERS TO SITA

SRI CHINMOY

RA 23. DRAMATIS PERSONÆ

RAMA
SITA (WIFE OF RAMA)
LAKSHMANA (HALF-BROTHER OF RAMA)
A LARGE AUDIENCE

MY RAMA IS MY ALL

RA 24. SCENE I

(Rama, Sita, Lakshmana and a vast audience. Sita is weeping with joy.)

RAMA   Sita, my heart is overflowing with joy to see you again. But, Sita, to me *dharma,* Divine Justice, is more important than my concern for you. You have stayed at the wicked Ravana's palace for several months. I am sure he has cast his lustful gaze on you. I am sure you are impure. My subjects will misunderstand me if I accept you now. Therefore, I am compelled to disown you. You must leave. You may go wherever you want to. Even if you want to have somebody else as the partner of your life, I will have no objection.

(Sita's tears become tears of grief.)

SITA   You speak like an ordinary human being, Rama. I thought that you were great, really great, but now I think that you are worse than any human being on earth. Can't you see with your occult vision whether or not I have lived an impure life at Ravana's palace? He tempted me with his wealth. He tried to force me to be his, but my inner strength protected and saved me. I wanted only you, and I still want only you, but now you discard me like a filthy rag. I am prepared to leave you, but before I leave, I wish to prove to you that I am Purity itself. I shall consign my body to fire and you will see what happens to me. *(To Lakshmana)* Lakshmana, with all your heart's magnanimity you have helped me millions of times. You have listened to me millions of times. You have always considered me as your mother. Listen then to one final request. Please light a blazing fire for me. This is my last request, my last prayer to you.

LAKSHMANA   Mother, not a prayer, not a request, but a fatal command. Rama, what am I going to do now?

RAMA   You have always pleased her. Now please her this time, too.

SITA   I know that fire is the cosmic Reality and Rama is the cosmic Reality. If I come out of fire unburned, then the world will know that I was pure — Purity itself. And if I do not come out of the fire, then I will enter into the cosmic Reality, which is my Rama.

MY RAMA IS MY ALL

RA 25. SCENE 2

(Lakshmana has lighted a blazing fire in the presence of a large audience.)

SITA   O Fire God, my husband Rama has every right to test me, and I have every right to prove to him that I was pure, I am pure and I forever shall remain pure. If I fail in this test, I shall go to my Divine Rama in Heaven. If I pass, I shall remain with my human Rama here on earth.

(Site walks slowly, steadily through the leaping flames and comes back to Rama. The all-consuming fire could do nothing to her. Her whole face is aglow. Rama receives Sita with all his love.)

RAMA   My Sita, the fire ordeal is over. The world now knows that you are Purity itself. You had the heart to prove yourself to my subjects. One part of my being wanted to please my subjects at your expense, with your sacrifice. It felt that the whole object of my stay on earth was to please them. Another part, which is divine, knew well that you were pure and felt that this was doing an injustice to you. But you and I are one. You have proved it. With your sacrifice you have shown your greatness before my subjects, and since we are one, you have made me great, also. What you have done for me and what we are doing for my subjects is right.

SITA   My Lord, you are right. You are always right. This existence of mine is only to please you, to prove to the world that I am only for you and that the illumination of the world depends only on your compassionate wisdom.

SRI CHINMOY

(Sita sings.)

*Saphal habe swapan amar saphal habe
samarpaner atma-hutir mahotsabe
tomar hasi tomar banshi
bijay ketan amar chetan
amar bhabe nachbe jani
amar bhabe*

(My dream will be fulfilled
In the great festival of my surrender's
    consecration-fire.
Your Smile, Your Flute,
Your Banner, Your Consciousness-Light,
In my world shall dance,
I know, I know.)

NO FAITH, NO SAFETY

SRI CHINMOY

RA 26. DRAMATIS PERSONÆ

HANUMAN (A GREAT DEVOTEE OF RAMA)
A MAN

MY RAMA IS MY ALL

RA 27. SCENE I

(Hanuman is at the bank of a river. It is raining heavily. A man passing by comes up to him.)

MAN   Ah, I have found someone who is also suffering from the rain. I thought that I would find nobody here. I came for the ferry, but no boatman is willing to carry me across to the other shore. All are afraid of this storm.

HANUMAN   I am not afraid of the storm. I am just thinking of my Lord Rama.

MAN   Hanuman! I have heard much about you. What has Rama ever done for you?

HANUMAN   Be quiet. What has Rama *not* done for me? Is there anything that he has not done for me? Or is there anything that he will not do for me? He has done everything and he will do everything for me. I have done hardly anything for him.

MAN   You have done so many things for him, Hanuman.

HANUMAN   True, but I still feel that I can please him much more than I have already pleased him.

MAN   O Hanuman, you are the incarnation of humility.

HANUMAN   I am the incarnation of sincerity. But if you say I am the incarnation of humility, I don't accept that. I *want* to be the incarnation of humility. How I wish I could do something really great for my Rama! It seems the rain will never stop. But I shall go to the other side,

(Hanuman starts walking on the water.)

MAN   Hanuman, Hanuman!

HANUMAN   *(coming back)* What is wrong with you?

MAN   I want to go with you.
HANUMAN   You want to go with me? Then come along.
MAN   But I am afraid.
HANUMAN   Don't be afraid. Do you have a pencil?
MAN   Yes.
HANUMAN   And a piece of paper?
MAN   Yes.
HANUMAN   Now close your eyes.

(The man closes his eyes. Hanuman writes on the piece of paper, folds it and gives it to him. He starts to open it.)

HANUMAN   No, hold it. Don't open it. I am going with you to the other side. But don't open this paper. If you open it and see what I have written, then you will not be able to walk on the water. You will sink.
MAN   No, no, I will never open it.
HANUMAN   Then come along.

(They begin walking together.)

MAN   O Hanuman, I do not know what you have written on this paper. It has such magic in it. I never imagined in all my life that I would be able to walk on water! You can do everything, Hanuman. You have all capacity. For me to walk on water without your help would have been simply impossible.
HANUMAN   Everything is possible by Rama's grace.
MAN   Where is Rama here?
HANGMAN   Rama is everywhere.
MAN   Hanuman, I am really curious to see what you have written there.
HANUMAN   Don't open it. If you open it you will sink.

MY RAMA IS MY ALL

MAN   If you are beside me, it is impossible for me to sink. You will help me. I'll open it. *(He opens the paper and looks at it. Inside is written the word "Rama".)*

MAN   "Rama!" it says. *(Laughing.)* Again Rama, even here!

(The man immediately sinks.)

MAN   O Hanuman, save me, save me!

HANUMAN   No. You sneer at my Rama, you ridicule my Rama. I won't save you. He who mocks my Rama, he who criticises my Rama, can never have my compassion. I repeatedly asked you not to open it. You disobeyed me, and then, what is worse, you sneered at my Rama. This is your punishment. I have no love for you. If someone does not care for my Rama, I in turn do not care for that person. Sink! Let your life end. For me, a life without Rama is a life of misery. I want you also to feel that a life without Rama is of no use; it is simply a life of destruction. In fact, you shall learn that a life without Rama is meaningless, useless, impossible. A life with Rama is a life of constant achievement, constant glory, constant bliss.

RAMA FAILS

SRI CHINMOY

RA 28. DRAMATIS PERSONÆ

RAMA
MINISTERS AND PRIESTS
A MAN OF VERY LOW CASTE
VASHISHTHA (PRECEPTOR OF RAMA)
MOTHER OF HANUMAN
HANUMAN (A GREAT DEVOTEE OF RAMA)

MY RAMA IS MY ALL

RA 29. SCENE I

(Rama's palace. Rama has invited all his ministers and priests to discuss a serious matter. Everyone has arrived except his preceptor, Vashishtha. Vashishtha has a special seat of his own. Suddenly a man of very low caste enters and deliberately sits on Vashishtha's seat.)

EVERYONE NEARBY Get up! Get up!
A MINISTER How dare you sit on this seat? This is Vashishtha's seat. He is the preceptor, the Guru of King Rama.

(Enter Vashishtha.)

VASHISHTHA Why is this man sitting on my seat? *(To the man.)* How dare you sit there? I shall kill you! Rama, if you are a true disciple of mine, you must kill this rascal.

(Rama gets his bow and arrow. The man runs for his life.)

VASHISHTHA Rama, you have to kill this rogue, this infidel! I can give you only three chances at most. If you fail in your first attempt, you can try two more times. And if you fail in your third attempt to kill him, I will think you are a useless archer.
RAMA You know I have killed Ravana, the King of the Demons. Is there anyone I cannot kill on the first attempt, O Vashishtha, O peerless Sage? I assure you, either I shall kill that fellow where I find him, or I shall bring him here.
VASHISHTHA No, Rama, I don't want you to bring him here. Just kill him wherever you find him. God knows where he is by now.

RAMA   With your blessing let me leave.

(Vashishtha blesses Rama. Exit Rama.)

MY RAMA IS MY ALL

RA 30. SCENE 2

(Rama is looking for the man. Finally he sees him at a distance. He gives chase, and the man runs for his life.)

RAMA Ah, I see he is entering into my Hanuman's house. The rogue is caught! He does not know that the house belongs to Hanuman, my dearest devotee. *(Shouts)* Hanuman! Hanuman!

(Enter Hanuman's mother.)

HANUMAN'S MOTHER O Rama, you have come. I am so grateful to you. Your presence has sanctified my home. O Rama, please wait for a few minutes. Hanuman will be coming immediately. He is getting ready to see you.

(Exit Hanuman's mother. Enter Hanuman with folded hands.)

HANUMAN Please tell me what I can do for you, my Lord.
RAMA Hanuman, where has he gone? Where is that rascal? Bring him out! He has insulted my Guru, Vashishtha. He sat on Vashishtha's seat. Vashishtha wants me to kill him. I have to fulfil Vashishtha's desire. Bring him out and I shall kill him.
HANUMAN O Rama, I am sorry but I cannot bring him out.
RAMA I can't believe my ears! Is this you, Hanuman, my dearest disciple? I was under the impression that you were ready to give your life for me at any moment.
HANUMAN That is true. I will give my life for you. But this is not my life. It is somebody else's life.

RAMA That means you won't listen to me, to my request, my demand, my command?

HANUMAN I am sorry. Forgive me. My mother has given him shelter. *Janani janmabhumishcha swargadapi gariyasi.* "Mother and Mother Earth are superior to Heaven itself."

RAMA But I am your Lord. Am I not superior to everything in your life?

HANUMAN That is true, but how am I going to break my mother's promise?

RAMA If you want to fulfil your mother's promise, then you are no longer my dearest disciple. I must come first in your life, Hanuman.

HANUMAN Yes, you do come first in my life. I have to break my mother's promise. I am prepared. To please you is to please God. Rama, how are you going to kill this man?

RAMA I am going to kill him with my arrows. Vashishtha has allowed me three attempts. He made me promise to try three times and then give up. But it will be a real disgrace if I cannot kill a human being in three attempts.

HANUMAN Please wait here. I shall bring the culprit right to you.

(Exit Hanuman.)

RAMA *(to himself)* I knew. The moment I saw the culprit entering into Hanuman's house, I knew it was his end. He could not escape me. The human emotions created some problem for my Hanuman; that is why he took his mother's side. But the divine in him is so strong, so powerful, that it has to come forward, and it did come forward. That is why he is bringing the culprit to me.

MY RAMA IS MY ALL

(Hanuman brings the culprit before Rama.)

HANUMAN   He is ready, Rama. You can satisfy yourself now.

(Rama aims at the culprit and shoots. The arrow drops without piercing his heart. Rama is wonder-struck.)

RAMA   What? How can this be? I killed Ravana, the most powerful demon on earth, and now my arrow fails. Let me try a second time. *(The same thing happens the second time.)* Only one more chance is left! Let me make my third attempt. *(The same thing happens the third time.)*

HANUMAN   Lord, you have to keep your promise now. You have three times tried to kill him, and three times you have failed. Now you can't try any more.

RAMA   No, I can't. I won't. But Hanuman, tell me: how could all this happen? I am the King of Kings, and my arrow fails today so miserably for the first time.

HANUMAN   I shall tell you the secret. I told the man to begin repeating in silence, the moment you drew back your bow, "Victory to Lord Rama." And the second time you drew it back, I asked him to repeat, "Victory to the consort of Sita." The third time, "Victory to Dasharatha's eldest son." So each time he prayed for your victory. Now if someone sincerely prays for your own victory, how can you kill that person? Your soul's divinity was pleased with him because he was praying for your victory. It was your vital and your mind that wanted to kill him. Naturally your soul's will shall always conquer the will of your vital and mind. You are the Lord of the gods. He prayed to you for your victory. Naturally your soul gave him protection, even though your mind and vital were begging for his destruction. The power of your soul is infinitely greater than the power of your vital desire.

RAMA   My dearest disciple, I accept my defeat with deepest joy and blessingful pride. I accept my defeat by you, my dearest devotee. You have taught me a lesson. My soul's will shall always conquer my vital and mental craving. I have failed in my outer attempt. But my body's failure is my soul's success. The success of my soul over my body is infinitely more meaningful and fruitful than my outer success.

HANUMAN   This knowledge that I have offered to you was granted to me by you. Is there anything I have that has not come from you? My knowledge, my power, everything that I have, everything that I am, has all come from you. In order to glorify me, in order to immortalise me, you are acting like my student. But I know that I am your eternal student. I know you are my eternal teacher.

(Hanuman sings.)

Janar age tomai ami henechhi
pabar age tomai ami jenechhi
debar age tomai ami peyechhi
taito tomai mor amire sanpechhi

(Before I knew You, I struck You.
Before I received You, I knew You.
Before I gave myself to You,
   I received You.
Therefore to You I have offered,
   sacrificed and surrendered
   my ego-reality's existence.)

BROTHER LAKSHMANA,
I SHALL FOLLOW YOU

SRI CHINMOY

RA 31. DRAMATIS PERSONÆ

RAMA
LAKSHMANA (HALF-BROTHER OF RAMA)
YAMARAJ (THE KING OF DEATH)
DURVASHA (A SAGE)
PRIME MINISTER
MINISTERS AND ELDERS

MY RAMA IS MY ALL

RA 32. SCENE I

(Rama and Lakshmana in a room.)

RAMA   Lakshmana, my dearest brother, you are my joy, you are my pride. The world admires me, adores me, but I know why I have become great, how I have become great and who has made me great. It is all because of you, my Lakshmana.

LAKSHMANA   O Rama, you are my eldest brother, but I have always considered you to be my father. To be with you, to be of service to you, is to live with the highest Goal.

(Lakshmana sings.)

Amar bhuban tomar charan lagi
amar jiban tomar swapan lagi
ogo asimer nirabata
ogo dyuloker amarata
eso eso eso e hiya rayechhe jagi

(My world is for Your Feet.
My life is for Your Dream.
O silence of Infinity,
O immortality of Heaven,
Come, come, come.
This heart remains awake.)

(Enter Yamaraj in the guise of a holy man.)

YAMARAJ   Rama, I would like to have a private interview with you. I have to discuss something most important with you,

something most urgent, and during our conversation I do not want anyone else to be present, only you and me.
RAMA   That can easily be done. I shall certainly do it, venerable Sir.

(Lakshmana is about to leave.)

YAMARAJ   Please wait. *(Lakshmana waits.)* O Rama, give me your promise that whoever enters, whoever comes here during our conversation, will be put to death.
RAMA   Yes, I devotedly agree to your proposal. Lakshmana, my dearest brother, do not allow anybody to enter into this room. Keep a rigid watch, and no matter who it is, do not allow anyone to intrude on our private talk.
LAKSHMANA   *(with folded hands)* Rama, I am at your supreme command.

(Exit Lakshmana.)

YAMARAJ   Rama, I am Yamaraj, the King of Death. I have been sent to you by Brahma, the Eternal Creator. He has asked me to tell you that your play on earth is done. You have fought very hard to establish the kingdom of *dharma* on earth, and you have succeeded. Now your time is up. You are needed in Heaven.
RAMA   I am happy to hear that my time has at last come. My Sita is no longer with me. Just to please the world I tortured her heart. I cared more for the world than for my dearest wife. Now she has left her body, cast off her mortal sheath, just to please me. I was such a rascal, such a wretched fellow. Now I shall meet her in the other world. I am so happy to go with you.

MY RAMA IS MY ALL

(Enter hurriedly Lakshmana.)

LAKSHMANA   Rama, Rama, my brother, the Sage Durvasha has come and he wants to see you immediately. I told him you were occupied and not available. He got furious and told me that in the twinkling of an eye he would destroy your whole family and your whole kingdom. I don't want him to destroy our family or our beloved Kingdom of Ayodhya. I know that nobody is allowed to come in here during your conversation, but I felt that I must sacrifice my life. It is better to die at the hands of my dearest brother Rama than to die at the hands of Durvasha.

YAMARAJ   Rama, we have not finished our conversation, and your brother has entered. That means he must die.

RAMA   It is true. It is true. Lakshmana, go and bring Durvasha here. In the meantime we will finish our conversation.

(Exit Lakshmana.)

YAMARAJ   So, are you ready? Soon you will be called away. Are you ready?

RAMA   Yes, I am fully prepared.

YAMARAJ   And what about your brother? He has violated your injunction.

RAMA   Yes.

YAMARAJ   And he will be put to death?

RAMA   He will.

YAMARAJ   I know you will keep your promise. May God bless you!

(Exit Yamaraj. Enter Lakshmana and Durvasha.)

RAMA   *(folding his hands)* O Sage, O Sage of the highest magnitude, forgive me, forgive me. I was having a most important private conversation with a guest, and that is why I could not see you immediately. Please forgive me. Now, please tell me how I can serve you. I am at your service.

DURVASHA   Rama, I am extremely hungry. I have not eaten for a long, long time. But today I want to eat your food. I don't want to eat anything else — only the food that is prepared for you.

RAMA   I am so proud that a great sage like you, Durvasha, wants to eat my food. Lakshmana, go and bring my food.

(Lakshmana goes and comes back with food. Durvasha eats with great satisfaction. When he is finished, he turns to Rama.)

DURVASHA   Rama, I bless you with all my heart and soul. You have satisfied my outer hunger, and I shall fulfil your inner hunger. Very soon you will be with your beloved Sita in the other world.

MY RAMA IS MY ALL

RA 33. SCENE 2

(Rama, Lakshmana and the ministers and elders.)

RAMA   What am I going to do? I have to keep my promise. Lakshmana is dearer than my life, but a promise is a promise.

LAKSHMANA   Rama, do not feel sorry. Do not weep. You have to keep your promise. You must kill me according to your promise. I will be happy to be killed by you. There can be no greater joy than to be punished by you. There can be no better death than to be killed by you.

PRIME MINISTER   O Rama, since it was your promise that you would put to death any intruder, I wish you to banish your brother from the kingdom. This punishment is equivalent to killing him.

RAMA   For me to live without my brother Lakshmana is also my death. To be away from him, not to see him around me, is my worst death.

LAKSHMANA   *(bowing)* Brother, Father, you are my All. I want the world to see that you are the Incarnation of Truth. You have established the kingdom of *dharma*. Your promise and your life can never be separated. They are one and inseparable. I am now leaving the palace. I will go and meditate on the bank of the Sarayu, and when the time comes I shall jump into the river and give up my life.

RAMA   O joy of my heart, O love of my heart, O power of my heart, you are leaving me. You are embracing death. Because of your constant sacrifice, this world knows me. And in the other world, I will also be known because of your sacrifice. I will be adored and worshipped. O brother of my heart and soul, O brother of eternity, you have followed me everywhere; wherever I have gone you have followed me like my own shadow. When Father sent me into exile, when I had to bring Sita back from Ravana, you followed me. But now, O Lakshmana, I shall follow you. I shall follow your life-breath. You go and reserve my place in the other world, in the world of the Beyond. I am coming.

(Lakshmana bows to his brother and begins to leave. Rama sings.)

*Deshe deshe cha bandhabah
tantu desha na pashyami
yatra bratha sahodara*

RAMA   In all countries there are wives, in all countries there are friends, but I shall not find a brother like Lakshmana anywhere in this world.

PART II

THE SINGER OF THE ETERNAL BEYOND

THE BABY KRISHNA AND
HIS FOSTER MOTHER, JASHODA

SRI CHINMOY

SI I. DRAMATIS PERSONÆ

JASHODA (FOSTER MOTHER OF KRISHNA)
KRISHNA (AS A YOUNG CHILD)

THE SINGER OF THE ETERNAL BEYOND

SI 2. SCENE I

(Jashoda is churning curd into butter. Krishna is playing near her.)

JASHODA   Krishna! What are you doing?

(Krishna smiles.)

JASHODA   Stop eating mud! Stop! You dirty fellow!

(Krishna smiles.)

JASHODA   Stop! Stop! Otherwise I shall strike you!

(Krishna smiles and Jashoda comes to him.)

JASHODA   Open your mouth! Spit it out!

(Krishna opens his mouth. She takes the mud out of his mouth.)

JASHODA   Oh! What do I see? I see the whole universe! I see earth, heaven, stars, planets, the sun, the moon, countless beings, all the beings inside you. My child, is this a dream? Is it only a dream? My child, close your mouth.

(Krishna closes his mouth.)

JASHODA   Now open it. *(He opens it.)* Again I see the universe: earth, heaven, stars, planets, the sun, the moon and countless beings. O Krishna, this time it is not a dream. This time it is not a mental hallucination. For the second time, I am seeing all this. O Lord Supreme, You have given me Nanda, my husband, who is all love for mankind. You have blessed me with Krishna, in whom I see the entire universe. Something within me tells me, O Lord Supreme, that my Krishna is none other than You, Yourself.

(Krishna smiles.)

DON'T WORSHIP INDRA BUT WORSHIP GIRI GOVARDHAN

SRI CHINMOY

SI 3. DRAMATIS PERSONÆ

KRISHNA
A RELATIVE
HIS PARENTS, OTHER RELATIVES AND NEIGHBOURS
INDRA (KING OF THE GODS)

THE SINGER OF THE ETERNAL BEYOND

SI 4. SCENE I

(Krishna's parents, relatives and neighbours are performing ceremonies in honour of the Lord Indra.)

KRISHNA Why are you worshipping Indra? Who is he?

RELATIVE Oh Krishna, you are just a child. You are eleven years old. That is why you do not know who Indra is.

KRISHNA I do not know, but I wish to know from you who he is.

RELATIVE Indra is the rain god. And he is King of the Gods.

KRISHNA That is why you are worshipping him? You should worship this hill. *(Points out the hill Giri Govardhan.)* Our cattle are being fed by this hill; everyone is being helped in one way or another by this hill. Indra does not help us in any way. If you want to know the Truth, if you care for the Truth, then I tell you that you should worship this hill, and not Indra.

RELATIVE Krishna, if we do it and something happens, your parents will feel miserable. And I am your relative, so I shall also feel miserable.

KRISHNA Nothing will happen. My parents will not feel miserable. You will not feel miserable. At least let's try this time, please. We shall not worship Indra any more.

(Indra is watching from Heaven. He is furious.)

INDRA How do they dare to listen to that little child, that rascal, Krishna! I shall show them! I shall teach them a lesson! I shall inundate the whole place with water!

(Rain begins to fall.)

RELATIVE   I knew this was going to happen! Now see this rain! God alone knows when this downpour will stop. Krishna, what do you have to say now?

KRISHNA   I never accept defeat. Never. Look! With one of my fingers I shall lift the whole hill, and it will serve as an umbrella. *(Lifts the hill.)* You can all be under the protection of the hill. Even if it rains for seven days, I will protect you. Giri Govardhan will protect us this way for seven days. And then Indra will have to accept defeat. Do not worry. You are all safe, protected under the hill.

RELATIVE   O Krishna, now we know who you are. From now on you will save us and illumine us.

RADHA AND KRISHNA ARE PURE

SRI CHINMOY

SI 5. DRAMATIS PERSONÆ

KRISHNA
RADHA (DIVINE CONSORT OF KRISHNA)
FIRST GIRL
SECOND GIRL
THIRD GIRL
OTHER DIVINE FRIENDS OF KRISHNA (MOSTLY WOMEN)

THE SINGER OF THE ETERNAL BEYOND

SI 6. SCENE I

(Krishna sits alone. Beside him is his flute.)

KRISHNA *(lifting his flute)* When I play on this flute, men and women, especially women, come to listen to my music. People criticise me because they feel that my association with these women is not pure. But I know how pure these women are, and I know what purity I embody. Poor Radha, she is my dearest *shakti*. She is Purity itself. But human beings, how will they understand divine Love? How will they understand divine Delight? I shall have to suffer criticism from people.

(Krishna sings.)

Je besechhe bhalo
ei dharanire
se peyechhe shudhu byatha
parane tahar dhelechhe abani
kuruper malinata
tabu nirbhay chale sei bir
pritthvir bojha niye
ahaba ante habe upanita
prabhur charane giye

(He who has loved this world
Has only got excruciating pangs.
The world has thrown on him all ugliness and filth
        and dirt, and impurity.
Yet the hero marches along,
Carrying the burden of the entire world.
At the end of his teeming struggles
He will go and stand at the Feet of the Lord
        Supreme.)

KRISHNA   I do not mind. I am above it all. But my Radha suffers, and I feel sorry for her.

(Enter Radha.)

KRISHNA   How do you feel today, Radha?

(Radha does not answer.)

KRISHNA   Yesterday you were in a sulking mood. It seems today you are worse. Radha, please tell me what is going on. Yesterday I asked you what was wrong with you, and you didn't answer. Today again I am asking you. I am begging you. Now tell me what is wrong with you. Has anybody insulted you?

RADHA   You are so pure, so divine. I come to you to listen to your music, to listen to your divine voice, to listen to your eternal Truth. I know you are divine, and my heart is all for you. But everybody criticises us, even my girl friends who also come here to listen to you. My girl friends are creating such gossip. It is unthinkable, unbearable.

KRISHNA   Do you know why they do it? Can you tell me why they act like that?

RADHA   Just because you show me special attention, they can't bear it. They are jealous of me. *(Krishna smiles.)* Can you not stop their jealousy?

KRISHNA   Human jealousy, Radha, is a very serious disease. I shall try to free them from jealousy. But it is a very difficult task.

RADHA   Either you have to free them from jealousy, or you have to make them feel that I am pure.

KRISHNA   To make them feel that you are pure — that is far easier. That I can do easily. I shall show you.

(Krishna begins playing soul-stirring music on his flute. All his divine friends come rushing to hear his music. Krishna plays for a few minutes.)

KRISHNA   Today I wish to play a special game. *(Speaking to the women.)* Most of you are married. I want you to prove today that you are all chaste. I want you to prove your purity.

(When Krishna says this, some of them immediately run away.)

KRISHNA   Look at this. I wanted them to prove their chastity and they have run away. You can imagine what kind of life they lead. So you people are remaining. I am so glad that you lead a chaste life. Now, here is a sieve and here is a bucket of water. One by one you come and pour the water into the sieve. If the water does not leak through when someone pours, that means that that woman is extremely pure and chaste.

(The girls line up. The first girl comes and pours water into the sieve. The water leaks through. The onlookers start laughing.)

ONLOOKERS Oh, she is not chaste. She is not pure.

(The girl hides her face in embarrassment. The next girl starts pouring, but again the water goes through.)

ONLOOKERS *(laughing)* She is not chaste, she is not chaste.
KRISHNA *(to a third girl)* Now come on.

(The third girl comes and suffers the same fate. The water leaks through the sieve. Everybody starts laughing.)

THIRD GIRL *(mockingly)* Oh, Radha should come. Let her try!
OTHERS Yes, Radha should come. Let Radha come. Let Radha try!
SECOND GIRL Why do you bother Radha? She is not chaste either. Have some sympathy for her. You know perfectly well what kind of life she is leading.
KRISHNA All right, she is not leading a life of purity. But let her try anyway. Radha, please come and see. You try, Radha. Come.

(Radha comes forward and is about to pour the water. The other women immediately start laughing.)

KRISHNA Be quiet. Let us see first.
RADHA Look, already they are laughing and mocking and criticising me. Why should I do it?
KRISHNA *(to the onlookers)* Do not mock. Do not laugh. This is not yet the time to laugh and criticise. You people have proved yourselves. You have proved that you are not chaste at all. You only know how to criticise and mock. Now, let Radha try. At least give her a chance.

(Radha pours the water. The water does not leak through the sieve. Everybody is astonished.)

KRISHNA   Now you can see who is chaste, who is pure. You people, look. You know how to criticise, how to mock. But you do not know how to lead a pure life. I am teaching you the eternal Truth. I am the Lord of the Universe. Radha comes to me for spiritual help, eternal Truth. Her love for me is divine. My love for her is also divine. Your minds are in the gutter. You remain in a filthy consciousness. You care for men, you care for earthly duties, you care for name, fame and so many things. But my Radha, I am always in her mind. She is also a married woman. She has her husband and everything else, just like you. But no matter where she goes, no matter with whom she speaks, her mind is always on my Transcendental Consciousness. She knows that I am the Lord of the Universe. *(Pauses.)* Whoever thinks of me has the purest heart on earth. Those who think of other things are not pure and can never be pure. Their purity today you observed. A day will come when the whole world will know who Radha is. The world will not only recognise her purity, but also receive from her divinity the purest delight that exists in the earth-consciousness. She is my delight; she is the delight of the Universe. Pray, meditate. All of you will one day have Radha's purity, Radha's consciousness. It will take time; it will take centuries, millennia. But it will be possible for you also to have Radha's height, Radha's consciousness, Radha's realisation.

(Radha soulfully looks at Krishna and the other girls listen quietly while the second girl sings.)

Kalo baran nai je kanu
jena kancha sona
bishwa ruper rup madhuri
jyoti diye bona
amar —
maner kali dhela pare
dekhai tare kalo
ta nahale priya je mor
sudhui ujal alo
alo andhar tahar gara
kanu bishwamoy
sabar sathe habe amar
naba parichay

(My Krishna is not black,
He is pure gold.
He Himself is woven
Into the universal Beauty, Light and Splendour.
He looks dark
Because I have spilled the ink of my mind on Him.
Otherwise, my Beloved is All-Light.
He created Light and Darkness,
He is within and without the Cosmos Vast.
With this knowledge,
I will have a new acquaintance
With the world at large.)

O KRISHNA, KEEP ME
IN CONSTANT SUFFERING!

SRI CHINMOY

SI 7. DRAMATIS PERSONÆ

KUNTI (MOTHER OF ARJUNA)
ARJUNA

THE SINGER OF THE ETERNAL BEYOND

SI 8. SCENE I

(Kunti is crying. Enter Arjuna.)

ARJUNA   Mother, Mother, why are you crying? Has anything happened to you?

KUNTI   Nothing, my son.

ARJUNA   You know that we are all right. Your children are all well. We Pandava brothers and all our wives are safe and well. Why are you crying? Mother, please tell me. Are you not feeling well?

KUNTI   No, my son, I am feeling perfectly well.

ARJUNA   Then why are you crying?

KUNTI   My son, you won't understand me.

ARJUNA   Perhaps I won't understand you, but you can make me understand. Tell me. Why are you crying?

KUNTI   I am crying for Krishna.

ARJUNA   You are crying for Krishna? Let me go and bring him here. He is all affection for you. He is all love for you and for all of us. Let me go and bring him. You don't have to cry for him. He will come. I will be able to bring him immediately.

KUNTI   No, I don't want you to go and bring him here.

ARJUNA   Then why are you crying for him? Either let me go and bring him, or stop crying, Mother. One of the two you must do.

KUNTI   Arjuna, people cry for name and fame; people cry for success and happiness. I cry only for one thing, only for one person, and that is my Krishna. I cry to him for one special thing. That is to keep me in constant suffering. When I have outer satisfaction, outer prosperity, I do not need Krishna and I forget him. And when I forget him, my life becomes unbearable. This morning I was praying to him, and I did not feel his presence inside my heart. A day I don't feel his presence inside my heart is a day of tremendous suffering. A day I don't feel his presence, I feel miserable; I feel that my real life has ended. That is why I am crying, Arjuna.

ARJUNA Mother, what kind of philosophy do you have? You don't have to suffer in order to feel Krishna's presence. His presence we can always feel. We don't have to be in sorrow in order to feel him. He is all joy, all love. Why do you cry for sorrow, Mother?

KUNTI Arjuna, your philosophy is different from mine. My philosophy wants constant suffering, constant sorrow. It is through constant suffering that I feel his presence. When I can feel Krishna in my heart, then I am happy. You are dear to me, just because I feel Krishna's presence inside your heart. All my children make me happy just because I feel Krishna's presence inside them. My real life is only to see and feel Krishna within me and around me. And in order to do that I need constant sorrow, constant suffering. *(Pauses.)* O Arjuna, my son, you stay with your philosophy. You remain with joy, continuous joy. You realise the Truth in your own way. I want to see, feel and become inseparably one with my Krishna, the eternal Life of the infinite Universe, in my own way.

(Kunti sings.)

THE SINGER OF THE ETERNAL BEYOND

*Dureo tumi kachheo tumi tabu bhabi dure
tripti je tai paina kabhu gahan hiya pure
basana mor purna hauk e nahe mor chaowa
tomar paye sanpi jena amar sakal paowa*

(You are afar, You are near.
Yet I think that You are always far, far away.
Therefore I get no satisfaction in the inmost re-
    cesses of my heart.
My wish is not to let my desire be fulfilled; that is
    not my wish.
My wish is to offer at Your Feet all desires con-
    ceived and achieved.)

KRISHNA, I NEED YOU ONLY

SRI CHINMOY

SI 9. DRAMATIS PERSONÆ

DURYODHANA (ELDEST OF THE KAURAVAS)
ARJUNA
KRISHNA

THE SINGER OF THE ETERNAL BEYOND

SI 10. SCENE 1

(The eve of the battle of Kurukshetra. Duryodhana has come to Krishna's abode. Krishna is fast asleep. Duryodhana enters Krishna's room and sits by Krishna's head on a chair. Soon Arjuna comes in and sits at Krishna's feet. Both of them are waiting for Krishna to wake up. Arjuna is looking at Krishna's feet most devotedly and soulfully. Duryodhana is looking at Krishna with tremendous confidence and assurance.)

DURYODHANA   *(to Arjuna)* Look at this Krishna! Why is he sleeping so much during the day? Has he not read the *shastras*? It is a great sin to sleep during the day. What is he doing?

ARJUNA   *(to Krishna)* For the first time, Krishna, I am seeing your feet. They are so beautiful. They are so divine.

(Arjuna touches Krishna's feet, appreciating and admiring their beauty.)

DURYODHANA   Yes, that is what you should do and must do. You should touch his feet, kiss his feet. You are meant for his feet and I am meant for his head. I shall touch his head.

(He is about to touch Krishna's head when Krishna opens his eyes and sees Arjuna.)

KRISHNA   Ah, my Arjuna, what brings you here? You are my joy, you are my pride, you are my love. What can I do for you?

DURYODHANA   Krishna, I came before him. I came before him, so you have to pay attention to me first. You have to fulfil my desire first.

ARJUNA   Krishna, I have come also with a desire.

KRISHNA   If both of you have desires, I shall fulfil your desires.

DURYODHANA   But I came first. You must fulfil my desire first.

KRISHNA   True, you came first, Duryodhana, but I saw Arjuna first. I have to fulfil his desire first. After all, he is younger than you. The younger one gets the first chance, always.

DURYODHANA   All right, Arjuna, you beggar, ask Krishna to fulfil your desire.

KRISHNA   Duryodhana, let us not quarrel here. This is my house. Both of you came here to have your desires fulfilled. I shall fulfil them. But here there should be no quarrel, no fight, no dispute. My place is all peace, love and harmony. Both of you are dear to me, and I assure you both that I shall fulfil your desires.

ARJUNA   O Krishna, you know that the battle is imminent. I want you to take my side.

DURYODHANA   Stop, Arjuna! I want Krishna on *my* side. *I* want him!

KRISHNA   If both of you want me, I have to choose one side. But I want to please both of you. Here is my suggestion: I shall be on one side, and my soldiers and warriors all will be on the other side. Now you make a choice. Arjuna has to make the first choice because I saw him first.

ARJUNA   O Krishna, I want you, I want you. I do not need your army. I want you only.

DURYODHANA   Krishna, are you sure? Will you keep your promise? You will be on one side and your army, your entire army, will be on the other?

KRISHNA   Duryodhana, my promise is my promise. Rest assured, I shall never break my promise. You take my entire army, and I will be on Arjuna's side.

ARJUNA   *(shedding tears of joy and gratitude)* O Krishna, you are so kind. To have you is to achieve victory. For me to have you is my supreme joy, supreme glory and supreme pride. O Krishna, you are so kind to me. My joy, my life is all gratitude to you.

DURYODHANA   I thank you deeply for your army. Your army is your real strength. Let Arjuna have your body's strength. I will have the strength of your entire army. But keep your promise. Keep your promise, O Krishna. All of your army must be on my side.

KRISHNA   O Duryodhana, I shall tell you something more. I shall not fight. I shall only give whatever help Arjuna asks of me.

ARJUNA   I want you to be my charioteer, O Krishna. Since you have taken my side, please be my charioteer.

KRISHNA   Of course, I will be your charioteer, Arjuna. But I shall not fight.

ARJUNA   No, you do not have to fight. Only be my charioteer.

DURYODHANA   *(overjoyed)* Krishna, so you will be Arjuna's charioteer! You cannot fight and you cannot have your army with you. This is your promise.

KRISHNA   Yes, this is my promise. You take my army with you and I shall be Arjuna's charioteer.

DURYODHANA   Tomorrow I shall come and take your army. Don't forget your promise, Krishna.

KRISHNA   Never.

(Exit Duryodhana.)

ARJUNA   I know that the creator is always infinitely greater than the creation. You are the creator of your army. Duryodhana has the creation, but I have the creator. I know, Krishna, that you are All. Your very presence is infinite strength for me. Your very presence is my victory.

(Arjuna sings.)

Ogo sundara ogo ananda
ogo mor prananath sasime asime peyechhi tomar
chetanar sakkhat rupantarer alor banshari
bajabo hriday bane
hasiya nachiya harabo
amare rakhal rajar dhane

(O my beautiful One, O my Lord of Delight,
O Lord of my life-breath,
In the finite and the Infinite I have met Your universal consciousness.
I shall play on the flute of transformation-light in the forest of my heart.
Smiling and dancing I shall lose myself in the wealth of Lord Krishna.)

(Krishna gives him a most soulful smile.)

KRISHNA   O Arjuna, you do not know how dear you are to my heart. Come, let us go.

KRISHNA AND ARJUNA

SRI CHINMOY

SI II. DRAMATIS PERSONÆ

KRISHNA
ARJUNA

THE SINGER OF THE ETERNAL BEYOND

SI 12. SCENE I

(Krishna and Arjuna on the battlefield.)

ARJUNA   Krishna, I have to fight now. I have to conquer my enemies. But Krishna, now that I am in the battlefield, I am nervous. You know I have never suffered from nervousness before.

(Arjuna sings.)

*Sidanti mama gatrani
mukham ca parisusyati
vepathus ca sarire me
romaharsas ca jayate*

(My limbs give way and my mouth is parched, my body quivers, and my hair stands on end.)

KRISHNA   Arjuna, you must never be nervous. This kind of thing I do not expect from you. You are a great hero, Arjuna. You must not be nervous.
ARJUNA   Krishna, please tell me what you actually want from my life. What do you expect from my life? Please tell me. What do you want from me? I am all yours.
KRISHNA   Do not be nervous. I have told you that you are the hero of heroes, the supreme hero. You have to fight. Fight for the right cause. I shall tell you all about the inner life, the spiritual life, the life of perfection, inner and outer. First I shall teach you the life of realisation and revelation. Then I shall teach you the life of perfection.

ARJUNA Krishna, you came into the world with a special purpose, I know. But please tell me, what is that purpose? I want to know from you.

(Krishna sings.)

Yada-hada hi dharmasya
glanir bhavati bharata
abhyutthanam adharmasya
tada 'tmanam srjamy aham
paritranaya sadhunam
vinasaya ca duskrtam
dharmasamsthapanarthaya
sambhavami yuge-yuge

(O Arjuna, whenever righteousness declines and unrighteouness prevails, Myself I embody and manifest. For the protection of the good and for the destruction of the wicked, and for the establishment of the inner code of life, I come into being from age to age.)

KRISHNA, I SEE DEATH-FORCES ALL AROUND ME

SRI CHINMOY

SI 13. DRAMATIS PERSONÆ

KRISHNA
ARJUNA

THE SINGER OF THE ETERNAL BEYOND

SI 14. SCENE 1

(Krishna and Arjuna on the battlefield.)

ARJUNA   Krishna, the battle is about to start. Alas, I see death-forces all around me.
KRISHNA   Stop, Arjuna. Your heart has always been a perfect stranger to fear.

(Krishna sings.)

Klaibyam ma sma gamah....

(Yield not to feebleness.)

ARJUNA   My Lord, please tell me something about death.
KRISHNA   Arjuna, this is a divine battle, so be not afraid of killing others, nor of being killed yourself. Here is my teaching with regard to death.

(Krishna sings.)

Vasamsi jirnani yatha vihaya
navani grhnati naro 'parani
tatha sarirani vihaya jirnany
anyani samyati navani dehi

(As a man casts off his worn-out garments and puts on new ones, so also the embodied soul casts off the worn-out body and enters into a new form for manifestation.)

ARJUNA   Is there anything that is not killed?
KRISHNA   Yes, Arjuna, the soul is not killed. The soul cannot be killed.

(Krishna sings.)

*Nai 'nam chindanti sastrani
nai 'nam dahati pavakah
na cai 'nam kledayanty apo
na sosayati marutah*

(Weapons cannot cleave the soul.
Fire cannot burn the soul.
Water cannot drench the soul.
Wind cannot dry the soul.)

Nimitta matram bhava savyasachin

(O Arjuna, become a mere instrument.)

ARJUNA   O Krishna, fear of death is gone. I shall be afraid neither of killing others nor of being killed by others. Fight I must, and conquer the forces undivine.

THE UNIVERSAL FORM

SRI CHINMOY

SI 15. DRAMATIS PERSONÆ

KRISHNA
ARJUNA

THE SINGER OF THE ETERNAL BEYOND

SI 16. SCENE I

(Krishna and Arjuna.)

ARJUNA   Krishna, I have a supreme desire.
KRISHNA   No true desire of yours will remain unfulfilled, Arjuna. Let me know what you want.
ARJUNA   My heart cries to see the Universal Form of God in you.
KRISHNA   Is that all. Behold!

(Arjuna, wonderstruck, sings.)

Pasyami devams tava deva dehe
Sarvams tatha bhutavisesasamghan
Brahmanam isam kamalasanastham
Rsims ca sarvan uragams ca divyan

(In Your Body, O Krishna, I see all the cosmic gods and numerous hosts of beings. I see Lord Brahma seated on his lotus throne and all the sages and celestial *nagas* [snakes].)

Tvam adidevah purusah puranas
tvam asya visvasya param nidhanam
vetta 'si vedyam ca param ca dhama
tvaya tatam visvam anantarupa
vayur yamo 'gnir varunah sasankah
prajapatis tvam prapitamahas ca
namo namas te 'stu sahasrakrtvah
punas ca bhuyo 'pi namo namas te

(You are the Primal God.
You are the Ancient Purusha.
You are the Supreme Haven of the Universe.
You are the Knower.
You are the Knowable.
You are the Supreme Abode.
By You pervaded is the entire Universe, O Being of infinite Forms.
You are Vayu, the wind god.
You are Yama, the cosmic destroyer.
You are Agni, the fire god.
You are Varuna, the sea god.
You are Shashanka, the moon god.
You are Prajapati, the grandsire of the Creation.
To You I offer my salutations, To You I offer.
A thousand times, and again and again, My salutations to You.)

KRISHNA, MY EXISTENCE
IS AT YOUR DISPOSAL

SRI CHINMOY

SI 17. DRAMATIS PERSONÆ

KRISHNA
ARJUNA

THE SINGER OF THE ETERNAL BEYOND

SI 18. SCENE I

(Krishna and Arjuna are together.)

ARJUNA   Krishna, on different occasions I have asked you for advice. Every time your advice has strengthened my heart and fulfilled my purpose. But today I am not in any specific difficulty. Today is the day for me to ask you what your supreme advice is.

(Krishna sings.)

Manmana bhava madbhakto
madyaji mam namaskuru....

(Oneness with My mind establish.
Devote your life to Me.
Sacrifice your breath to Me.
Before Me prostrate.)

Sarvadharman parityajya
mam ekam saranam vraja
aham tva sarvapapebhyo
moksayisyami ma sucah

(All duties give up.
In Me alone take refuge.
From all sins you I shall liberate.
Grieve not.)

ARJUNA   Krishna, my Lord....

SRI CHINMOY

(Arjuna sings.)

*Nasto mohah smrtir labdha
tvatprasadan maya 'cyuta
sthito 'smi gatasamdehah
karisye vacanam tava*

(My delusion is now destroyed for good. Through your boundless Grace and Compassion I have recognised the Truth. All my doubts are dispelled. To your Will I surrender my life unconditionally. My existence is totally at your disposal.)

KRISHNA Arjuna, you are dear to me in my role. You are dearer to me in my soul. You are dearest to me in my Goal. In you is my supreme Realisation. With you is my supreme Manifestation.

ASK VISHMA, O ARJUNA

SRI CHINMOY

SI 19. DRAMATIS PERSONÆ

VISHMA (GRANDSIRE OF THE PANDAVAS AND THE KAURAVAS)
KRISHNA
ARJUNA

THE SINGER OF THE ETERNAL BEYOND

SI 20. SCENE I

(Vishma is lying down on a bed of arrows made by Arjuna. Arjuna and Krishna have come to pay him their last respects. Vishma suddenly bursts into tears.)

ARJUNA Krishna, Krishna, please tell me why my grandfather is shedding tears? He has read and studied the Vedas. He has read and studied all our Indian scriptures. He knows perfectly well that death is not the end. Why, then, is he afraid of death? It was he who told us how to kill him, despite the fact that he was our adversary in this war. Who else on earth would tell his opponents how to kill him? He has shown the world the zenith of the heart's nobility and magnanimity. His soul is the height of sacrifice. O Krishna, is there anything on earth that you do not know? Tell me, O Krishna, what can I do for him? I will do anything for my grandfather. We lost our father when we were quite young. Vishma replaced our father with his constant love and concern. His sacrifice for us was unparalleled. Now, Krishna, do tell me why he is crying and weeping.

KRISHNA I do not know, Arjuna. You can ask him. He will tell you.

ARJUNA Grandfather, please tell me why you are weeping. What can I do for you?

VISHMA My child, I am weeping not because I am afraid of death. I am shedding bitter tears for one simple reason: because your Pandava family has suffered so much. The Kauravas have been torturing you right from the beginning. Krishna is the Lord of the Universe, yet your suffering has no end. I do not know how it is that you have suffered so much when Krishna has been with you all the time. How is it possible for him to observe your suffering? His heart is all love and concern for you. I do not understand his game; that is why I am shedding tears.

KRISHNA *(smiling)* O Vishma, O man of wisdom, my mystery is unfathomable. You know that my heart has been suffering with Arjuna's family. My soul is one with them. Both my divine existence and my human existence are one with them.

VISHMA O Lord, you are dearer to me than my life itself. You made a solemn promise that you would not take weapons, that you would not fight, yet twice you left your chariot to kill me. On the third day and on the ninth day of the battle, you came out of your chariot to kill me. I was so filled with joy, for it was by you, my Lord, that I wanted to be killed. To die in your presence, to be killed by your weapons, means to go to Heaven immediately. Nothing can be more glorious than to be killed by the Lord Himself. O Krishna, when you came out of the chariot to kill me, I wanted to embrace you in the battlefield, but Arjuna pulled you back into the chariot. Arjuna, you have done me a terrible disservice.

ARJUNA I wanted Krishna to keep his promise, Grandfather. He promised he would not fight, that he would only be my charioteer.

VISHMA *(to Krishna)* I know, Krishna, that you are now with me. The end of my life is fast approaching. You have many times blessed me, O Krishna, with your divine presence. But this time please bless me in a different way: place your ever-compassionate hands on my head, and let this blessing of yours carry me into the highest plane of Peace.

(Krishna blesses Vishma. Vishma sings.)

THE SINGER OF THE ETERNAL BEYOND

Shanti shanti hridaye shanti
Parane shanti raje
Chira manohar kanur banshari
Dyuloke bhuloke baje
Ghor danaber hingshar chhaya
Andhar nishar agyana-maya
Hariye phelechhi amar e tanu
Mana prana antare
Akuti amar taba kripa nire
Nirabadhi santare

(Peace, Peace,
Peace within my heart reigns supreme.
The soul-stirring flute of Lord Krishna
Is being played in my Heaven
And on my earth.
The destruction-shadows of dark demons
And the ignorance-delusion of sombre night
Lie long-buried in the depths of my body, mind,
    heart and life.
My aspiration-flames ever swim across the expanse
    of Your Compassion-waters.)

KRISHNA   Vishma, the world knows about your supreme promises and supreme sacrifices. To fulfil your father's desire you did not marry, you did not take the throne. The Kauravas supported you. Morality-bound, you fought for them. The human in you fought with the human, the undivine. The divine in you fought with the divine for the divine. The human in you fought against the Pandavas. The divine in you told the Pandavas how to kill you. Arjuna has listened to your advice, and now you are dying. Your life is now a matter of a few hours. I offer to you all my heart's boundless

Love, Peace and Bliss. Here on earth you are immortal, and there in Heaven you are immortal. Your promise is the pride of Mother Earth and your sacrifice is the pride of Father Heaven.

UTANKA

SRI CHINMOY

SI 21. DRAMATIS PERSONÆ

UTANKA (A SAGE)
KRISHNA
CHANDALA [UNDERTAKER]

THE SINGER OF THE ETERNAL BEYOND

SI 22. SCENE I

(Utanka's ashram. Utanka is meditating. Enter Krishna.)

UTANKA   Krishna, Krishna, you have come. I am so happy, so delighted, so grateful. Give me some news.

KRISHNA   News? Have you not heard about the Kurukshetra battle?

UTANKA   No, I have been praying and meditating here all the time. I have heard no news. I do not know anything about the Kurukshetra battle. What happened? Tell me, Krishna, tell me.

KRISHNA   Oh, it's a long story.

UTANKA   But tell me what has happened.

KRISHNA   Utanka, all one hundred brothers of Duryodhana were killed on the battlefield.

UTANKA   Duryodhana's brothers killed? What had they done?

KRISHNA   You know that they were very unspiritual, very undivine. You know how they tortured the Pandava family and me all the time. You know that.

UTANKA   I know, I know, but that doesn't mean that they had to be killed. Who has killed them?

KRISHNA   The Pandavas, with the help of their friends.

UTANKA   I can't understand this. Tell me, were you there?

KRISHNA   Yes, I was there. I was Arjuna's charioteer. I did not fight.

UTANKA   You did not fight, but your very presence was a great help to them. You gave them inspiration and strength. Krishna, I shall curse you. You are responsible for ruining such a big family. I am sure that many, many, many people were killed.

KRISHNA True, many people were killed and Yudhishthira is now the King of Hastinapura. He is a very pious King. You know he and sincerity go together, he and purity go together, he and all virtues go together.

UTANKA I don't deny it. He will make a good King. But so many people were killed, so many people from the Kaurava family were destroyed. You have just seen it. What kind of news are you giving me, Krishna?

KRISHNA I tried my best. I went there personally to avert the war, but the Kaurava princes wouldn't listen to me. They mocked me. They insulted me.

UTANKA Now, I see. That is the reason you entered into this battle, because they insulted and mocked you. Why didn't you tell me that that was the reason?

KRISHNA No, that is not true. It was not because they insulted and mocked me, but because I saw that the time had come for them to be destroyed. In every way I tried to prevent the battle, avert the war. I asked that they give the Pandavas only five villages, but they wouldn't do it. So it was the Will of God that they be destroyed.

UTANKA Will of God! Will of God! It was the will of Krishna the rogue! *(All of a sudden.)* Wait, Krishna, wait!

KRISHNA What is wrong?

UTANKA I hear a message from within. Allow me to concentrate on it. *(He concentrates.)* Ah, Krishna. I shall not curse you, but you have to fulfil my desire.

KRISHNA Let me know what your desire is.

UTANKA My inner voice says that you showed your Universal Form to Arjuna before the Kurukshetra battle. Is it true? Is it true? I have been longing to see the Universal Form in you for such a long time, Krishna. Krishna, I shall not curse you. Please, please show me your Universal Form.

KRISHNA Oh, Utanka, all right. I do not want to be cursed by you. I shall show you my Universal Form.

(Krishna shows his Universal Form. Utanka touches Krishna's feet.)

UTANKA O Krishna, I have seen in you an infinite sky; hundreds of suns, stars, planets; all the creatures and human beings. They are all taking birth, living and dying within you, under your supreme guidance. Inside you all the universal forces are functioning. O Krishna, forgive me! Forgive me, O Lord of my existence, O Lord of the world.

KRISHNA I have forgiven you, Utanka. I did not want to be cursed by you. That is why I have fulfilled your desire. Now, do you have any more desires to be fulfilled?

UTANKA O Krishna, after seeing your Universal Form, can there be any other desire?

KRISHNA Think it over. I have much to do at home. Is there anything else you want before I leave?

UTANKA O Krishna, since you are all-powerful, all-loving, please give me one boon.

KRISHNA What kind of boon do you want, Utanka?

UTANKA This place is a dry desert. There is no water here at all. I wish to have water. Please supply me with water, O Krishna.

KRISHNA That is very easy. Whenever you want to have water, just think of me and water will be supplied.

(Utanka, with deepest gratitude, touches Krishna's feet. Exit Krishna.)

SI 23. SCENE II

(Utanka is very thirsty, and there is no pure water in the house. He invokes Krishna.)

UTANKA   O Krishna, fulfil your promise. I need water, pure water. Let me see if you come, or how the water will come.

(Immediately, a Chandala [undertaker] comes forward with a glass of water and offers it to Utanka.)

UTANKA   You untouchable! How dare you come to me with water! True, I am thirsty, but I will never take water from an untouchable. Get away from here! I don't need you. I will die of thirst before I drink anything that you have touched.

(Exit Chandala.)

UTANKA   O Krishna! You rogue! True, I wanted water. I am practically dying of thirst, but did you have to send an undertaker, an untouchable, with my water? This is how you insult me. I don't need that kind of water. Either bring me the water yourself, or I don't need any water from you. I shall manage my life as I did before you gave me that boon, you rogue. *(Enter Krishna.)* Krishna, you didn't keep your promise. You didn't give me water, at least not pure water that I could drink.

KRISHNA   Water! I sent Indra himself to you, not with water, but with divine nectar.

UTANKA   Indra?

KRISHNA   Yes, in the garb of a Chandala. He wanted to test you, to see whether you have conquered the feeling of superiority and inferiority, purity and impurity, whether you have gone beyond that after having seen my Universal Form.

UTANKA You know, Krishna, that I am a Brahmin. I thought that he was a Chandala. He came in that garb. How can I drink water from a Chandala? Why did he deceive me?

KRISHNA He did not deceive you, Utanka. He came to see whether you had really gone beyond caste. Brahmin, Kshatriya, Vaishya, Shudra and Chandala all go together. They are all in the Heart of God, in the Heart of the Supreme.

UTANKA O Krishna, forgive me. Now it is too late. What am I going to do? What can I do?

KRISHNA Utanka, I have forgiven you. From now on whenever you are in need of water, you will be supplied with water in another way. You invoke me and with my occult power, I shall form clouds in the sky and cause rain. Then you will have no dearth of water. This plot of land will always have enough water. And the clouds that form in the sky will be called *Utanka megh* from now on. In the future, those who stay in this land, when they see these rain clouds, will call them *Utanka*.

UTANKA Krishna, you are all forgiveness. You are a constant miracle. You are constant joy. You are constant fulfilment. This ungrateful heart of mine is at your compassionate feet.

NOT HOW MANY HOURS YOU MEDITATE,
BUT HOW YOU MEDITATE

SRI CHINMOY

SI 24. DRAMATIS PERSONÆ

KRISHNA
ARJUNA
CARTMAN

THE SINGER OF THE ETERNAL BEYOND

SI 25. SCENE I

(Krishna and Arjuna are walking along the street. All of a sudden they see a man drawing a cart loaded with flowers.)

ARJUNA   Krishna, look! A man is drawing a cart loaded with all kinds of flowers. Are they not beautiful?
KRISHNA   Yes, they are really beautiful.
ARJUNA   *(to the cartman)* What are you doing with these flowers, my friend? Where are you going?

(The man pays no attention to Arjuna. He continues pulling the cart. Exit cartman.)

KRISHNA   Arjuna, let us follow him.
ARJUNA   That's a nice idea.

(Exeunt Krishna and Arjuna.)

SRI CHINMOY

SI 26. SCENE II

(The cartman has reached his destination. Enter Krishna and Arjuna.)

ARJUNA What are you going to do with all these flowers? It seems to me that you have already brought a few cartloads of flowers here. What a huge pile of flowers I see! What are you doing with so many flowers?

MAN I have no time to speak to you. I am now employed in serious business. I can speak only to one person on earth, and that is Bhima, the second Pandava.

ARJUNA Why?

MAN Don't argue with me. He is the greatest spiritual seeker of all. When he meditates just for a minute or two before his meals, saying, "O Mighty Lord Shiva," he offers thousands of flowers to the Lord. His concentration is most intense; his meditation is most sincere. Look, in his family he has a brother named Arjuna, who only offers one flower at a time to Lord Shiva. He just shows off, meditating for hours. God alone knows when Arjuna will come to realise that his meditation, his power of concentration, is nowhere near his brother Bhima's.

ARJUNA Krishna, enough humiliation! You are humiliating me in every way! Why do you humiliate me so badly?

KRISHNA This is not humiliation, my dearest Arjuna. This is illumination. I am teaching the world through you. I wanted to teach you that it is not how many flowers you offer or how many hours you meditate that counts, but rather your power of concentration, your power of dedication. You pray to this god and that god. You want to please all the gods. You collect many flowers and offer them to Lord Shiva one by one, for two hours every day. Each time, while offering

THE SINGER OF THE ETERNAL BEYOND

a flower, you utter the name of Lord Shiva. You think that, since you offer many flowers to Lord Shiva and the other gods for so many hours, you are the best seeker. This is your pride, O Arjuna. It was my boundless love and compassion for you that wanted to shatter your pride. O Arjuna, again and again I tell you, you are my dearest disciple, my dearest friend. You have established your eternal oneness with me.

(Arjuna sings.)

Ami tomar phul tumi amar kul
ami tomar dhenu tumi amar benu
ami tomar gan tumi amar pran
ami tomar khama tumi amar rama

(I am Your flower,
        You are my Golden Shore.
I am Your divine cow,
        You are my Flute, Divine Flute.
I am Your song, celestial song,
        You are my Life, Eternal Life.
I am Your forgiveness,
        You are my Beauty, Inner Beauty.)

THESE ARE MY PSYCHIC TEARS

SRI CHINMOY

SI 27. DRAMATIS PERSONÆ

A SCHOLAR
A BRAHMIN

THE SINGER OF THE ETERNAL BEYOND

SI 28. SCENE I

(A scholar is walking along the street. He sees a Brahmin holding a copy of the Bhagavad-Gita and weeping.)

SCHOLAR   O Brahmin, your eyes are swimming in a sea of tears. My heart is all sympathy for you. I clearly see that you have been unable to understand the teachings of the Gita. But I shall gladly help you. Tell me, where do you find it difficult? Which particular *shloka* don't you understand? I shall explain it to you.

BRAHMIN   There is a special reason why I am weeping.

SCHOLAR   Yes, I am sure you have a special reason. Why don't you be frank with me? Tell me straight away which particular shloka you find difficult to understand.

BRAHMIN   You will not understand me. You will not believe me.

SCHOLAR   I *will* understand you. I *will* believe you. Tell me why you are weeping. I have not much time, for I am now on my way to my school, where my students are waiting for me. Please don't waste my time. Please tell me.

(Brahmin sings.)

I am a fool, they say.
Am I, am I a fool?
I go to my inner School;
God's Eye my eternal Day.
To help my Lord in His Play,
To found His Smile on earth,
My divinely human birth.
Yet I am a fool, they say.

BRAHMIN I am weeping, I am weeping because....
SCHOLAR Please don't waste my time. Don't weep, don't weep. Just let me know what you can't understand and I shall immediately help you.
BRAHMIN I am weeping because I see the Lord Krishna right in front of me. No matter which page I turn to, I see Arjuna's charioteer, Krishna. These are my psychic tears. I see my Lord in all the pages. I see Sri Krishna in His chariot. That is why I am shedding tears. It is not that I do not understand the teachings of the Gita.

(The scholar bows to the Brahmin.)

SCHOLAR I have studied the Gita hundreds of times. I have taught thousands of people the Gita, but none of them have said that they have seen Lord Krishna. They haven't seen even a spark of Sri Krishna's light. I have personally talked and talked about the Gita. I have taught and taught the Gita, but I have never seen Sri Krishna on the pages, or before my eyes in a mental vision. I have never felt his presence deep in my heart. *(Pauses.)* O Brahmin, forgive my arrogance, forgive my impertinence. Today I am not going to school to teach. Today is the end of my teaching career. Today begins my life of aspiration, my life of the inner cry. From now on I shall only pray to Krishna instead of explaining Him. Instead of speaking about Him I shall meditate on Him, and like you, I am sure, one day I will be able to see Krishna, my beloved Lord. My life of outer teaching now ends, and my life of inner searching begins.

TWO DIVINE LIARS: ARE THEY REALLY SO?

SRI CHINMOY

SI 29. DRAMATIS PERSONÆ

KRISHNA
SATYAVAMA (HIS WIFE)
DURVASHA (A GREAT SAGE VERY DEVOTED TO KRISHNA)

THE SINGER OF THE ETERNAL BEYOND

SI 30. SCENE I

(Krishna's palace. Krishna and Satyavama are together.)

SATYAVAMA   How is it that people think you are full of compassion? I see that you have no compassion at all. Look at your greatest devotee. He is repeating your name so devotedly and so soulfully! But you do not care for him. All he eats is a blade of grass now and then, because there is nobody to feed him.

KRISHNA   What do you want me to do?

SATYAVAMA   Why don't you ask someone to look after him? You have so many admirers and devotees. Why don't you ask someone to bring food to Durvasha every day, so that he can continue his meditating and still have proper food to eat.

KRISHNA   He does not need that kind of food.

SATYAVAMA   *(becoming angry)* He does need it, but you don't supply it.

KRISHNA   No, no. His food is different, entirely different.

SATYAVAMA   I am sure that if I take him some proper food, delicious food, right now, he will eat voraciously.

KRISHNA   Well, perhaps you are right. You can try it. Go to him on the other side of the Jamuna, and then come back and tell me what he says about the food.

SRI CHINMOY

SI 31. SCENE II

(Satyavama, having prepared a most delicious meal, goes to the River Jamuna, and tries to cross it. The Jamuna is a tiny river that is usually knee deep, but when there is a flood or a storm, it has to be crossed in a ferryboat. Satyavama sees that the water is raging like the surges of the sea. The boatman refuses to take her across because of the danger. Satyavama, depressed and angry, returns to the palace.)

SATYAVAMA Krishna, I went to cross the river to take food to your dearest disciple, but the river was hostile to me. Do something!

KRISHNA All right. Go and say this to the river: "If my Lord Krishna has not seen the face of any woman other than me, then calm down."

SATYAVAMA How can I say this? I know how many women friends you have. I cannot say to Jamuna that you have never seen the face of any woman but me. It is all lies! Jamuna will never calm down. You have seen the faces of millions of women. To say that you have only seen my face is ridiculous!

KRISHNA Go. Go and say what I have told you to Jamuna and see what happens.

SI 32. SCENE III

(Satyavama stands at the edge of the raging river.)

SATYAVAMA   O Jamuna, if my Lord Krishna has not seen the face of any woman but me, then please calm down so that I may cross.

(The river subsides and she crosses.)

SATYAVAMA   *(thinking aloud)* I am sure the Jamuna has allowed me to cross just to please Krishna.

(She comes to the place where Durvasha is meditating. He is in a high trance, but slowly opens his eyes when she approaches him.)

SATYAVAMA   O Durvasha, I have observed that for many weeks now you have been repeating my Lord's name with deepest devotion, and you have taken almost no food. Today, I have brought you food which I myself have prepared for you.

DURVASHA   *(still in a meditative mood, touches the feet of Satyavama)* Mother, your compassion is food enough for me. Yet I am supremely grateful that you have thought of me and brought me food.

(Satyavama has to feed Durvasha herself as he is still in a trance-like state. When he has finished the food, Durvasha bows and touches Satyavama's feet.)

SATYAVAMA   Now I am going home. I am happy that you are pleased with my meal.

(Exit Satyavama. Durvasha resumes his deep meditation, and a little later Satyavama returns.)

SATYAVAMA   O Durvasha, please do something for me. There is no boatman at the river and my Lord is on the other side. I cannot cross because of the storm. While I was coming here it was also stormy, but my Lord made the river subside. But now my Lord is not here. Please tell me what I should do.

DURVASHA   This is very easy, Mother. I will tell you. Go and say this to the river: "If Durvasha has not eaten anything but a few blades of grass for many years, then you must calm down, O Jamuna."

SATYAVAMA   You fool! You liar! I have just fed you a most delicious meal with my own hands, and now you are asking me to say this!

DURVASHA   Mother, please tell the river what I have told you. I will come with you.

(Exeunt Durvasha and Satyavama.)

SI 33. SCENE IV

(Satyavama and Durvasha at the river.)

SATYAVAMA *(sarcastically, to the river)* If Durvasha hasn't taken anything to eat for several years except a few blades of grass, then please, Jamuna, calm down. *(The waters subside. Satyavama is surprised and angry.)* Durvasha, your Lord is a liar and you are a liar! I am caught between two liars. But at least I am able to go home.

(Exit Satyavama.)

SI 34. SCENE V

(Krishna's palace.)

SATYAVAMA   Krishna, you are a liar and you have taught your dearest disciple also how to tell lies.

KRISHNA   What lies have we told?

SATYAVAMA   You said that you have never looked at any woman's face in your life except mine. How can it be? Millions of women you have seen. We have so many relatives, including your own mother, your sister and many others around us. So how can you say that you have not seen any other woman's face?

KRISHNA   Satyavama, you do not understand my spiritual knowledge. You are my dearest. You and I are one. When I look at any woman, immediately I see your face in that person. All women to me are represented by you. When I look at any woman's face, physically it is different, but according to my inner wisdom, inner light, I see that it is you who are that particular person. You are the Divine Mother and I am the Divine Father. So I see my female part, you, inside everyone. How, then, can I say that I am seeing somebody else? It is you I see in different forms, in different shapes.

SATYAVAMA   *(satisfied)* I see. You are dealing with your universal consciousness. You are the Lord and I am your divine *Shakti*. But what about this liar Durvasha? He is your devotee. I fed him a delicious meal with my own hands. And immediately afterwards he said that he had not eaten anything but a few blades of grass for several years!

KRISHNA   Dearest Satyavama, all the while you were feeding him, Durvasha was in trance. He always remains in trance.

And in trance what he eats is delight, ecstasy. That is his only food. He has practically lost all outer consciousness. On rare occasions he comes down to the earth-consciousness. Most of the time he is in his highest transcendental Consciousness, where he is communing with me. I feed him Peace, Light and Bliss. When he told you that he had taken only blades of grass, he was speaking the truth. He ate your food, true, but he didn't get any taste from the food you gave him. He was only drinking my divine nectar all the time. Before he entered into this rigorous discipline, this austere life, he decided that he would eat only blades of grass after beginning serious meditation. That particular idea is still in his mind, and he still thinks that he is eating only grass and nothing else, for he is not aware of outer things, earthly things. He has lost the consciousness of the outer world. So if you give him delicious earthly food, he gets no more taste from your meal than he gets from grass. That is why he could say that he had not eaten anything other than a few blades of grass for many years.

SATYAVAMA You have convinced me, my Lord. I am most grateful to you. I withdraw my charges.

(Krishna smiles.)

HER COW MUST DIE TOMORROW

SRI CHINMOY

SI 35. DRAMATIS PERSONÆ

KRISHNA
ARJUNA
A WOMAN (VERY DEVOTED TO KRISHNA)

THE SINGER OF THE ETERNAL BEYOND

SI 36. SCENE I

(Evening. Krishna and Arjuna are walking along the street. It is quite dark. A woman sees them.)

WOMAN   It seems to me that both of you are lost in the dark, and that both of you need a place to stay tonight. I shall be happy to have you as my guests tonight.
ARJUNA   That is a splendid idea.
KRISHNA   Let us stay at her place.
WOMAN   I shall be happy to have you as my divine guests.

(Exeunt omnes.)

SRI CHINMOY

SI 37. SCENE II

(The woman's home. Enter all three.)

ARJUNA   How many children do you have?
WOMAN   Oh, I have no children.
ARJUNA   What does your husband do?
WOMAN   I have no husband. My husband died long ago. I am all alone.
ARJUNA   Then how do you support yourself? I am sorry that we have come here to burden you.
WOMAN   Oh no, no. Do not feel sorry. I am quite rich. My Lord Krishna supports me. I have a cow. The cow gives milk, and I sell the milk and thus maintain my life on earth. So, I am very glad to receive both of you. Let me feed you with what little I have.

(She brings food and offers it to them. Arjuna and Krishna eat happily.)

KRISHNA   Most delicious food!
WOMAN   All thanks to Lord Krishna. He is my Lord; he is my all, my Lord Krishna. I feel that both of you are very nice and spiritual. Whom do you pray to?
ARJUNA   We also pray to Krishna. He is very great.
WOMAN   I am so happy that two devotees of Krishna have come here. I am so happy and proud that we three are together.

THE SINGER OF THE ETERNAL BEYOND

SI 38. SCENE III

(The following morning Krishna and Arjuna are leaving.)

KRISHNA   I am very grateful to you for your generosity.
ARJUNA   I am also grateful for your generosity.
KRISHNA   May Krishna bless you. May Krishna guide you.
ARJUNA   May Krishna protect you, and may you get a vision of Krishna.

(Exeunt Krishna and Arjuna.)

SRI CHINMOY

SI 39. SCENE IV

(Krishna and Arjuna are walking together.)

ARJUNA O Krishna, this woman is so poor. Why don't you do something for her? I could not tell her you were Krishna because I did not have your permission. But you can see, Krishna, how she suffers. She has nobody on earth. Her only means of support is her cow. She has only the cow and nothing else on earth. How can she live, Krishna? Please give her something. Give her a boon, I beg of you. Grant her a boon so that she can lead a better life.

KRISHNA I have already granted her a very big boon.

ARJUNA What is your boon?

KRISHNA The boon is that her cow will die tomorrow.

ARJUNA Krishna, she fed us and this is your boon? What! This kind of boon you give! Are you so ungrateful, so cruel? She has no other means of support, and you want her cow to die! I can't understand you, Krishna. I can't understand you at all.

KRISHNA True, Arjuna, you do not understand Me. Now listen. She always thinks of the cow. The cow has to be fed; the cow has to be milked; the cow has to be bathed, and so forth. I want her to think only of Me, and when she has nobody on earth, not even the cow, she will think of Me all the time, devoting herself to Me twenty-four hours a day. If her cow were to remain alive, she would linger on earth and constantly think of the cow, and not of Me. She would not make as much progress. But since I am now taking her cow, soon the time will be right for Me to take her away from this world, and after a few years I will give her a better and more fulfilling incarnation.

THE SINGER OF THE ETERNAL BEYOND

ARJUNA   *(bowing)* O Krishna, you are right. You are always right. Your ways are inscrutable, but I see you are always right, perfectly right, once I understand you. You are always right, my Krishna.

THINK OF GOD:
HE WILL NOT ONLY THINK OF YOU, BUT HE
WILL THINK OF YOUR DEAR ONES AS WELL

SRI CHINMOY

SI 40. DRAMATIS PERSONÆ

A POOR BRAHMIN
HIS WIFE
SRI KRISHNA
MEN AND WOMEN SERVANTS
A SERVANT
A BYSTANDER

THE SINGER OF THE ETERNAL BEYOND

SI 41. SCENE I

(A Brahmin and his wife inside their cottage.)

WIFE   My Lord, you always speak of your friend, Krishna. If he really is your friend, how is it that you do not go to him and get some money to relieve our poverty? You happened to be a very close friend of his when you were both boys. Now he has become King of Dwaraka, a very opulent, powerful King ruling a vast territory. But your fate is otherwise. You are extremely honest, sincere, moral and spiritual, but you are extremely poor. Sri Krishna is so rich, and you always speak highly of him. Why don't you go to him for help?

BRAHMIN   I do not want to ruin our friendship now that I know Krishna is not an ordinary man. He is a King in the outer world, and he is also a King in the inner world. I think of him, meditate on him and pray to him. He gives me much joy, much inner treasure. Although I do not have a lot of money and I do not wallow in the pleasures of riches, inwardly I am very happy. If I take money from him, then perhaps our friendship will come to an end. That is why I do not want to go to him.

WIFE   No, you should go. He is not an ordinary man, and he is very generous. He will give you a large sum of money. And I assure you that he will maintain his same old friendship with you.

BRAHMIN   I really can't do it. *(Pauses.)* All right. Since you have been insisting on my going for a long time, I will go there. I will kill two birds with one stone. I will please you by listening to your request, and I will please myself by seeing my intimate childhood friend whom I haven't seen for a long time. I will go and see him, but not to ask for money. I will see him, my Lord Krishna, so I can be filled with inner joy. And at the same time, I will be fulfilling your request that I go to his palace. Give me some food. Krishna, if he is still the same old Krishna, may ask me for something home-made.

WIFE   I have a small quantity of popped rice that you can tie in the corner of your *dhoti*.

BRAHMIN   Thank you. I shall leave for his palace right now.

THE SINGER OF THE ETERNAL BEYOND

SI 42. SCENE II

(The Brahmin and Sri Krishna at Sri Krishna's palace.)

KRISHNA I am exceedingly glad to see you, my old friend. Please tell me about your present life.

BRAHMIN I am very happy, and my wife is very nice. And you, Krishna, you are a Lord now — an inner king and an outer king. Even so, you are showing me the utmost kindness, sympathy and friendship.

KRISHNA What have you brought from home? I am eager to eat something of yours.

BRAHMIN *(aside)* Krishna is the King here. He has hundreds of slaves, and his palace is most luxurious. All divine and earthly things are at his command. What can I do? I am too embarrassed to give him this small quantity of popped rice.

(Sri Krishna snatches away his popped rice and starts eating.)

KRISHNA Delicious, most delicious! For a long time I have not been blessed with this kind of food. I left Brindavan, and now I am King. Here I get food, but it doesn't have in it the real affection, the boundless affection, that is in this food you have brought from your wife. Now that I am in a city, I miss real affection, real concern.

BRAHMIN *(aside)* How I am enjoying Sri Krishna's presence! Divine Joy, divine Peace, divine Light is pouring forth from him, and I am drinking in his divine Nectar. I am so happy. Oh, now I am really pleased. I have fulfilled my desire, and my wife's desire I have also fulfilled in a way, since I have come to Sri Krishna. But I will not be able to ask my beloved Krishna for earthly wealth. I can't. How can I ask him for earthly things, fleeting things, ephemeral things, when out of his infinite bounty he has given me divine things, eternal things?

THE SINGER OF THE ETERNAL BEYOND

SI 43. SCENE III

(The Brahmin is on his way home the following day filled with utmost inner and outer joy. He sings.)

> *Amar bhuban tomar charan lagi*
> *amar jiban tomar swapan lagi*

(My world is for Your Feet.
My life is for Your Dream.)

(Suddenly, a heaviness attacks him.)

BRAHMIN   I am spiritual; that is why I am in a position to cry for divine things. But my wife does not care for spiritual things; she needs earthly things. Perhaps I made a mistake. I ought to have asked Krishna to give her something. She likes candy. I should have asked him to give me some candy for her. I feel sorry, but now it is too late. I do not want to go back to my friend, but I know she will be angry with me. What can I do?

SI 44. SCENE IV

(The Brahmin enters his village and approaches his home. Many men and women servants are moving around.)

BRAHMIN   Oh God! Where is my cottage? Standing where my home, my tiny cottage, was, I see a big building, a huge palace. I see servants and maids. *(Looking in.)* From here I can see that it is full of expensive furniture, and it is decorated with elaborate ornaments. *(Turning to one servant who is passing by.)* What happened to the cottage that was here?

SERVANT   Oh, don't you know? The owner is now wallowing in riches.

BYSTANDER   He went to his friend, Krishna, and Krishna gave him all this wealth.

BRAHMIN   Ah! Now I know the whole story. *(His wife appears briefly in the doorway, dressed in costly garments and jewels.)* Now my wife is decked in a most expensive, beautiful dress, and I see a flood of joy in her face. Hundreds of servants are waiting to attend me. But an inner pang shoots through me. O Lord Krishna, you have deceived me! Now how can I think of you? You pleased me when I was with you. Now you have pleased my wife. But here is temptation. My wife did not care for the spiritual life. Now that she is rich it will be worse; she will never care for it! Perhaps my spiritual life will come to an end as well. I will become involved in these ordinary earthly things, ephemeral glittering things.

(Suddenly Krishna appears before the Brahmin in a vision.)

BRAHMIN   O Krishna, feed me only with inner wealth. I want to live in you and receive your inner wealth, not this outer wealth. O my eternal friend, beloved Krishna, keep me inside your heart and feed me with your Compassion, Peace, Light and Bliss. And I pray to you to transform my wife's consciousness so that she will also realise that earthly wealth is no wealth — only inner wealth is worth having.

KRISHNA   My childhood friend, do you think I would betray you? You sought only inner wealth, and I have given you all that I am. Your wife sought outer wealth, and I have given her all that I have. After a while she will get tired of this outer wealth, she will see that it does not satisfy her, and then she too will cry for Light, Peace and Bliss. And then you both will run side by side to your Goal: my Infinity's Breath and my Eternity's Life.

HE EATS GRASS BUT CARRIES A NAKED SWORD

SRI CHINMOY

SI 45. DRAMATIS PERSONÆ

KRISHNA
ARJUNA
ASCETIC

THE SINGER OF THE ETERNAL BEYOND

SI 46. SCENE I

(Krishna and Arjuna.)

KRISHNA   Arjuna, I am in the mood to go out for a walk. Would you like to accompany me?
ARJUNA   Certainly! It is a great joy, a great honour to walk with you.
KRISHNA   Come, let us go.

(Exeunt omnes.)

SI 47. SCENE II

(Krishna and Arjuna are walking together along the street. All of a sudden they see an ascetic.)

ARJUNA   Look, there is an ascetic meditating.
KRISHNA   Yes, let him meditate. Let us not bother him.
ARJUNA   But look, Krishna, something is very strange.
KRISHNA   What is it? I do not see anything.
ARJUNA   Look, he is eating a tiny blade of dry grass. I see green grass all around, but he is eating dry grass.
KRISHNA   It is certainly strange, Arjuna.
ARJUNA   But that is not the thing. It is something unthinkable, unbelievable! The man has a naked sword by his side. Krishna, it is really incredible! On the one hand he will eat only dry, lifeless grass, because he does not want to destroy life. His compassion for living things is so great that he won't even eat green grass. But at the same time, he is carrying a naked sword. Tell me, Krishna — why is he behaving like this? What is wrong with the fellow? It seems to me that his life is a life of contradiction. A blade of grass and a naked sword do not go together.
KRISHNA   Yes, you are right. To eat only dry grass and carry a naked sword is certainly incongruous. Why don't you go and ask why he does this? I shall wait for you.
ARJUNA   No, please come with me.
KRISHNA   All right, I am coming. I am following you.

(They go up to the ascetic.)

ARJUNA   Please tell me, venerable sir, why you act this way? I see that you are leading a simple life, an austere life, a pious life. But why are you carrying this sword? Please tell me the reason for this strange behaviour.

ASCETIC   The reason is very simple. I have four persons to kill with this sword, four unpardonable rascals.

ARJUNA   Who are they? I may be of some help to you if they are so bad.

ASCETIC   I don't need your help. Thank you anyway.

ARJUNA   May I please know their names? Such bad people must not stay on earth. They should be killed if they are really so bad. You say you do not need my help, but in case you change your mind, I am the person who can be of service to you.

ASCETIC   Thank you. I am happy to hear it. I shall tell you their names after all. The first is Narada.

ARJUNA   Narada! What has he done? What has he done to you?

ASCETIC   All the time Narada sings the glories of my Lord Krishna. He never shuts up. He does not even give my Lord time to take his rest. All the time he has to sing, and Krishna has to hear his songs. With his constant singing, singing, singing, he is always disturbing my Lord's sleep. I shall kill that wretched Narada if I see him!

ARJUNA   May I know who the second person is?

ASCETIC   The second rascal is Draupadi, the wife of the Pandavas. As soon as she got into a difficult situation she had to cry, "Lord, save me! Save me!" My Lord had to go and use his force in order to save her modesty. What kind of audacity she had! Who asked her husband to mix with bad people and play dice with the Kauravas? If her husband did something wrong, she should have to pay the penalty for it. Why did she have to call on my Lord Krishna to save her modesty? He had to waste his precious time and energy just to save her modesty. I hate her. I hate her for that, and I shall kill her as soon as I see her!

ARJUNA   What are you talking about? How do you know that story? You are an ascetic.

ASCETIC   Do you think that I do not care for the world's news? I know what is happening in the world. Listen: The story of Draupadi is very simple. Draupadi's husband, Yudhishthira, lost to Duhshasana in a dice game. And his last promise, unthinkable, was that he would give his wife, Draupadi, to the winner. Naturally Duhshasana defeated Draupadi's husband, that senseless man. She had to stay with the Kauravas, their enemies. They wanted to undress her in front of their kings and potentates. Draupadi tried to hold fast to her sari, but finally she surrendered and said, "O Krishna, save me, save me!" Immediately my Lord had to grant her an endless stretch of material. They went on and on pulling at her sari, but it was endless. That is why I hate Draupadi. As for Yudhishthira, it is beneath my dignity even to think of him. He was the real culprit. Anyway, it was Draupadi who invoked my Lord to help her. I hate her. In season and out of season, at any time, she calls on him. When the Pandava family was in the forest, do you know what happened?

ARJUNA   I do not know what happened.

ASCETIC   You don't know? That means you don't read, then.

ARJUNA   Oh, I am an illiterate person. I do not read books, but I would be very happy to hear from you what happened. I have great fondness for the Pandava family. I like the Pandavas better than I like the Kauravas.

ASCETIC   Yes, they are nice people. My Lord Krishna always takes their side. But they have no sense. They exploit my Lord Krishna. When the Pandava family was in the forest, it happened that the sage Durvasha came to visit them with all of his followers and disciples. The Kauravas, the enemies of the Pandavas, had sent Durvasha to pronounce a curse on the Pandavas. Durvasha had once gone to the Kauravas, where he was given princely honours by the eldest of the Kauravas, Duryodhana. Now, since he was very highly pleased with Duryodhana, Durvasha said he would grant him any boon. So Duryodhana asked him to go into the forest where the Pandavas were and cause them trouble. My Lord Krishna had given the Pandavas a pot out of which any number of people might be fed. But this miracle could take place only before Draupadi had taken her last meal of the day. After Draupadi had eaten her last meal, the Pandavas could not feed a single person on earth. Duryodhana asked Durvasha to go there one day after Draupadi had finished her last meal. Durvasha listened to Duryodhana's request. He came after Draupadi had finished her meal, only to torture her. When he came in he said, "I am very hungry, very hungry. I and my followers are going to bathe in the Ganges, and when we return you must feed us." Draupadi knew that she could not feed them. But she also knew that if she did not feed them he would curse her and her husbands. So she invoked my Lord Krishna for help. My Lord Krishna — do you know where he was?

ARJUNA   No.

ASCETIC   He was seated on his throne. He was nowhere near the forest, but immediately he had to use his occult power to come physically to save her. Sri Krishna said, "Please give me something to eat. I am very hungry, Draupadi." Draupadi answered, "You are hungry? O Krishna, I have invoked you to help me because I have no food, and you have come here to torture me. How am I to feed you? I have no food here." Lord Krishna said, "You have to give me food. Examine your pot." She replied, "There is nothing left, O Krishna. I am not telling you a lie. We have all eaten, and there is nothing left. I can show the pot to you." She brought the pot before Krishna. To her surprise there was a grain of rice in it. He ate it. Then he said, "I am satisfied. Now ask me anything. I am pleased with you." She said, "Then save me. The sage Durvasha is coming. He has gone now with his thousands of disciples to bathe in the Ganges, and when he comes back he will want food." With his spiritual power, Krishna immediately made food for thousands of people. But Durvasha, with his yogic vision, came to know that Sri Krishna was there. He said, "It is useless for me to go there, because now they will be able to feed us. I don't want to go there. I am satisfied." So look how Draupadi caused problems for my Krishna. My Lord Krishna had to save her again. I shall kill her! I won't let her go on like this, exploiting my Lord.

ARJUNA Who is the third person, please?

ASCETIC The third person is that Prahlada. Whenever there is any danger, immediately Prahlada says the name of my Lord Krishna, who goes to save him. Prahlada has no right to bother my Lord so often. He has to be punished.

ARJUNA Please tell me who Prahlada is.

ASCETIC Oh, you don't know Prahlada? He claims to be one of the greatest disciples of Krishna, which is absolutely untrue. Prahlada's father used to hate Krishna. The very name of Krishna used to irritate him. His son was just the opposite. Constantly he was all love, all admiration for Krishna. So what did his father do? His father took Prahlada and threw him into a tub of boiling oil. On another occasion, he knocked him onto the ground in the path of a mad elephant, all because his son was worshipping Krishna. But the boiling oil did not kill the boy, nor did the elephant crush him. Sri Krishna, my Lord, was there to save him. Sri Krishna's presence saved him every time. I hate Prahlada! I

ARJUNA shall punish him. I shall punish him for wasting my Krishna's time. All these three that I have mentioned I shall kill.

ARJUNA Now may I know who the fourth person is?

ASCETIC The fourth! He is the worst of all! The wretched, wretched Arjuna! I want to kill him here and now. If I see him anywhere I will kill him, without delay.

ARJUNA Arjuna! What has he done?

ASCETIC That third Pandava has brought disgrace to his family and to the whole world!

ARJUNA How? Please tell me how Arjuna has brought disgrace to his family and to the world?

ASCETIC Look at his audacity. He asked my Lord Krishna to be his charioteer on the battlefield. Sri Krishna is not only my Lord, he is the Lord of the Universe. And Arjuna asked him to be his charioteer! Look at his audacity! I shall kill him! I shall kill him! Until I kill him I shall not leave this earth.

ARJUNA *(smiling)* You are absolutely right. I am sure that one day you will meet these four and you will be able to kill them.

ASCETIC I am so happy to hear these words from you. Yes, I shall certainly do it.

(Exeunt Krishna and Arjuna.)

KALI AND KRISHNA ARE ONE

SRI CHINMOY

SI 48. DRAMATIS PERSONÆ

WIFE (A DEVOTEE OF LORD KRISHNA)
HUSBAND (A DEVOTEE OF MOTHER KALI)
THEIR SON
ANGEL

THE SINGER OF THE ETERNAL BEYOND

SI 49. SCENE I

(The home of two devotees, husband and wife.)

WIFE   Kali, Kali, all the time Kali! What has Kali ever done for us? She has only created untold problems.

HUSBAND   Krishna, Krishna, all the time, all the time! What has Krishna done for us? He has only deceived the world, and he is deceiving you.

WIFE   Krishna has deceived the world? My Krishna has deceived the world? My Krishna is all love, all love for mankind. Your Kali is ruthless. She kills people, she destroys people. She is called destruction. I have lost my only daughter because of her. When she was seriously ill you prayed to Kali. You assured me that Kali would cure our daughter. Now we have lost our only daughter. *(Cries.)*

HUSBAND   Why didn't you pray to your Krishna? If he is so kind, so generous, so compassionate, why didn't you call on him? Why didn't you pray to him to cure our daughter?

WIFE   I didn't invoke Krishna because I did not want to conflict with your prayer. I thought that since you were praying most ardently to your Kali, your Kali would cure our dearest, sweetest daughter. We have lost our daughter because of Kali. Now if our son gets even a headache I will not allow you to pray to Kali. I will pray to Krishna, my Krishna. He will cure our son. There is no danger on earth which I cannot conquer with my prayers to Krishna. Our son will remain on earth, happy and prosperous, all by Krishna's Grace. Our son will become great, very great. And I know it is Krishna's Grace that will make him great.

HUSBAND   I also want our son to be happy and great. If you feel that your Lord Krishna will make our son happy and great, then you pray to Krishna and I shall remain silent. I shall silently pray to my Kali to give me joy, to give me peace of mind, so that I can bear your constant scoldings and insults.

WIFE   If I scold you, then you have to know that you deserve it. You are callous, useless, hopeless in every way.

HUSBAND   Let us not quarrel. Let us not fight in front of our son. I wish you to be happy; I wish my son to be happy; I wish my Kali to make me happy.

SON   How I wish I could do something so that all our problems would be solved! Father is fond of Kali; Mother is fond of Krishna. I do not know of whom I am fond. No, I do know of whom I am fond. But if I say I am fond of Krishna, Father will be displeased; and if I say I am fond of Kali, Mother will be displeased. So I won't say.

WIFE   All right, keep it secret.

HUSBAND   Even if you say you are fond of Krishna, I will not be displeased. You are free to choose.

WIFE   I also want to tell you, my son, that if you are fond of Kali, you must not think I will be displeased with you. You have a free choice. But it is better for you to be fond of one particular deity, to have total faith in him and love and adoration for him. You should worship only one deity, and that deity will make you really happy, great and prosperous.

THE SINGER OF THE ETERNAL BEYOND

SI 50. SCENE II

(Night. The son is sleeping. He suddenly awakens.)

SON   What a strange dream I had! I dreamt that I struck the statue of Kali which is in my father's room and broke it to pieces. I was so happy to inform my mother that now there is only one statue in the house. All along I have been inwardly, secretly praying to Krishna. I am fond of Krishna and not of Kali. Let me go and see if the statue is broken or not.

(Opens the door to his father's room and sees a statue of Krishna, not of Kali. He is wonder-struck.)

SON   How can it be? How can it be?

(Goes to his mother's room and looks in. Her own statue of Krishna is still there.)

SON   Now we have two statues of Krishna! But perhaps I was mistaken. Let me go again to Father's room and see. Maybe Father has replaced Kali's statue. Perhaps he has given away Kali's statue and bought a statue of Krishna so that Mother will be happy. Perhaps he does not want to quarrel with Mother any more.

(He goes to his father's room and sees that the statue of Krishna is still there. He wakes his father.)

FATHER   What are you doing here at this hour?

SON Why have you replaced Kali? Why do I see Krishna's statue?

FATHER Krishna? Krishna? How did Krishna get here? Has your mother brought her statue here and put it in my room?

SON No, the same Krishna statue is in her room. I was just there.

FATHER Let me go into your mother's room and see.

(Father and son go into the mother's room and see the same statue of Krishna there.)

MOTHER What is the matter? What are you doing here at this hour? What are you doing in my room?

SON Mother, Mother, now there is only Krishna in our family! In your room is Krishna and in Father's room is Krishna.

MOTHER What? Is it true? I can't believe my ears! That means your father has now become Krishna's devotee. I am so glad. I am so glad that at last you have replaced Kali with Krishna.

FATHER I have not done it. I don't know how Krishna's statue got into my room.

MOTHER Then how could this happen?

SON Father, this must be a miracle. Since it is a divine miracle, let us meditate together. Let the three of us meditate together and see what we can learn from within.

(They sit down to meditate. An angel appears.)

ANGEL It was your son's prayer that we heard. Your son has always been suffering from your quarrels. One of you cries for Krishna, the other is all for Kali. Although he was fond of Krishna, your son felt miserable because each of you was always fighting for his own chosen deity. In order to prove to you that Kali and Krishna are one, Kali has taken the form of Krishna. From now on there will be no quarrel between you, no dispute between husband and wife, for you know that Kali and Krishna are one. Now Krishna is in both rooms because both wife and son like Krishna. Let there be no more disputes about which deity is better. You two may worship Krishna directly, and you *(addressing the husband)* may worship Kali inside Krishna. She is most certainly there. They are one.

(The angel disappears and the whole room is flooded with light.)

PART III

SIDDHARTHA BECOMES THE BUDDHA

WHO IS THE OWNER:
THE LIFE-SAVER OR THE LIFE-TAKER?

SRI CHINMOY

SB I. DRAMATIS PERSONÆ

PRINCE SIDDHARTHA
DEVADATTA (COUSIN OF SIDDHARTHA)
JUDGE

SIDDHARTHA BECOMES THE BUDDHA

SB 2. SCENE I

(Prince Siddhartha is walking in the garden in a contemplative mood. All of a sudden a bird falls down in front of him.)

SIDDHARTHA   Ah, poor bird! My heart is bleeding for you. Who has done this? Who has hurt you? Who has aimed this arrow at you? Poor, innocent bird! Let me take the arrow out of your body. *(He removes the arrow.)* Now let me try to cure you.

(Enter Devadatta.)

DEVADATTA   Siddhartha, this is my bird. What right have you to keep my bird? Give it to me!

SIDDHARTHA   No, this is my bird, Devadatta.

DEVADATTA   Your bird! I shot this bird. It belongs to me. This is my arrow. I aimed at the bird and it fell down here. It is mine, mine, my property, my possession.

SIDDHARTHA   Devadatta, if I had not removed the arrow from the bird, it would have died by this time.

DEVADATTA   The point is not whether the bird would have died or would not have died. The bird is alive, and it is my possession. It was my power, my skill, my capacity that brought the bird down to earth. You cannot have it. Everybody appreciates and admires you for your heart, for your kindness. But now let the world appreciate my capacity, my skill. You be satisfied with what you have: love. And I shall be satisfied with what I have: power. My power, my skill at archery deserves this bird, not your love.

SIDDHARTHA   O Devadatta, you have the power to kill, and I have the power to love. But since I have this animal, this poor innocent bird, you shall not get it back.

DEVADATTA   Siddhartha, there is a time to listen to your philosophy, and there are people to listen to your philosophy. But this is not the time, and I am not the person. You can advocate your philosophy to others who want to be like you, who want to live in the moon-world and have no practical sense. Life has to be practical. Life needs strength, life needs vigour. But your life is a life of laziness and false kindness. You should be strong. You are the Prince, and soon you will have to rule your kingdom. This kind of false attitude will not help you in any way. What I have done today, you will do millions of times more. I was about to kill a bird. You will one day kill men. At that time your philosophy will change.

SIDDHARTHA   No, Devadatta, my philosophy will always remain the same. My philosophy is the philosophy of compassion, and not the philosophy of destruction.

DEVADATTA   You stay with your philosophy, and let me stay with mine. My philosophy is power. Your philosophy is compassion. Well and good. Now give me my bird.

SIDDHARTHA   Sorry, I will not give it to you.

DEVADATTA   Are you prepared to go to the court to fight for this bird?

SIDDHARTHA   Yes, I am fully prepared.

SIDDHARTHA BECOMES THE BUDDHA

SB 3. SCENE 2

(The court.)

JUDGE   Prince, why do you keep a bird which belongs to somebody else? True, you have compassion, you have love for the bird. You have love for everything. But justice says the bird belongs to Devadatta. It was he who brought the bird down to earth. It is his possession.

SIDDHARTHA   O venerable Judge, I do not know anything about justice, but my heart tells me that he who saves life is the owner, not he who takes life. My heart was bleeding for the bird and I saved it. I am prepared to give my own life for this bird.

DEVADATTA   Siddhartha, you know how to talk. You know perfectly well that no one will kill you in place of this bird. Don't show your false compassion.

JUDGE   Devadatta, I am the Judge. Let me hear more from him.

SIDDHARTHA   O sir, I feel that this bird belongs to me because I have saved its life. Devadatta practically killed the bird. Please tell me who is more important, the life-saver or the life-destroyer?

JUDGE   Prince, I agree with you. The life-saver is infinitely more important than the life-taker. You have saved the bird's life; therefore it is you who can claim this bird. The bird is yours. He who saves life or gives new life is the real owner, and not he who takes life or destroys life. Today you have offered your life for a bird. A day will come, I clearly foresee, when you will offer your life for all of humanity. Your heart will cry to save the bleeding heart of humanity. Your heart will cry to illumine the unlit mind of humanity. Your soul will cry to elevate the consciousness of humanity.

DEVADATTA   Siddhartha, today your love-power has won the victory, but a day will come when I shall conquer you with my destruction-power. You will see that power conquers love.

SIDDHARTHA   Devadatta, you are wrong. Love will always conquer, for Love is the Almighty Power.

PRINCE SIDDHARTHA LEAVES THE PALACE

SRI CHINMOY

SB 4. DRAMATIS PERSONÆ

PRINCE SIDDHARTHA
CHANNA (HIS CHARIOTEER)
AN OLD MAN
A SICK MAN
A DEAD MAN
A SPIRITUAL MAN

SIDDHARTHA BECOMES THE BUDDHA

SB 5. SCENE I

(Channa, Siddhartha's charioteer, is driving the Prince through the streets.)

SIDDHARTHA   Channa, I am so happy today. For the first time I have come out of the palace. I smell now the real fragrance of life. Look at this panoramic view. My entire being is in deep ecstasy.

CHANNA   O Prince, in your happiness is my happiness. I am always at your disposal.

(All of a sudden Siddhartha sees an old man before him.)

SIDDHARTHA   Channa, who is this man? He can't even walk. How strange — his hair is white. My hair is black, and yours is, too. Everyone in the palace has black hair. What is wrong with this man's hair?

CHANNA   Prince, he is an old man; therefore he is very weak. That is why he cannot walk properly. Old people have white hair. One day you and I also will grow old.

SIDDHARTHA   Me? I shall become old? Impossible! I feel miserable for that old man. Channa, I don't think that I shall ever have to become old.

CHANNA   Prince, how I wish that you would never become old! But, unfortunately, nobody can escape old age.

SIDDHARTHA   Channa, I feel really miserable for that old man, who is so thin and weak. Let us go back to the palace. I hope that tomorrow I shall not have to see an old man.

CHANNA   Oh, no. Tomorrow I shall drive you along another road.

SIDDHARTHA   The very idea of becoming old in the future is making me sad.
CHANNA   Me too, O Prince.

SIDDHARTHA BECOMES THE BUDDHA

SB 6. SCENE 2

(The following day Channa is driving Siddhartha in the chariot along a different road.)

SIDDHARTHA   Life outside the palace is really beautiful, Channa. Here everything is fresh, charming and soulful.

CHANNA   I am glad that you are enjoying your ride.

SIDDHARTHA   Inside the palace it is all luxury. Outside the palace it is all beauty, nature's beauty, life's beauty. *(All of a sudden Siddhartha sees a man lying in the street.)* Channa, who is this man? He can't even sit properly. He is lying down in the street. He is pressing his head with one hand and pressing his stomach with the other. His eyes are deeply sunken. He is moaning and shedding bitter tears. What is wrong with him? It seems that he is finding it difficult to breathe.

CHANNA   Prince, that man is sick. He is suffering from severe pain in his head and stomach. Perhaps he has other ailments, too. Prince, everyone falls sick once in a while.

SIDDHARTHA   No! I have never fallen sick. I feel such sorrow for that man. Can I be of any help to him?

CHANNA   No, you cannot be of any help to him, Prince. Only a doctor can help him. I am sure that soon some of his friends will take him to a doctor. Prince, we should move away from this place. As it was yesterday, today also your joy is ruined. The world is full of misery.

SIDDHARTHA   I see. I was totally ignorant of this. Tomorrow we must take another road and drive around the kingdom.

CHANNA   Certainly. Tomorrow we will drive through other streets.

SB 7. SCENE 3

(The next day. Siddhartha and Channa are in the chariot. Channa has taken a new road.)

SIDDHARTHA   Beauty, beauty! Today I see and feel real beauty on earth. We have covered a long distance. We are passing through a series of beautiful spots. *(All of a sudden Siddhartha sees some people carrying a man on their shoulders. Tears are running down their cheeks.)* Channa, what is wrong with that fellow? Why should others have to carry him? And why are they crying?

CHANNA   Ah, that man is dead.

SIDDHARTHA   What do you mean?

CHANNA   There is no life in him, Prince. His play on earth is over. Everybody has to die one day. Everybody has to go away from this world. Everybody has to suffer from death.

SIDDHARTHA   Not me! I don't want to die. My beloved wife also has to die? My darling Rahul also has to die? No, that can't be. I shall not be able to bear such a loss.

CHANNA   Prince, whoever lives on earth has to die eventually. Nobody can live forever.

SIDDHARTHA   Channa, I can't believe it. I don't want to believe it. I must conquer death, not only for myself, but for everybody. Channa, please tell me if there is anything more powerful, more destructive than death.

CHANNA   No, Prince, there is nothing more powerful and destructive than death. Death conquers everybody. We are all slaves of death.

SIDDHARTHA   Not me!

CHANNA   We are all at the mercy of death.

SIDDHARTHA BECOMES THE BUDDHA

SIDDHARTHA   Not me! Channa, now that I have seen an old man, a sick man and a dead man, I think that I have seen everything bad that the world can show me. But something within me tells me that there are still things that I have not seen as yet. I want to come out tomorrow again.

CHANNA   If you want to come out of the palace again, I shall be more than happy to drive you, O Prince.

SB 8. SCENE 4

(The next day. Siddhartha and Channa are in the chariot driving along the streets.)

SIDDHARTHA   Channa, we have covered a very good distance. Today everything is fine. Today I don't have to see an old man, a sick man or a dead man. Today I shall see and enjoy only nature's beauty, nature's lustre, nature's love, nature's heart and nature's soul.

(All of a sudden he sees someone meditating beneath a tree.)

SIDDHARTHA   Who is that man, Channa? What is he doing at the foot of that tree? Why are his eyes closed? What is he doing with a garland of beads?

CHANNA   I am answering your questions one by one, O Prince. Who is that man? He is a spiritual man. What is he doing at the foot of the tree? He is praying and meditating. Why are his eyes closed? He thinks that his prayers will be more sincere and his meditation will be more intense if he keeps his eyes closed. What is he doing with a garland of beads? He is repeating the name of God, and counting the number of chants on the beads.

SIDDHARTHA   I believe all that you say, but what will he get by leading this kind of life?

CHANNA   He will get infinite Peace and infinite Joy.

SIDDHARTHA   Infinite Peace? Infinite Joy? I must go and talk to him. Channa, come along. Let us go and speak to this peculiar man.

CHANNA   Indeed, that's a nice idea.

SIDDHARTHA BECOMES THE BUDDHA

(They leave the chariot and approach the spiritual man.)

SIDDHARTHA   May I know your name? What do you do for your living? *(No answer from the spiritual man.)* Do you know that I am Prince Siddhartha? My father owns this kingdom; he is the Lord of this kingdom. You are ignoring his son. I can do anything to you that I want. For God's sake, don't waste my precious time!

(No answer from the spiritual man.)

CHANNA   Prince, forgive me. I must tell you something. He is a spiritual man. He is praying to God; he is meditating on God. We should not disturb him. Who knows what is happening inside him? Perhaps God and he are talking inwardly. Perhaps God is telling him how he can have infinite Peace and Bliss.

SIDDHARTHA   I need that. I need infinite Peace and infinite Bliss, Channa. Do you think I will ever have that kind of Peace and Bliss?

CHANNA   Why not? Why not? Without fail you will have infinite Peace and infinite Bliss if you pray and meditate like this spiritual man.

SIDDHARTHA   Channa, then tomorrow a new life for me begins. I shall pray and meditate all day and night. My present life of luxury is no longer for me. I shall welcome the life of poverty. I shall embrace the life of renunciation. I shall put an end to suffering in this world. I know ignorance is the root of all suffering. I shall uproot the huge ignorance-tree, Channa; I shall exterminate it. The first day I saw an old man; the second day I saw a sick man; the third day I saw a dead man; today, the fourth day, I see a spiritual man. Either tomorrow, or in the near future, or in the distant future,

I shall see another man, who has infinite Light, infinite Peace and infinite Bliss. My life is meaningless and useless without eternity's Light, infinity's Peace and immortality's Bliss. The human in me ends its role today, Channa. No more for me this life of pleasure. The divine in me shall begin its role tomorrow. For me, from now on, only the life of universal Peace and transcendental Bliss.

SIDDHARTHA BECOMES THE BUDDHA

SRI CHINMOY

SB 9. DRAMATIS PERSONÆ

SIDDHARTHA (LATER, THE BUDDHA)
SUJATA (A DEVOTEE)
FIRST ASCETIC
SECOND ASCETIC
THIRD ASCETIC
FOURTH ASCETIC
FIFTH ASCETIC

SIDDHARTHA BECOMES THE BUDDHA

SB 10. SCENE 1

(Siddhartha is sitting under a tree in high meditation. Enter five ascetics.)

FIRST ASCETIC   O Siddhartha! Siddhartha! Look at Siddhartha!

SECOND ASCETIC   I am sure he will soon realise the highest Truth.

THIRD ASCETIC   Without fail.

FOURTH ASCETIC   We have also been crying for our realisation. We have been praying to God and working so hard in our inner life. But still the realisation of God is a far cry for us. I am happy that at least one person will realise God.

FIFTH ASCETIC   At least Siddhartha will reach the highest Truth. It does not matter who reaches the Truth first; I want people to be free from ignorance.

FIRST ASCETIC   Let us not disturb him. He is in deep meditation, in trance. Let us not disturb poor Siddhartha. May God bless him. He has not been eating at all. He drinks only water. He is so weak, so weak. Poor fellow! Such a hard, austere life! I am sure God will soon grant him illumination.

SECOND ASCETIC   He could have enjoyed all the pleasures of the world. He was the Prince, and in every way he could have lived a life of pleasure.

THIRD ASCETIC   He knows that the life of pleasure cannot give him abiding satisfaction.

FOURTH ASCETIC   But it is very difficult to overcome vital movements, vital pleasure.

FIFTH ASCETIC   God has something special to do with Siddhartha's life. I can clearly see it.

(Enter Sujata, who bows down to Siddhartha and places before him a bowl of sweetmeats. Siddhartha opens his eyes and accepts food from Sujata.)

SUJATA   O Sage, I am so grateful to you that you have accepted my food. For days you have not eaten anything. Your body has become so weak, so thin. Now I shall bring food for you regularly. You pray to God; I shall serve you. I am so glad, so grateful that you will accept my devoted service.

SIDDHARTHA   I have come to understand that starvation is not right. The extreme path is not the right way. The middle path is by far the best. To reach the highest Truth one need not stop eating altogether. One has to eat a moderate amount of food. The food that is necessary for health, to keep the body fit, one must eat. But at the same time one must not be a voracious eater. When I realise the highest Truth, mine will be the middle path.

FIRST ASCETIC   Shame, shame! Look at Siddhartha! He is eating food!

SECOND ASCETIC   Look who is serving him! Such a beautiful girl!

THIRD ASCETIC   Well, what can you expect? How long can one control his vital life?

FOURTH ASCETIC   Alas, Siddhartha has fallen.

FIFTH ASCETIC   He does not deserve our appreciation and admiration. He has taken sweetmeats from such a beautiful girl. He is serving his senses and he is feeding his body. See, the life of pleasure has already started. A woman is enough to destroy a man's aspiration no matter how sincere, how devoted he is. One beautiful woman is enough to take even such a great aspirant from the path of Truth. Let us go.

FIRST ASCETIC   Whom to blame? The girl or Siddhartha?

SIDDHARTHA BECOMES THE BUDDHA

SECOND ASCETIC   I blame the girl. She has ruined Siddhartha's aspiration.

THIRD ASCETIC   I blame Siddhartha. Who asked him to be so weak? If he had been strong in his mind he could have rejected her.

FOURTH ASCETIC   Well, we must remember that it is a difficult task to conquer the wrong movements of the vital.

FIFTH ASCETIC   It is difficult also to pray to God, to meditate on Truth.

FOURTH ASCETIC   But since he made an attempt to realise the Highest, he should have continued.

FIFTH ASCETIC   I feel sorry for him. At the same time I feel that he can be of no use to us now. I thought that he would illumine us as soon as he got his own illumination.

THIRD ASCETIC   I thought the same. But now it is impossible. Let us leave, let us leave. Siddhartha has failed, Siddhartha has fallen.

Exeunt the five ascetics. All this time Sujata is feeding Siddhartha and showing her loving, soulful gratitude to him. Tears of gratitude are flowing from her eyes.)

SIDDHARTHA   Sujata, don't pay any attention to them. They are ignorant people. From ignorant people we can expect only ignorance. You have come to feed me, and I am grateful to you. My blessingful joy you will always feel.

SUJATA   O Sage, I don't pay any attention to those ascetics. They are fools. They do not see your utmost sincerity. They do not see your burning cry for Truth, for God. It will take them thousands of years to realise God, but I clearly see that very soon you will reach your goal. I see that the day of your realisation is fast approaching.

SIDDHARTHA They came, and now they have left. They saw something in me, and that is why they wanted to stay. But when they saw me take food from you, they left. They left just because their minds are still impure; just because their vitals need more purification; just because they could not identify their lives with my aspiring consciousness and your dedicated consciousness. Your dedication knew and felt the depth of my aspiration. And my aspiration feels the depth of your dedication. Sujata, I bless you with all my heart and soul. Here I shall sit, here at the foot of the Bodhi tree. Here I shall realise the Truth. I shall not move from this spot any more. Even if I suffer from cold or hunger or thirst, or from anything else, I shall not move. Here at this very place my Illumination must take place. And I shall put an end to sorrow.

(*Sujata bows to Siddhartha and leaves. Siddhartha sings.*)

Hihasane shushyatu me shariram
twagasthi mangsam pralayancha jatu
aprapya bodhing vahukalpa durlabham
naivasanat kayamatah chalishye

(Here on this seat may wither my body;
Skin, bone and flesh may be destroyed.
Without getting the supreme Wisdom
Attainable only with difficulty
In myriad aeons,
Definitely I shall not move from this seat.)

SIDDHARTHA BECOMES THE BUDDHA

(Siddhartha meditates. He is having visions of life. The life of pleasure, vital movements, sex forces — all are trying to enter into him.)

SIDDHARTHA   Ah, these lower vital movements are trying to enter into me. No, I shall not permit them. I have my inner strength, indomitable strength. I shall fight against them.

(Siddhartha meditates with tremendous determination. Suddenly his whole being is flooded with Light. He starts to sing.)

> *No more my heart shall sob or grieve.*
> *My days and nights dissolve in God's own Light.*
> *Above the toil of life my soul*
> *Is a Bird of Fire winging the Infinite.*
> *I have known the One and His secret Play;*
> *And passed beyond the sea of ignorance-Dream.*
> *In tune with Him, I sport and sing,*
> *I own the golden Eye of the Supreme.*
> *Drunk deep of Immortality,*
> *I am the root and boughs of a teeming vast.*
> *My Form I have known, and realised,*
> *The Supreme and I are one — all we outlast.*

(All of a sudden his body begins radiating a golden Light and Siddhartha becomes the Enlightened One, the Buddha.)

BUDDHA   I know, at last I know the Truth! I know the way. I know the way to end sorrow, to exterminate the tree of suffering. From today I shall serve humanity with my inner Light. I have seen the Truth, and this Truth every human being on earth will achieve. My Truth is for all. My Love is for all. My Realisation is for all. I am for all. This life of mine, this dedicated life of mine, is for humanity's use.

SRI CHINMOY

Now that I have the Transcendental Light within me, I shall go out into the world to teach others.

(Exit the Buddha.)

SIDDHARTHA BECOMES THE BUDDHA

SB II. SCENE 2

(The five ascetics are meditating. Enter the Buddha.)

BUDDHA   Now I have come to Benares, a sacred place. *(He sees the five ascetics)* Ahhh! Here are the five ascetics who came to me and left me.
FIRST ASCETIC   Look, here is Siddhartha again.
SECOND ASCETIC   But this time he cannot fool us.
THIRD ASCETIC   Certainly not. He cannot fool us any more.
FOURTH ASCETIC   But look at him. He looks different.
FIFTH ASCETIC   I see something in him, something strange.
FIRST ASCETIC   Well, I seem to see some Light in him.
THIRD ASCETIC   His whole face is glowing.
FOURTH ASCETIC   His face? His entire body is glowing!
FIFTH ASCETIC   He is illumined, totally illumined!

(The Buddha approaches them. One by one they touch the Buddha's feet. The Buddha, with his compassionate smile, blesses them.)

SECOND ASCETIC   Siddhartha, you are no more Siddhartha.
THIRD ASCETIC   You are the Enlightened One.
FIRST ASCETIC   O Buddha, we are bathing in the sea of your Light.
FOURTH ASCETIC   O Buddha, we are your first disciples.
ALL TOGETHER   With us the journey of your manifestation begins. With us the manifestation of your mission begins.

(The Buddha gives them a smile of compassion, joy and pride.)

BUDDHA   You have my Compassion. You have my Light. You have my Bliss, my children, my sweet children.

FATHER, GIVE ME MY SHARE, PLEASE

SRI CHINMOY

SB 12. DRAMATIS PERSONÆ

THE BUDDHA
DISCIPLES OF THE BUDDHA
RAHUL (SON OF THE BUDDHA)

SIDDHARTHA BECOMES THE BUDDHA

SB 12. SCENE 1

(The Buddha with his disciples. Enter Rahul, his son. The disciples are all excited to see the Buddha's young son.)

RAHUL Father?

BUDDHA Yes, my son?

RAHUL Mother says that you have given joy to hundreds of people. Now I also want to have joy from you.

BUDDHA My son, tell me what kind of joy you want from me.

RAHUL I want my share of your wealth, your property. Everybody has become rich with your wealth. Now I want to be rich, too.

BUDDHA My son, my wealth is of a different type. I have no money. I have no material wealth. I have only inner wealth, which is Peace, Light and Bliss.

RAHUL Father, I know Mother has told me about your wealth. You have Infinite Peace, Infinite Love, Infinite Joy, Infinite Bliss. I want to have my share. I am your son. I want to follow your path.

BUDDHA But you are a child, you are a little boy. How can you accept the path right now?

RAHUL Father, what is wrong? Is your spirituality meant only for grown-up people and not for children? Is the Truth you have achieved only for the elderly? Is Truth not for everybody? Is God not for everybody, Father?

BUDDHA Wonderful, my child, wonderful, my son! I accept my defeat. Truth is for all. And my Love, my Peace, my Light you can share, as others already share. I share with you my Joy, my Peace, my Illumination.

RAHUL Father, have you accepted me as your disciple?

BUDDHA   Yes, I have accepted you with all my heart and soul, my son.

RAHUL   Then you have to accept another also. There is one more seeker you have to accept as your disciple.

BUDDHA   Who? Whom have I to accept, my son?

RAHUL   My mother. My mother wants to be your disciple.

BUDDHA   *(pauses)* My son, I do not accept women as my disciples, my real disciples.

RAHUL   Father, why not? Are women not meant to realise the highest Truth? Your heart is big. Everybody says the Buddha's heart is as vast as the infinite ocean. If your heart is so big, how then do you deny women the Truth that you have realised? Father, that is unfair. You have to accept my mother. And the day you accept her, you must accept all women.

BUDDHA   My son, I am truly proud of you. You are still a child, you have not yet seen even eleven summers, but your inner knowledge is profound. My son, your knowledge of Truth has given me enormous joy and pride. The world listens to me. I have hundreds of disciples and they listen to me with devotion. I listen to you with my heart's pride and my soul's joy. Go and tell your mother that I have accepted her also as my true disciple. Today I take both of you into the *sangha*, my spiritual community.

THE BUDDHA NEEDS A FEW MUSTARD SEEDS

SRI CHINMOY

SB 13. DRAMATIS PERSONÆ

THE BUDDHA
KRISHA GAUTAMI (A DISCIPLE)
LADY
MAN
LITTLE GIRL

SIDDHARTHA BECOMES THE BUDDHA

SB 14. SCENE I

(The Buddha is in deep meditation with his eyes wide open. Enter Krisha Gautami, carrying her dead child. She places the child at the feet of the Buddha.)

GAUTAMI   O Sage, O Master, O Lord, O Light of the World, please, please bring back life to my child. He is my only child.

BUDDHA   Gautami, don't cry, don't weep. Just do as I say.

GAUTAMI   O Master, I shall do anything that you want, immediately. Only bring back my child's life.

BUDDHA   Gautami, I wish you to bring me a few mustard seeds. But they must come from a family that has not been visited by death. Remember, you must bring me the mustard seeds only from a house that has not been visited by death.

GAUTAMI   O Master, that is so easy. I shall go and bring mustard seeds for you. Then will you be able to cure my son?

BUDDHA   Yes, Gautami, I shall be able to do it if you can bring me mustard seeds from a house where there has not been any death.

SB 15. SCENE 2

(Gautami is going from door to door.)

GAUTAMI   O Mother, please give me some mustard seeds. My only child has died and the Buddha has told me that if I bring him some mustard seeds he will bring life back to my child.

LADY   Don't worry. I will bring them to you.

GAUTAMI   O venerable lady, please wait. First tell me, has anybody died in your family?

LADY   When?

GAUTAMI   Any time.

LADY   Just last year I lost my husband.

(She begins to weep.)

GAUTAMI   Then I cannot take your mustard seeds.

(Gautami sheds bitter tears and goes to another house. A man opens the door.)

GAUTAMI   My Lord, please give me a few mustard seeds. I need them badly.

MAN   Certainly, I will give you mustard seeds. I shall get them for you.

GAUTAMI   First, please tell me, has anybody died in your family?

MAN   Ah, just last week I lost my wife, my dearest on earth.

GAUTAMI   Ah, then I cannot take the mustard seeds from you.

(Gautami again sheds bitter tears and goes to another house. A young girl opens the door.)

GAUTAMI   My child, you are so beautiful. Please bring me a few mustard seeds. Please go and ask your mother to give me some mustard seeds.

LITTLE GIRL   I know where my mother keeps mustard seeds. I will bring them for you.

GAUTAMI   Please tell me what your father does?

LITTLE GIRL   My father? *(Starts crying.)* My father is in Heaven. Just two months ago my father died all of a sudden.

GAUTAMI   My child, I cannot take your mustard seeds.

(Weeping, Gautami goes to another door.)

SB 16. SCENE 3

(Gautami returns to the Buddha.)

GAUTAMI   O Master, I have been to many places. Each family has lost someone. It seems that there is no family that has not suffered from death.

BUDDHA   Gautami, you are right. No family on earth can say that death has not visited it. You are suffering, and like you many, many others are suffering. Many have suffered and many will suffer. Not just many, Gautami — all. Everyone has to suffer from death. We came from Light and we shall go back to Light.

GAUTAMI   But, Father, he was my only child. How can I be consoled? Who will console me?

BUDDHA   Who will console you, Gautami? I will console you.

GAUTAMI   Please console me, Father. You are the only one who can do it.

BUDDHA   Gautami, as long as there is life there will also be death. Birth is bound to be followed by death, and death is bound to be followed by birth. Now, Gautami, I shall tell you the cause of sorrow. You have lost your only child. Your life is overwhelmed with sorrow. But the cause of your sorrow is not death. The cause of sorrow is desire. The day you conquer desire you conquer sorrow, too. Pray and meditate. You will conquer desire, and at that moment you will see that Light and Delight have become your constant friends.

GAUTAMI   O Sage, you are my Master. Today I know you. I have nobody on earth, nobody. I have no husband, I have no child — nobody but you. You are my All. You have consoled me. Now what I need from you is inner illumination. I shall dedicate my entire life to you unconditionally, wholeheartedly. It is through my dedicated service to you, Master, that I shall achieve my illumination.

BUDDHA   Gautami, you are right, absolutely right. My child, your life is destined to enter into the realm of eternal Bliss. Meditate on God. Meditate on Truth. You will attain Peace, Joy and Bliss.

THE MEETING PLACE OF
EXISTENCE AND NON-EXISTENCE

SRI CHINMOY

SB 17. DRAMATIS PERSONÆ

KING PRASENJIT
KSHEMA (A GREAT DISCIPLE OF THE BUDDHA)

SIDDHARTHA BECOMES THE BUDDHA

SB 18. SCENE 1

(King Prasenjit and Kshema.)

KING   Kshema, you are a great disciple of the Buddha. He is proud of your wisdom and I am fascinated by your spiritual insight. You have been at my palace for a few days, and you have given much wisdom to all the members of my royal family. I offer you my deepest gratitude.

KSHEMA   O King, I am so happy that I have been able to serve my Lord Buddha in your royal family.

KING   Kshema, tell me in a few words about Buddha's philosophy. You have to forgive me, but I do not have much time. My work in the kingdom is simply killing me. I am overburdened, but I am deeply interested in Buddha's philosophy. Tell me in a few words.

KSHEMA   Your Majesty, Buddha's teaching is very simple. He gives us the message of renunciation. He gives us the message of compassion. It is through renunciation and compassion that one can enter into Nirvana.

KING   One thing more, O Kshema.

KSHEMA   Tell me.

KING   Why has Buddha not spoken about the soul? We Hindus all believe in the existence of the soul. Nothing can be done without the soul.

KSHEMA   True, he has not spoken about the soul, but he has spoken about the inner Light. What is that inner Light if not the soul? He has not used the term soul, but what he speaks of as the inner Light is nothing but the soul.

KING   He has not used the term God. We Hindus believe in God.

KSHEMA   True, he has not used the term God. But he has used the term Truth. What is Truth? Truth is God. God is Truth. The moment you realise the Highest Truth, you will realise God the Infinite.

KING   It seems to me that Buddha has not spoken about life after death or about life after Nirvana.

KSHEMA   True, Buddha has not spoken about life after death and life after Nirvana, but he has told us why death exists, and he has told us a little about Nirvana. He has given us the message of peace. Death exists when there is no peace. When you have peace, there is no death. As for the life after Nirvana, first we have to know what Nirvana is. Nirvana is infinite Delight. What can there be after infinite Delight?

KING   I don't understand your philosophy, Kshema.

KSHEMA   Let me try to make it clear to you. From your palace you can see the Ganges?

KING   Yes.

KSHEMA   You can see the sand on the bank of the Ganges. Now send whomever you want from your kingdom to count the number of grains of sand. Or send somebody to measure the weight of the ocean. Can anybody from your kingdom do it, your Majesty?

KING   I am sorry, I do not think anybody can count the number of grains of sand on the shore, or measure the weight of the ocean.

KSHEMA   True. Nobody can count the grains of sand on the bank of the Ganges or weigh the water in the ocean. Similarly, when you enter into Nirvana, there Bliss is infinite. It cannot be measured, weighed or counted. It is unfathomable. In that highest realm of Bliss we see the meeting place of existence and non-existence. There non-existence and existence are inseparable, indescribable.

HERE AND NOWHERE ELSE

SRI CHINMOY

SB 19. DRAMATIS PERSONÆ

THE BUDDHA
SEVERAL DISCIPLES
ANGULIMAL (A DACOIT)
KING PRASENJIT
KING UDAYAN OF KAUSHAMBI
MAGANDIYA (HIS WIFE)
GATEMAN
ANANDA (DEAREST DISCIPLE OF THE BUDDHA)

SIDDHARTHA BECOMES THE BUDDHA

SB 20. SCENE I

(The Buddha with his disciples. One disciple stands up.)

DISCIPLE   O Lord, I wish to preach your teachings.
BUDDHA   Certainly you may, but I would like to ask you a few questions first. I am sure you will be able to answer them.
DISCIPLE   It is by your grace that I will be able to answer them.
BUDDHA   Tell me, if somebody speaks ill of you, what will you do?
DISCIPLE   My Lord, I shall keep silent.
BUDDHA   Tell me, if he strikes you, what will you do?
DISCIPLE   I shall not raise my hands. I shall remain silent.
BUDDHA   If he wants to kill you, what will you do?
DISCIPLE   I shall keep silent. I know that death is inevitable. Everybody has to die. I shall also have to die one day. I shall not invoke death, and at the same time I shall not avoid death.
BUDDHA   I am most pleased with your answers. You can preach my philosophy. You have my blessings. *(To all the disciples.)* Today I would like to walk in the forest. Those who want to follow me can come along.

(All the disciples eagerly follow the Buddha.)

SB 21. SCENE 2

(The Buddha and his disciples are in the forest. All of a sudden a dacoit named Angulimal enters.)

ANGULIMAL   Stop! Stop!

BUDDHA   I have already stopped. It is you who have not stopped. You have killed hundreds of people. You wear a garland of thumbs around your neck. I have already stopped; I am stationed in the Infinite Consciousness forever. But you are still roaming in the world of vital desires and trying to destroy the world. You have not yet come to a halt. In my case, I am already in the static silence of the Ineffable.

(Angulimal pulls out a knife and attempts to stab the Buddha, but the Buddha's Light captures him. He falls at the feet of the Buddha.)

ANGULIMAL   O Buddha, forgive me. Forgive my ignorance. Forgive me for what I have done to the world, and for what I was going to do right now to you.

BUDDHA   I have forgiven you. I have forgiven your past; I have forgiven your present.

ANGULIMAL   If it is true that you have forgiven my past and my present, then I wish you to prove it.

BUDDHA   How do you want me to prove it?

ANGULIMAL   Accept me as your disciple. If you accept me as your disciple, then I will believe that you have truly forgiven me, O Lord.

BUDDHA   You are my disciple, Angulimal. I accept you.

SIDDHARTHA BECOMES THE BUDDHA

SB 22. SCENE 3

(The Buddha with his disciples. Enter King Prasenjit.)

PRASENJIT Master, I am so sorry that I have not been able to come to you for such a long time. My body remains in the palace, but my heart remains with you.

BUDDHA Yes, my son, I know. Your heart of dedication and aspiration is here, but your physical body is needed by your kingdom.

PRASENJIT Master, the world is so corrupt. But your dream will one day be fulfilled, and then this world will have no suffering. One day the world will come to know that the cause of suffering is desire. Now people are still quarrelling, fighting and killing each other. I have some sad news for you: just last week a member of the royal family was stabbed to death by Angulimal, the dacoit. I am sure you have heard about Angulimal. He removed the right thumb of my relative and is now wearing it around his neck. How hard my soldiers are trying to capture him! But that criminal will never be caught. This is very sad news for me. Master, I pray to you to do something for my relative in the inner world.

BUDDHA I shall certainly do something for him.

PRASENJIT I am sure, Master, that a day will come when even a murderer like Angulimal will be transformed by your Light and Compassion.

(Angulimal is now a disciple. He is seated among the other disciples, listening to this conversation. He is clean-shaven and wears the ordinary simple dress of a mendicant.)

BUDDHA   Prasenjit, Angulimal's transformation has already taken place.

PRASENJIT   How? When? Where?

BUDDHA   *(pointing to Angulimal)* There is Angulimal.

PRASENJIT   This is Angulimal? He who has killed hundreds of people? This is Angulimal? This is the murderer? I see light around his face! How can it be?

BUDDHA   His transformation has already taken place.

SIDDHARTHA BECOMES THE BUDDHA

SB 23. SCENE 4

(King Udayan of Kaushambi and his wife, Magandiya.)

UDAYAN   Magandiya, why do you always speak ill of Buddha?
MAGANDIYA   I hate him! I hate him! I hate him! He has insulted me! I must take revenge!
UDAYAN   How strange, how strange! Buddha, of all people, has insulted you? How? When?
MAGANDIYA   Before I married you I loved him most dearly. But he rejected my love brutally.
UDAYAN   I am surprised. I am sure he rejected your love gently and not brutally.
MAGANDIYA   Say whatever you want to say; to me Buddha is not a man of compassion. To me he is a man of cruelty. He creates frustration in others' hearts. He creates destruction in others' lives.
UDAYAN   But now that you have married me, are you not happy with me, my darling?
MAGANDIYA   Yes, I am, but an insult is an insult. Neither can I forget Buddha's insult nor can I forgive him.

(Enter Gateman.)

GATEMAN   *(salutes the King and Queen)* Buddha and his disciples are anxious to see you, your Majesty.
UDAYAN   Please bring Buddha and his disciples in. I am so happy that on his own Buddha has come to my palace.

(Exit Gateman.)

MAGANDIYA Buddha! Buddha! Think of the devil and the devil appears. I can't stand Buddha. I can't stand him at all! You stay with your Buddha, but I am leaving!

(Exits angrily, breaking a vase. Enter the Buddha and his disciples. Udayan offers him a soulful salutation.)

UDAYAN Buddha, please be seated on this throne.
BUDDHA King Udayan, I prefer to sit on the floor. *(He sits.)*
UDAYAN If you sit on the floor, then my seat must also be on the floor, Lord Buddha. *(Sits.)*
BUDDHA My children, sit down. *(All the disciples sit.)* Where is the Queen?
UDAYAN She is extremely busy. I am afraid she will not be able to join us.
BUDDHA I understand, King Udayan. For some time you will be occupied in listening to my spiritual teachings, and she will be occupied in insulting and cursing me.
UDAYAN O Buddha, nobody can hide anything from you. You are all knowledge.

(The Buddha smiles.)

ANANDA O Lord, why do you come to this kingdom of Kaushambi where the Queen is so hostile to you? On our way to the palace so many people mocked you, insulted you and threatened you. You know perfectly well that it is the Queen who has been instigating them for the last few years to say and do all these undivine things to you.
BUDDHA Ananda, my most devoted disciple, tell me one thing: if we go to some other place and are insulted there, if we are criticised and threatened the same way we have been treated in this kingdom, what would you suggest we do then?

ANANDA   Lord, we should immediately move to some other place.

BUDDHA   And in the new place also if we meet with the same problem, what should we do?

ANANDA   Then, Lord, we should go to some other place.

BUDDHA   Ananda, if the same thing happens over and over everywhere we go, what will you do?

ANANDA   Each time we are criticised and insulted, I think we should to go a new place to observe our fate.

BUDDHA   O Ananda, most loving child, if we move from one place to another with the idea of finding a better place for manifesting the Truth, we shall never be successful. Truth has to be manifested here where we are, and not elsewhere. Once the Truth is established here, in the twinkling of an eye the Truth will be founded everywhere. Either here or nowhere the Truth must be established. Again and again I must tell you, Ananda, the Truth has to be seen, felt and realised within, and then manifested here on earth, wherever we are, and nowhere else.

BUDDHAM SARANAM GACCHAMI

SRI CHINMOY

SB 24. DRAMATIS PERSONÆ

GATEMAN
DEVADATTA (COUSIN OF THE BUDDHA AND A CLOSE FRIEND OF
    AJATASHATRU)
AJATASHATRU (THE PRINCE, LATER KING)
DR. JAIVAKA (PHYSICIAN OF KING AJATASHATRU)
THE BUDDHA
DISCIPLES OF THE BUDDHA

SIDDHARTHA BECOMES THE BUDDHA

SB 25. SCENE I

(King Bimbisara's palace. Enter Devadatta.)

GATEMAN May I know whom you want, sir?
DEVADATTA Yes, please go and tell Prince Ajatashatru that his friend Devadatta is here.

(Exit Gateman. Enter Ajatashatru.)

AJATASHATRU Come in, come in. I am so happy to see you.
DEVADATTA I wish to have a private audience with you. May I?
AJATASHATRU Yes, come into my chamber, come into my room. Nobody is there.

SB 26. SCENE 2

(A most beautiful room. Enter Ajatashatru and Devadatta.)

DEVADATTA   Ajatashatru, my friend, tell me frankly: are you jealous of anybody?

AJATASHATRU   I don't think so.

DEVADATTA   I am. I am so jealous of Buddha. But my jealousy does not help me at all. He now has thousands of disciples, while I have only a few. And even those few disciples are leaving me and going to him. I hate him! I want to kill him!

AJATASHATRU   Oh, now it seems to me that I am also jealous of someone.

DEVADATTA   Ah, you are also jealous of someone? Please tell me who.

AJATASHATRU   I am jealous of my father, the King. Everybody touches his feet; everybody adores him. He has so much power and wealth.

DEVADATTA   You see, you have as much reason to be jealous of your father as I have to be jealous of Buddha. But we can easily solve your problem.

AJATASHATRU   If you solve my problem I will also try to solve your problem, Devadatta.

DEVADATTA   Ajatashatru, your father is old. This is the time for him to take rest and retire, but these old men never give way. Even until the last moment they want to enjoy the world, they want to lord it over the world. In every way you have surpassed your father. You have strength; you have power. Just throw the old man into prison and then you will become King. You can rule his kingdom peacefully and bravely. Who is there to stop you? I shall help you.

SIDDHARTHA BECOMES THE BUDDHA

AJATASHATRU   It is an excellent idea, an excellent idea! I shall do it. And when I become King, I promise you, Devadatta, I shall help you kill Buddha.

DEVADATTA   Be sure you don't eat your promise, Ajatashatru. Now you are the Prince, but you will soon be King. And it is on the strength of my advice that you will become King.

AJATASHATRU   I am not a mean fellow. I shall remember your help. I want to become King, and with your advice I shall fulfil my desire. Then I shall help you get rid of Buddha.

SB 27. SCENE 3

(Months later. King Ajatashatru is consulting his physician, Dr. Jaivaka.)

AJATASHATRU   Why have I begun to suffer from all kinds of diseases and ailments since I have become King? When I was Prince I was always healthy and robust. But now I have lost all my health. Is it because of the pressure of my work?

DR. JAIVAKA   No, King, it is not that which is causing your suffering.

AJATASHATRU   Why, then, am I suffering?

DR. JAIVAKA   Your disease, King, is psychological. You have an inner disease.

AJATASHATRU   What kind of inner disease? What do you mean by inner disease, Dr. Jaivaka? How will you cure me?

DR. JAIVAKA   O King, I will not be able to cure you because your disease is not physical. Your disease is mental, psychological, spiritual. Only Buddha can cure you.

AJATASHATRU   Buddha? Lord Buddha? Do you know that Devadatta and I are intimate friends, most intimate friends?

DR. JAIVAKA   Yes, I know it. And I also know that Devadatta helped you become King.

AJATASHATRU   Certainly he did. And I promised him that I would help him get rid of Buddha.

DR. JAIVAKA   That also I have heard. I am fully aware of it.

AJATASHATRU   Then why do you say that Buddha can cure me? That is impossible.

DR. JAIVAKA   O King, do you want me to tell you the truth, or do you want me to flatter you? No ordinary doctor can cure you. Only Buddha the Doctor can cure you. Your heart is extremely pure. Your heart is feeling miserable for what you have done to your father and for what you have been doing to Buddha, the innocent Buddha, the Light of the world. Once you rolled a big stone towards him while he was meditating on his disciples, but it veered away before hitting him. On another occasion, you set a mad elephant to destroy him. But Buddha just looked at the elephant and it bowed down to him. Instigated by Devadatta, in various ways you have tried to kill him, but each time you have failed, and you will always fail. Buddha has realised the highest Truth. Your heart is crying for the highest Truth. This is your disease, the disease of your spiritual heart. If you really want to be cured, go to Buddha. He is the Divine Doctor, the Doctor Supreme. Nobody on earth but Buddha can cure you. He can and he will.

AJATASHATRU O human doctor, you are sending me to the Divine Doctor. I am grateful. My life of vital desire has ended. My life of soul's aspiration is beginning with your divine advice.

DR. JAIVAKA Your soul is more than ready to accept the Buddha's Light. Buddha the infinite Light will transform Ajatashatru, the King of ignorance, into Ajatashatru, the Light of immortalising Bliss.

SB 28. SCENE 4

(The Buddha with hundreds of disciples. Enter King Ajatashatru. All the disciples are excited. Ajatashatru prostrates himself before the Buddha.)

AJATASHATRU   O Lord of the world, out of our stupendous ignorance my friend Devadatta and I tried to kill you several times, but we failed, badly failed. Today I am at your august feet, to be killed immediately by your wisdom-sun.

BUDDHA   O King....

AJATASHATRU   Master, I am not your King. You are the King of my heart and soul. You are the Lord of my heart and soul. I am your undeserving slave.

BUDDHA   You are not my slave, you are my son, my chosen son. My compassion-sun forgives your ignorance-night. My wisdom-sun illumines, liberates and immortalises your heart's cry.

(Enter Devadatta. Falls at the feet of the Buddha.)

DEVADATTA   Siddhartha, while we two were quite young I fought with you over the possession of a bird. The strength of my unruly, undivine vital had to surrender to the strength of your all-loving heart. You won the bird. I told you that one day with my vital love of power I would conquer your heart's power of love. Since then I have tried in hundreds of ways to humiliate you, to ruin your mission and to kill you, but I have failed. You forgave me then, O Siddhartha. Now, O Buddha, my shameless life desperately begs your forgiveness.

BUDDHA   Devadatta, forgiveness is granted.

DEVADATTA   O Buddha, if you have really forgiven this inhuman creature, then do me another favour out of your infinite bounty. Your heart of compassion took care of that innocent bird. Now I pray to you to take care of the crying, bleeding bird inside my heart. And also I pray to you to take care of its cage, this body.

(Devadatta sings three times.)

Buddham saranam gacchami
dhammam saranam gacchami
sangham saranam gacchami

(I go to the Buddha for refuge.
I go to the Dharma for refuge.
I go to the Order for refuge.)

SARIPUTRA, YOU ARE A FOOL

SRI CHINMOY

SB 29. DRAMATIS PERSONÆ

THE BUDDHA
SARIPUTRA (A DISCIPLE)

SIDDHARTHA BECOMES THE BUDDHA

SB 30. SCENE I

(The Buddha and his disciple Sariputra.)

SARIPUTRA   O Lord Buddha, I am sure that you are the greatest of all spiritual Masters. Nobody before you attained to your height, and nobody after you will be able to equal you. You are unparalleled. You will always remain unparalleled. Nobody has come near your realisation, and nobody will ever come near your realisation.

BUDDHA   Sariputra, how do you know that nobody before me has ever attained to what I have attained? And how do you know that nobody will surpass me in the future? How can you make this kind of utterance? Do you know anything of the past? Do you know anything of the future?

SARIPUTRA   O Lord, I do not know anything about the past or the future, but I know everything about you.

BUDDHA   Sariputra, you are a fool. You know very little about me. A spiritual Master of my calibre cannot be known totally by anybody on earth. You see my outer history, my outer life. But my inner life you do not see, you cannot see. In my outer life I do perhaps ten things a day. In my inner life I am doing millions of things daily. The inner life of a spiritual Master will always remain a mystery. The outer life of the Master may be observed, but it will not always be understood. Very often it will be misunderstood. So, Sariputra, about my outer life you know practically nothing, and about my inner life you know nothing at all.

SARIPUTRA   I know nothing, true. But I know who you are. You are my liberation and you are my All.

BUDDHA   Sariputra, do not think of the past. Do not think of the future. Think only of the present. The past we have left behind. The future has not yet arrived. To think of things that we have left behind is useless, and to think of things that have not yet happened is equally useless. Forget about the past. Forget about the future. Think only of the present. It is today that you have to aspire. It is today that you have to realise. It is today that you have to manifest. It is today that you have to conquer all your desires. It is today that you have to bring to the fore all your aspiration. It is today that you have to become what you inwardly are, the Light. It is today that you have to give to the world at large what you are, the Light.

THE BUDDHA AND ANANDA

SRI CHINMOY

SB 31. DRAMATIS PERSONÆ

THE BUDDHA
ANANDA (HIS DEAREST DISCIPLE)
A GROUP OF A FEW INTIMATE DISCIPLES

SIDDHARTHA BECOMES THE BUDDHA

SB 32. SCENE I

(The Buddha and Ananda.)

BUDDHA   Ananda, I am now an old man. I am eighty years old. Ananda, for fifty years I have been teaching and preaching. The time has come for me to depart from this world. I am weak. I am an invalid. My whole body is shattered, Ananda. This body can be of no more use here on earth.

ANANDA   *(shedding tears)* No, Master, no. You have to stay with us for quite a long time more. Your very presence is a great blessing to humanity. This *sangha* is not yet well established. This sangha needs your physical presence.

BUDDHA   Ananda, do you mean to say that the sangha expects something new from me? Do you mean to say that I have not spoken in clear terms what I have to say about this *dharma*? I have not kept anything hidden from you people. Never have I shown any sign of reticence, nor any indifference. Besides, I never thought that I would have to conduct and manage the sangha, and that it would always depend on me. So why should I stay? Why should I be involved any longer in the activities of the sangha? Ananda, from now on be self-sufficient. Have faith in yourself. Lead a spiritual life. You will realise the highest Truth. He who follows the dharma, he who takes refuge in the dharma, will alone enter into the world of Bliss, and nobody else.

ANANDA   O Lord Buddha, what you say is perfectly true, but our hearts cannot live without you. We need you. We shall eternally need you.

BUDDHA   Ananda, you need me. I need you. Again, the Truth Eternal needs us both. The Truth Eternal needs me in the world of the Beyond, and the same Truth needs you here on earth. My life has come to an end. All the experiences of the world I offer to the world. Yesterday I ate at Chunda's house. Since then I have been feeling weaker, but I wish to assure you that this weakness is not due to his food. I am suffering, true, but it is not his fault at all. He gave me food with utmost love and devotion. Nobody should blame him when I die. I offer him my deepest blessings. Before I was illumined, before I became the Enlightened One, Sujata's food helped me to live on earth. Her food made it possible for me to meditate. And now Chunda's food is helping me to enter into the highest Nirvana. I see no difference between Sujata's food and Chunda's food. Each has served a special purpose of its own.

(Enter a few intimate disciples.)

ANANDA   Look! Look! Today the Buddha's whole body is flooded with Light. This Light we have never seen around him. Such celestial Light!

THE DISCIPLES   Yes, Lord, today we see something totally new in you which we have never seen before. Your whole face is inundated with Light and Delight.

BUDDHA   Ananda, today reminds me of my days at the foot of the Bodhi tree. Just before I entered into Nirvana this body had the same Light, the same Delight. Today once again this body is flooded with Light and Delight. You are seeing it for the first time. But I am seeing it for the second time. The day ends, and my earthly sojourn ends along with it. Therefore, all of you are seeing this Light in me and around me.

(Ananda bursts into tears and is about to leave.)

SIDDHARTHA BECOMES THE BUDDHA

BUDDHA Ananda, stay here. Don't go away. My life can now be measured in minutes. Ananda, do not cry for me. I tell all of you not to cry for me. Ananda, I have told you repeatedly that everything is transient on earth. There is nothing everlasting here. Anything that comes into life will have to give up life. You have served me, O Ananda, most devotedly, most soulfully, and for that I offer you my last blessings. Proceed on your inner strength, and you will receive liberation. You will have your liberation in due course. My spiritual journey began with renunciation and compassion, and today, at the end of my journey's close, I offer to the world the same message: renunciation and compassion. O Ananda, do not grieve.

(The Buddha dies.)

PART IV

THE SON

THE SON

SRI CHINMOY

TS I. DRAMATIS PERSONAE

THE FATHER
THE SON — JESUS
MARY (MOTHER OF JESUS)
ANGEL
ELIZABETH (MOTHER OF JOHN THE BAPTIST)
JOSEPH (FATHER OF JESUS)
THREE SHEPHERDS
KING HEROD
THREE WISE MEN
TEACHER OF JESUS
STUDENTS
JOHN THE BAPTIST
DISCIPLES OF JOHN THE BAPTIST
DISCIPLES OF JESUS
JUDAS, PETER, PHILIP, THOMAS (OTHER DISCIPLES OF JESUS)
MARY MAGDALENE
KRISHNA
RAMA
BUDDHA
THE CHRIST

THE SON

TS 2. SCENE I

(In Heaven.)

FATHER   My son, I have an excellent plan. I wish to share it with you. I want you to descend to earth and play the most significant role.

SON   Father, my Father, indeed that is a splendid idea.

FATHER   You know, to work for earth, to work for the transformation of the earth-consciousness, is an unimaginably difficult task.

SON   But Father, I do not want to miss this unique opportunity. Besides, I know pretty well that You, my Father, will inundate my earthly pilgrimage with capacity. Since I have no hesitation whatsoever, Father, I cannot brook any further procrastination.

FATHER   *(with a broad smile)* Son, you will be on earth for thirty-three years!

SON   Only thirty-three years! How, then, am I going to fulfil my task?

FATHER   Son, you can and you shall. Son, on earth some people walk, while others march and still others run. In your case, you will not only run the fastest but also manifest the highest. Son, your body will remain on earth for thirty-three years. But your Consciousness shall guide the earth-consciousness forever and forever. Son, you will tell the world that you are the way and you are the Goal.

SON   Father, you have just thrown me into a sea of confusion.

FATHER   Why, my son? How, my son?

SON   Krishna, Buddha and others have preceded me, Father. And I am sure, after my departure, there will be others to succeed me. Such being the case, how can I tell the world that I alone am the way and the Goal?

FATHER My son, when I said *you*, what I actually meant was aspiration. When I said *you*, what I actually meant was salvation. You embody aspiration, the way. You embody salvation, the Goal. It is you the aspiration and you the salvation who will serve Me, manifest Me and fulfil Me on earth. Son, is My philosophy clear to you now?

SON More than clear. Needless to say, it is Your Compassion that has made it so clear to me.

FATHER I am glad that you have understood Me. I am glad that you are going to reveal Me on earth. I am glad that you are going to manifest Me on earth. I am glad that you are going to fulfil Me on earth. Remember that you are My instrument. *Nimitta matram bhava savyasachin.*

SON Father, what language are You speaking? It sounds quite strange, yet so charming.

FATHER Ah son, don't you know this language? It is Sanskrit. And what I have just said was your brother Krishna's lofty utterance. He said to his dearest disciple, "O Arjuna, become my mere instrument." You will also tell your disciples and dear ones to become divine instruments. Son, I tell you something which will fascinate you or, at least, amuse you. During your stay on earth, you will go to that part of the world where scriptures in Sanskrit are being taught. You will learn much from them. You will be in that part of the world for a year. That year in your inner life will be most rewarding.

SON How strange is Sanskrit! How sweet is Sanskrit! Father, will You kindly repeat what You have just said in Sanskrit?

FATHER *Nimitta matram bhava savyasachin.*

SON Thank You, Father. I know I am just a humble instrument of Yours. That's all.

THE SON

FATHER   Son, you know the supreme secret, and that supreme secret is humility. It is your humility that will crown you with the transcendental triumph. Son, you understand Me and I understand you. But the world will misunderstand you. You will give to humanity what you have and what you are: Love, Concern and Compassion in infinite measure. Yet the world will misunderstand you badly. Some unlit, undivine and unthinkable human beings will kill you.

SON   They will kill me! Why? How?

FATHER   Why? Because they are ignorant. How? They will crucify you.

SON   Crucify me? Are you serious, Father?

FATHER   Son, I am. Unfortunately, I am. But son, you know perfectly well that it is only the body that is destroyed, not the soul. The soul is immortal. The soul-bird will naturally fly back to its divine Source when the cage is smashed.

SON   Father, they are such ungrateful people!

FATHER   Son, gratitude has not yet been born on earth, and I do not know if it will ever take birth on earth soil. But you must not think that I have forsaken you at the time of your crucifixion. The human in you will think so, but not the divine in you. Since you are taking human incarnation, you have to act like a human being at times. Otherwise, there will be no game. Otherwise, people will always see a yawning gulf between your life of purity and luminosity and their lives of impurity and obscurity. Noticing this, they will never attempt to transcend their earth-bound consciousness. Light must descend into darkness. Only then can Light transform and illumine darkness. There is no other way. To transform the consciousness of humanity you have to become one with humanity. You have to become part and parcel of humanity. You have to act at times on their own level, according to their limited understanding. My son, there is no other way.

At the end of your journey the human in you will say, "Father, why hast Thou forsaken me?" The divine in you will say, "Father, forgive them, for they know not what they do!" I assure you, My son, the dying human in you will immediately be comforted by Me and will be well taken care of by Me. The illumining divine in you will not only immortalise you, but will also hasten My full manifestation on earth.

THE SON

TS 3. SCENE 2

(Mary's home. Enter an angel.)

ANGEL Mary, Mary, I have a most special message for you from Above.
MARY Special in what sense?
ANGEL Special in a divine sense, in an illumining sense.
MARY Ah, then tell me, do tell me.
ANGEL Mary, the Lord is growing inside you.
MARY The Lord?
ANGEL The Lord of the Universe.
MARY I don't believe you. I simply can't believe my ears. Don't torture me, for God's sake!
ANGEL Am I torturing you, Mary?
MARY Yes, you are. A torrent of fear is torturing my heart. A volcano of doubt is torturing my mind.
ANGEL Be not afraid, for that does not become you. Be not wedded to doubt, for neither does that become you, Mary. I will tell you a secret: Infinity you embody; Eternity is your heart; Immortality is your life. Jesus, the son of God, is inside you, Mary. He shall save his people. He shall rule the length and breadth of the world forever. Do you want to know how?
MARY How?
ANGEL He will not rule the world with the sword-power. He will rule the world with his heart-power, with his love-power.
MARY Heart-power and love-power: are they two different things?
ANGEL No, they are one. Heart is love. Love is heart.

MARY   At last I am really happy. You have given me the supreme message. What can I give you in return?
ANGEL   Nothing. Just believe what I have said.
MARY   I believe you now. I accept your message most gratefully.
ANGEL   Mary, your acceptance of my message is my highest reward. Mary, you are immaculate. You are great. You are divine. Mary, before I leave I give you another piece of good news. Your cousin Elizabeth, too, will have a child.
MARY   Wonderful, wonderful! I shall visit her shortly.
ANGEL   That is a splendid idea, indeed.

(Exit Angel.)

MARY   O Lord, You are giving me Your beloved son. I am an ignorant woman. I know nothing. But I do know that You are all Forgiveness, all Compassion and all Love.

(Mary sings.)

Ah! simple to learn my Supreme's Message-Light,
Easy to do His glowing and fulfilling Task.
In me now sings and sports His Nectar-Day.
In His Glory's sky, my Goal and I shall bask.

THE SON

TS 4. SCENE 3

(Elizabeth's home. Enter Mary.)

ELIZABETH   Mary, Mary, I have heard. But I must not call you Mary anymore. From now on I must call you Mother, Mother of my Lord Supreme. Blessed and unparalleled are you among women. Blessed and unparalleled is your son among men.

MARY   May the divine Mother, Mother of the universe, bless me, my little heart. May Her Universal Consciousness guide me, my humble life. May Her Transcendental Light illumine me, my small world.

ELIZABETH   I assure you, She will. The Mother of the universe will fulfil all your desires, and more.

MARY   Thank you. Thank you. Ah, I forgot to ask you the most important thing. The angel has told me that you too are being blessed with a divine child. Is it true?

ELIZABETH   Yes, it is true. But mine is no match for yours. That does not mean jealousy will take shelter in my heart. No, never shall I allow jealousy to darken my heart's door. My son shall be the harbinger of your son's supreme arrival. My son shall tell the world who your son is. My son shall lead the world safely to your son, the Abode Supreme. He is your son, but he will be my Lord. He will be my Supreme. He will be my All.

(Elizabeth sings.)

SRI CHINMOY

God is a Man,
I love His Face.
His blue-gold Love,
My Heaven-bound race.

MARY   O God, do grant me three boons. I wish to see my son always the way Elizabeth sees him. I wish to feel my son always the way Elizabeth feels him. I wish to treasure my son always the way Elizabeth treasures him.

THE SON

TS 5. SCENE 4

(Nazareth. Joseph the carpenter is having a dream. Enter an angel.)

ANGEL   Joseph, you are the most fortunate person on earth, Your wife Mary will soon have a child.
JOSEPH   Stop, Angel! What you say is absurd. First of all, I am not yet married to Mary. And if it is true that she is with child, in spite of my deepest love for her I am not going to brave the waves of merciless public criticism by marrying her. After all, who wants to submit himself to wild scandals?
ANGEL   Mary's child will be a divine child. You must marry her. Since he is the Lord's beloved son, his divinity can easily set aside all human laws and principles. I warn you, Joseph, do not act like a rank fool. Accept Mary. Marry her. Claim her as your very own. Your son's name will be Jesus. That means salvation. Her son, who is equally your son, shall be the King of Israel. He shall illumine the entire world.
JOSEPH   I bow to your deep wisdom, Angel. Mary and I shall become one and inseparable. But, you know, I am just a simple man, a sincere man and a humble man.
ANGEL   Joseph, I like your simplicity, I love your sincerity, I adore your humility.
JOSEPH   Angel, I wish to ask you something. Please give me a sincere answer. How often do you see God?
ANGEL   I see God on rare occasions.
JOSEPH   I was under the impression that you saw God daily.
ANGEL   Oh, no. We angels are not so lucky as the cosmic gods. They see God daily.
JOSEPH   What do you and your angel comrades actually do?
ANGEL   We do quite a few things both for God and man. We bring down God's messages from the cosmic gods and

offer them to aspiring human beings. We inspire human beings secretly with deep inspiration and kindle the flame of aspiration in them.

JOSEPH   Tell me clearly, if possible, what you angels actually are.

ANGEL   We are of God's strong Love and we are for man's high promise.

JOSEPH   How great you are!

ANGEL   You are wrong, Joseph. Just say how fortunate we are. God consciously appoints us to serve Him in man. Man unconsciously invokes us to show him the way to God's Transcendental Abode.

JOSEPH   Sorry to change the subject.

ANGEL   That's perfectly all right.

JOSEPH   Do you really think and feel that my son Jesus will be the King of Israel?

ANGEL   No thinking, no feeling! I clearly see that your son Jesus will be the King of Israel. Something more. He will be the divine Emperor of the whole world. And he will forever rule the earth-consciousness with his love-power. *(Joseph folds his hands and bows to the angel. The angel blesses him.)* May God, the author of all good, bless your devoted heart.

THE SON

TS 6. SCENE 5

(A stable in Bethlehem.)

JOSEPH   Alas, this place is over-crowded. All the inns and the hotels are full. There is no room for us. You are soon going to be the mother of a child. And, since we believe in the Angel Gabriel, we can unmistakably say that the child will be the Lord of the entire world. However, here we are now beggars, and beggars cannot be choosers. So let us be satisfied with the stable that they have given us to stay in. Alas, here the cattle are kept and here our baby will be born in a day or two. Needless to say, when our baby is born we shall have to lay him in the manger along with the cows and oxen. Indeed, this is a supreme irony of fate — that the Lord of the Universe begins his earthly sojourn with animals and humble creatures. I am really worried.

MARY   Everything will be all right. Don't bury yourself in unnecessary worries. Our Lord Supreme is always merciful.

TS 7. SCENE 6

(The night is far advanced. Some shepherds are tending their sheep in a field near Bethlehem.)

FIRST SHEPHERD   Look, look, dear friends! What a bright and powerful light is in the sky!

SECOND SHEPHERD   Look, look! An angel of the Lord is fast approaching us.

THIRD SHEPHERD   Look, the angel is standing right before us.

THE THREE SHEPHERDS   Alas, some unknown fear is torturing our hearts.

ANGEL   O sweet, simple and sincere shepherds, cast aside your baseless fear. I have come to you with news of great joy. Today and just today, is born the Saviour. He is born in Bethlehem, which is quite near to us. The newborn divine baby is lying in the stable of an inn. He is the Christ, the Lord, the anointed King. Look up and see what my comrade angels are doing.

SHEPHERDS   Ah, they are dancing, praising and singing: *Glory to God in the Highest. And, on earth, peace among men, in whom God is well pleased.* It is wonderful, wonderful! Let us hurry to Bethlehem and see this wonderful thing.

(Exeunt omnes.)

THE SON

TS 8. SCENE 7

(King Herod's Palace.)

HEROD Unbearable! Unthinkable! Impossible! I shall not allow anyone else to be the King. I am the King, the only King of Judea. The priests and scribes have told me that this little baby King is in Bethlehem. I just want to be sure if it is true that he is there in Bethlehem. If he is, then I shall kill him. I shall send him to God. I shall remain King as long as I am allowed to live on this earth.

(Enter the three wise men.)

HEROD *(greeting them)* I am so happy to see you. I have heard much about you. You three are exceptionally wise men. You have come from the far East. You have studied the stars, and I understand that a star is leading you to the new King. Please go and see the divine child and come back with some information about him. Then I shall personally go and worship him.

(Exeunt the three wise men.)

TS 9. SCENE 8

(Mary and Joseph are in the inn.)

MARY Joseph, I told you not to worry. Now we have a nice room in a big inn. We are no longer in a stable. Here you and I will be able to look after our sweet divine baby quite easily.

JOSEPH Mary, you were right. You are right. You are always right.

MARY What you and I need is patience. That's all.

(Enter the three wise men.)

WISE MEN *(bowing to the baby)* O King, O Lord of the world, we are not on earth today. We are now in the seventh heaven of delight. No divine gifts have we to offer you. Be pleased to accept our earthly gifts of gold, perfume, frankincense and myrrh.

JOSEPH O divine guests, please spend this night here.

WISE MEN Thank you, Joseph. It is most kind of you.

(Mary feeds them. They go to sleep in one corner of the room, Joseph in another corner and Mary and the child in a third corner. After a few moments a divine voice awakens the three wise men.)

VOICE Go home. Don't go back to Herod.

(Exeunt the three wise men. An angel appears and awakens Joseph and Mary.)

ANGEL   Joseph, you, your wife and your child must leave immediately for Egypt. Otherwise Herod will soon find your little child here and kill him.

(Mary takes the baby in her arms. Exeunt omnes.)

(Jesus, Mary and Joseph at home in Nazareth.)

JESUS Mummy, Mummy, what is that in the sky?

MARY That is the moon.

JESUS The moon! It is so beautiful!

MARY You are much more beautiful, my child.

JESUS No, I am not. Mummy, I want to go to the moon and bring it down.

JOSEPH You don't have to go to the moon. The moon will come to you.

JESUS What for?

JOSEPH To play with you.

JESUS With me! How nice! *(To Joseph.)* You know, Daddy, in my dreams I see some most beautiful people. They come and play with me. They love me dearly.

MARY Do you know who they are?

JESUS No Mummy, but they like me a lot. They are my best friends.

MARY They are called angels.

JESUS Angels, angels! But Mummy, I don't see them during the day. Where do they hide during the day?

MARY During the day they hide in the skies.

JESUS Ah, I shall fly to the skies and catch them.

MARY You don't have to fly and catch them. They themselves will come to you. One of them has told me and your father that you are the beloved son of God.

JESUS What does he mean by that?

MARY He means that our Lord who is in Heaven loves you most. You are His darling.

THE SON

JESUS Am I, am I God's darling? Then I must go to see Him. Please take me to His House.
MARY We shall take you to me Temple of the Lord on Mount Moriah tomorrow.
JESUS Thank you, Mummy. Tomorrow I shall go to see our Lord's House. Tomorrow I shall see the Lord. Thank you, Mummy, thank you.

TS II. SCENE 10

(Nazareth. Several years later. Joseph is extremely ill. Mary is nursing him.)

JOSEPH   Mary, did you inform Jesus about my illness?

MARY   Yes, I did. Two months ago when sickness was entering into your body I asked an India-bound caravan to inform Jesus about your sickness.

JOSEPH   How long does it take for a caravan to reach India?

MARY   At least three months.

JOSEPH   Alas, even if he has heard about my sickness and even if he has left India....

MARY   It goes without saying that if he had heard about your illness he would have immediately left for home.

JOSEPH   But, my dear, it will take him three long months to reach us. You know quite well that my days on earth are very few.

MARY   No, I do not agree with you. You must stay on earth until our beloved son comes back.

JOSEPH   Who does not want that? But my life-boat is sinking fast. Jesus, my beloved son, my boat is sinking, but your boat will soon ply between the shores of earth's excruciating pangs and Heaven's ever-increasing Delight. I shall watch from Heaven with my soul's boundless pride as your white-red boat sails towards the shores of my ever-transcending Beyond. Jesus, my son!

(Joseph closes his eyes and dies.)

THE SON

TS 12. SCENE II

(Benares. A school for religious study. Several students, including Jesus, are seated in a semi-circle.)

TEACHER   Today I shall teach you something new. I have already taught you the *Chandi* and the *Yoga Vashishtha*. Today I shall start with a new book, the *Bhagavad-Gita,* the song celestial. The *Gita* is our Bible. So, dear Jesus, I am sure you have read your Bible. Beginning today, you will be studying our Bible. Jesus, my goodness! What is wrong with you? Why are you so sad and depressed? Is anything wrong with you? Has anything happened?

JESUS   Nothing particular, sir.

TEACHER   Tell me, tell me what is torturing your heart.

JESUS   *(bursting into tears)* I have received news from home that my father has died.

TEACHER   Your father! When? Where?

JESUS   Three and a half months ago my father died. He died in Israel. Sir, you have been extremely kind to me. I am most grateful to you. You have taught me some of the Hindu scriptures with tremendous love and care. But unfortunately, tomorrow I shall have to leave for home.

TEACHER   How will you go back home, my son?

JESUS   I shall go back the way I came. I came to India with a caravan and I shall go back with another caravan. Tomorrow I shall start. I have been in India for about a year. Here everyone has been extremely kind to me. I shall carry with me India's love, India's concern, India's compassion to offer to my people.

TEACHER   Dear son, thousands of students have passed through my hands, but none can come near you. You are a real genius.

You are unparalleled. Today you are badly suffering from the loss of your dear father. How I wish I could be of some consolation to you. Ah, a brilliant idea has flashed across my mind. I shall read out a few verses from the *Gita*.

> *Vāsāsi jīrāni yathā vihāya*
> *navāni ghāti naro 'parāi*
> *tathā śarīrāi vihāya jīrāny*
> *anyāni sayāti navāni dehī*

> (As a man casts off his worn-out garments and puts on new ones, so also the embodied soul casts off the worn-out body and enters into a new form for manifestation.)

> *Nai 'na chindanti śastrāi*
> *nai 'na dahati pāvaka*
> *na cai 'na kledayanty āpo*
> *na śoayati māruta*

> (Weapons cannot cleave the soul. Fire cannot burn the soul. Water cannot drench the soul. Wind cannot dry the soul.)

Would you like to recite with me?

JESUS   Certainly. I will be happy and grateful if I can join you.

(The teacher and Jesus recite together. The other students listen to them with rapt attention. Jesus' eyes are beaming with joy.)

JESUS   Sir, I am so grateful to you. These divine words from the *Gita* have consoled my heart completely.

THE SON

TEACHER I have always seen and felt something special in you. Outwardly I have never told it to anyone, but you are my most favourite student. I cherish your sincerity, your humility and your purity. Now Jesus, since you will not be able to study the *Gita* with me I wish to tell you something which will undoubtedly inspire you. You know that the *Gita* is the colloquy between the Lord Krishna and his dearest disciple-friend, Arjuna. The Lord taught his disciple something unique. He said God is the real doer. Human beings are mere instruments. Whether we are here on earth or there in Heaven, it is God who acts in and through us. We are mere instruments: *Nimitta matram bhava savyasachin.*

JESUS I have heard this before. I have heard this somewhere else. Alas, I can't recollect it. *(After a pause.)* Ah, I know! My Supreme Father told me about this mantra just before I left Heaven.

(All the students burst into a roar of laughter.)

A STUDENT *(in a mocking manner)* His Supreme Father in Heaven! What else? You fool, how can you remember what happened in Heaven? Today you are no longer our Jesus, but the King of Imagination.

TEACHER You rascals, keep quiet! Hide your ignorance in silence. What is strange about remembering one's existence in Heaven? You fools have not yet read the *Gita*. That is why you are behaving like brainless sheep. In the *Gita* the Lord clearly says that all of us have gone through many, many incarnations. This is not our first and last life. In the *Gita* the Lord tells Arjuna all about his previous incarnations.

A STUDENT   Our Lord Krishna can do that kind of thing. We believe in Krishna. But for our Jesus, the King of Imagination, to act like our Lord Krishna is absurd.

TEACHER   You fools! Today you are calling my Jesus the King of Imagination. You are making fun of him. I tell you, one day you will come to know who he is. Your King of Imagination will become not only the King of Israel but also the King of the world. My heart tells me that he is not a mortal like us. He is a world-saviour. He is another Krishna.

(Jesus comes and touches the feet of his teacher with utmost humility.)

JESUS   Sir, I am all gratitude.

TEACHER   Today you are touching my feet with all your heart's humility. In the near future not only I, but the entire world, will touch your feet and worship you.

THE SON

TS 13. SCENE 12

(John the Baptist alone by the Jordan River.)

JOHN   This world is not meant for me. I am sick of this world. I tell people something repeatedly, yet they won't believe me. They just go on bothering me and harassing me. I tell them that I am *not* the Messiah. I am *not* Elijah. I am not the Prophet. They ask me why do I then baptise people? I tell them that I have been commanded by the Lord from Above to baptise. I also tell them that I baptise with water, but soon after me somebody will baptise with the Holy Spirit. I am no match for him. I am not good enough even to untie his sandals.

(Enter some of his disciples.)

DISCIPLE   Master, we just overheard you. You were saying that you are not good enough even to untie his sandals. Who is that great man? Nobody can be higher than you.

JOHN   Children, there can be and there is one higher than me, and he is Jesus. I am just a voice that shouts in the desert. I am trying to make a straight path for the Lord Jesus to travel.

DISCIPLES   Master, you feel anything you want to. You say anything you want to say. It is up to us to believe you or not. You are inferior to none.

JOHN   You impossible fools! Your stupidity constantly pains me. Ah, look, look! He is fast approaching me. There is the Lamb of God. There is the Son of God. There is the one about whom I have been talking all along.

(Enter Jesus.)

JESUS I wish to be baptised by you, John.

JOHN O, Jesus, how can I baptise you? I know who you are. You are the Son of God. You are His beloved Son.

JESUS Let us not break the order. Let us do everything in order. It is by you that I must be baptised. You have recognised me. Therefore, John, you are divinely great. You are making the road ready for me. Therefore you are supremely good. Your mother, Elizabeth, was divinely great and supremely good, too, for she recognised me and inspired my mother immensely even before I was born.

JOHN O Son of God, you are seeing me and my mother through your own transcendental greatness and universal goodness. I have just one more thing to do on earth and that is to place all my disciples at your feet as I place myself at your feet.

(He touches Jesus' feet.)

DISCIPLES *(shocked)* You can touch his feet, but we will not. He may be greater than you in your view, but we will have nothing to do with him. We shall offer you our loyalty constantly. You are our Master, our only Master.

JOHN You fools. You should be loyal only to the Highest. Only the best should be your Master. And I want to tell you something more. I am not guiding you to someone who is a little better than I. I am leading and guiding you all to the one whose greatness is nothing other than God-greatness, whose goodness is nothing other than God-goodness. I tell you once and for all, to please him is to please God the Father. To have him is to have God the Father. He is

Heaven's most beautiful flower and earth's most nourishing fruit.

JESUS *(smiling at John's disciples)* Your name is the Lord's ever-illumining and ever-fulfilling Vision. O children of John, I am deeply moved by your unprecedented loyalty to your Master. Your Master has had the Vision of the Ultimate Reality. Needless to say, he will lead, guide and perfect you on your journey to the Transcendental Goal. My heart deeply admires your love for your great Master. My soul sincerely admires your Master for his unflinching love for Truth.

TS 14. SCENE 13

(Jesus and Mary at home.)

JESUS   Mother, I beg to be excused.
MARY   Son, you have not done anything wrong. Why do you need my forgiveness?
JESUS   Mother, yesterday at the wedding party I was unnecessarily rude to you. When they ran short of wine you requested me to do something. I was so hostile to you. I said, "Woman, what matters it to you and to me? My hour has not yet come."
MARY   But you did listen to me, after all. So how can I be displeased with you? My son, you transformed water into wine. What a miracle! Jesus, it was your first miracle. I am sure you will do many more. But this much I tell you, my son, if you are going to perform fifty miracles in the outer world, then rest assured you will perform fifty thousand miracles in the inner world. All your inner world activities, your divine Father in Heaven and my simple soul on earth, will know. Jesus, yesterday at the wedding party I asked the servants to listen to you. Today I ask the whole world to listen to you, and it certainly will.
JESUS   You think too highly of me, Mother.
MARY   Son, your supernatural height is not only far beyond the domain of my experience, but also far beyond my imagination's flight.
JESUS   I know, Mother of mine. You want only my divinity to come to the fore. I am the sun. You are the moon. I am rising; therefore cheerfully and unconditionally you are going to hide yourself. From now on you have decided to remain in the background. Such is your love for me. Such

THE SON

is your oneness with me. Mother, I may become great one day. But you are good. To me greatness is no match for goodness.

TS 15. SCENE 14

(Jesus and his disciples.)

JESUS   Lazarus, my dear friend, you are no more. O soul of Lazarus, to you I offer my heart's immense gratitude, for it is you who are helping me reveal the Glory of God. Martha, Mary, dear ones, I am coming to your house to revive your dead brother. Children, let us go to Judea.

DISCIPLES   Judea! What for? Have you forgotten that just the other day they wanted to stone you?

JESUS   Don't worry. I know who I am. This time they will see my light. My dear friend Lazarus died four days ago. My Father wants me to go to Lazarus and revive him.

DISCIPLES   But by this time he is buried. What can you do now?

JESUS   I can do nothing. I have done nothing. I will be able to do nothing. But my Father did, does and will do everything in and through me.

DISCIPLES   Lord, we give glory to you. You give glory to your Father. You stay with your Father. We stay with you, our Father.

JESUS   Amongst you there are still some who do not believe in me. When I revive Lazarus, their belief will grow. I am grateful to Lazarus. I am grateful to the non-believers, for they are helping me to reveal the Lord's divine Glory on earth. Come, don't delay. Let us go and bring joy to the bereaved and stricken family.

THE SON

TS 16. SCENE 15

(Jesus on the Mount. He is rapt in trance. Enter Father. The face of Jesus glows.)

FATHER   Son, I wish you to offer a series of aphorisms as special advice to your disciples. Your disciples may ask you for their meanings. Therefore I shall tell you the meanings as well, First, blessed are the poor in spirit, for theirs is the Kingdom of Heaven.

JESUS   How wonderful is Your advice, Father!

FATHER   It means that the Kingdom of Bliss is for those blessed people who have devoted dedication to their inner and spiritual life and who have nothing to do with pride.

JESUS   I see. Thank You, Father. Next?

FATHER   Blessed are those who mourn, for they shall be comforted.

JESUS   Wonderful, Father.

FATHER   Son, it means that the true spiritual life of a seeker begins when he has a real sense of loss. His loss is the loss of his inner wealth: peace, joy, love and bliss. This loss creates in him an inner cry which may outwardly be known as mourning. Naturally a seeker of this type will be given back the peace, joy, love and bliss which he is crying to recover.

JESUS   I see. Thank You, Father. Next?

FATHER   Blessed are the meek, for they shall inherit the earth.

JESUS   Wonderful, Father.

FATHER   Son, it means that if a man has a tremendous sense of superiority, he will lord it over others, but if the same man feels that he is weak and helpless without Me, then he will develop a deep sense of humility. This humility will make him one with all human beings on earth. His universal oneness is the strength that will enable him to claim the earth divinely and supremely.

JESUS   I see. Thank You, Father. Next?

FATHER   Blessed are the pure in heart, for they shall see God.

JESUS   Wonderful, Father,

FATHER   Son, it means that purity alone has the capacity to receive and achieve Divinity. A pure heart is a peerless manifestation of My divine Reality.

JESUS   I see. Thank You very much, Father. Next?

FATHER   Blessed are the peacemakers, for they shall be called sons of God.

JESUS   Wonderful, Father.

FATHER   Son, it means that My divine children are those who aspire for Light and who are surcharged with Light. Light, in the process of its manifestation, becomes the all-nourishing and all-fulfilling Peace.

JESUS   I see. Thank You, Father. Next?

FATHER   If any one strikes you on the right cheek, turn to him the other also.

JESUS   Wonderful, Father.

FATHER   Son, it means that forgiveness is by far the best quality both in Me and in all human beings. If ignorance has struck you once and you have forgiven ignorance, there is no guarantee that it will not strike you again. But if you tell ignorance that if it wants to strike you again you are more than prepared to answer it with your forgiveness-weapon, ignorance comes to realise that your weapon is infinitely stronger than its weapon. Your weapon has Light and spreads Light; whereas its weapon, which is darkness, is all confusion. Remaining in utter and constant confusion, how can it continue to fight against its opponent, Light, which is all-loving and all fulfilling?

JESUS   I see. Thank You, Father, thank You. Next?

FATHER   When you give alms, do not let your left hand know what your right hand is doing.
JESUS   Wonderful, Father.
FATHER   Son, it means that man gets a great sense of satisfaction if he sees that someone is watching while he is giving something to others. The satisfaction that results from a public show immediately creates unnecessary pride. What is pride, if not immediate and total self-destruction?
JESUS   Thank You, Father, thank You. Next?
FATHER   For today it is enough, My son. I am a bit tired. Some other day I will give you more advice.

SRI CHINMOY

TS 17. SCENE 16

(Jesus with his disciples.)

JESUS   I am a Jew, but the Jews do not accept me. They hate me, even though I came to save them. Such is my fate. Yet I know that the whole world will one day accept me, love me and adore me. I know that I am not for a tiny section of humanity only. I am for the whole of humanity. But those who accept me and claim me as their own are undoubtedly my beloved ones. My days are numbered. I have twelve disciples. Among them, Judas will betray me. He will put me into the hands of the enemy. And then they will crucify me.

(All the disciples are shocked.)

DISCIPLES   Judas! Judas! Judas will betray our Lord!
JUDAS   Impossible, impossible! *(Touching Jesus' feet.)* Lord, is there anything that I can do without your knowledge or without your approval or, at least, without your acquiescence? I know, Lord, your words will prove true. But Lord, it seems to me that it is you who have chosen me to play this unthinkable part in your cosmic play.
JESUS   *(smiles and blesses him)* Judas, you are right. True, the world will hate you. But the world does not know that everything is predestined. So Judas, do your part well when your hour strikes.
DISCIPLES   Lord, our hour has already struck. We want to do our part well.

THE SON

(They all grab Judas and start striking and kicking him.)

JESUS   Stop! Stop, or I shall leave you all immediately! Judas is doing the right thing. His betrayal is predestined. What can he do now? And what can I do now? Only our Father in Heaven knows what is best for Judas and what is best for me and what is best for all of you.
DISCIPLES   We know what is best for us!

(They start striking Judas again.)

JESUS   Stop! Stop! If not, I shall leave you for good!
PETER   Lord, you are great. You are divine. For you it is easy to forgive a filthy betrayer and a scoundrel like Judas. But we are mortals, ordinary human beings. How can we forgive him?
JESUS   Peter, the same way I shall forgive you. Peter, one day you will deny me — not once, not twice, but thrice. Three successive times in one short day!
PETER   Me? Impossible! When? Why?
JESUS   Yes, Peter, it is you and nobody else who will deny me. You think it is impossible. But I tell you, Peter, it is not only possible; it is inevitable. It is all predestined. Do not cry, do not weep, Peter. I loved you most. I shall always love you most. Again, when the hour strikes, it is you who will carry my banner of Truth and unlock my heart's door so humanity can see my Father's Light. You love me most dearly. Therefore I wish you to take care of my other disciples who are my lambs, my sheep.
PETER   Lord, I shall. I shall without fail. Lord, you are the Lord of Love. You are the Lord of Compassion. You are the Lord of Forgiveness,

JESUS   No, no. I am just the son of fulfilment. My Father is the Lord of Love. My Father is the Lord of Compassion, My Father is the Lord of Forgiveness.

PHILIP   Lord, will we ever see your Father?

JESUS   Certainly you can. Philip, shall I tell you the supreme truth? He who has seen me has seen the Father, for I and my Father are one.

Children, I wish to tell you a funny story:

> There were once three sons of the same father: the youngest, the middle and the eldest.
> The youngest son said: "Father is in Heaven."
> The middle son said: "The Kingdom of Heaven is in your heart."
> The eldest son said: "I and my Father are one."
> To the youngest son, the Father said: "Son, thank you for your vision."
> To the middle son, the Father said: "Son, thank you for your mission."
> To the eldest son, the Father said: "Son, thank you for your union."

My sweet children, Father asked me to go into the world. I obeyed Him. He asked me to show the world His Light. I obeyed Him. I have fulfilled all His demands. He has fulfilled His dreams through my dedicated and surrendered life. Now He wants me to go back to Him. Therefore I am prepared. Children, my Father gave you all to me. Now, at my earthly journey's close, I am returning you all to Him. I am nothing. He is Everything. He is for everything. He is All. He is for all.

Judas, come here, please.

THE SON

(Judas goes and sits at the Master's feet.)

JESUS   *Nimitta matram bhava.* Be thou a mere instrument.

(Judas sings.)

Today, today, today
Alone with God I stay;
Tomorrow and forever
With His Compassion-Ray.

JESUS   Peter, come here, please.

(Peter goes and sits at the Master's feet.)

JESUS   *Nimitta matram bhava.* Be thou a mere instrument.

(Peter sings.)

An ant like me to save
You came into this world of dust and clay.
A beggar like me to love
And give me a role sublime in Your Cosmic Play.

JESUS   Children, be the instruments of the Lord. We are all His instruments. Him to embody we came into the world. Him to reveal we came into the world. Him to fulfil we came into the world.

SRI CHINMOY

TS 18. SCENE 17

(Evening. Jesus alone in a small garden.)

JESUS Yes, I have performed miracles and my miracles have been many and varied. I have stilled storms. I have cured physical maladies. I have given sight to the blind. I have even raised the dead to life. But the world will never believe that I consider my miracles to be of secondary importance, to say the least. I came into the world to reveal my Lord, my Father who is in Heaven. If anybody believes in me for my own sake, then he is infinitely greater than those who believe in me only for my miracles. Again, because of the people's lack of faith, I did not want to perform miracles at Nazareth. It would have served no purpose. To me, each miracle is a manifestation of God's Power-Light. And if it is not properly accepted it only feeds man's curiosity; it does not help elevate man's consciousness at all. Therefore, it is absolutely necessary that God's Power-Light be well regulated by God's Wisdom-Height. But who will believe that I have the power to perform miracles in the face of all unbelievers, disbelievers and stark atheists? Alas, nobody understands me. Nobody comes to me to fulfil my Lord in His divine Way.

(Jesus sings.)

None came to me, none came and none shall come.
Only my supreme Beloved came, only He.
I cried for His smile and He, for my selfless love.
Sleepless in me He grows His Vision-Tree.

THE SON

TS 19. SCENE 18

(Jesus and Mary.)

JESUS   Mother, please sing me a song, How I wish I could have a singing voice like yours.
MARY   Son, how I wish I could have an illumining heart like yours.
JESUS   Mother, please sing.

(Mary sings.)

My life began with duty's pride,
My life shall live with beauty's light,
My life shall sport with reality's soul,
My life shall end with Divinity's Height.

JESUS   Mother, in Heaven I shall miss your stirring voice. In a few days I shall be crucified.
MARY   Oh no, impossible! I shall not allow that to happen. My beloved son, will you not use your divine power to save yourself? Please do it, my son. I shall be so happy, so proud and so grateful.
JESUS   To please you, Mother, I performed my first miracle at the wedding party. I transformed water into wine. To please you again at the end of my journey's close I shall perform another miracle, the Miracle of miracles. Since my Heavenly Father wants me to come back to Him, I shall have to go back. But three days after my death, I shall appear once again and see you all. This miracle will have no parallel in the history of our Lord's creation.

So, Mother, Mother of my heart, I shall please you in a different way. I shall not save my body, but I shall prove to the world that I am deathless, that I am eternal. Although the body is perishable, the soul is immortal. This body has played its role. Why keep it on earth any longer? Mother, soon you too will join me in Heaven.

MARY   Shall I? How I wish, son, we could go together.

JESUS   Mother, your hour has not yet struck, but soon it will.

(Enter Mary Magdalene, weeping.)

MAGDALENE   Lord, last night I had a terrible dream, in my dream I saw you being crucified. On the cross you asked for a drink and they gave you some wine. You drank the wine, then bowed your head and said, "It is all finished." My dream was so vivid. Lord, this dream is ruthlessly tearing at my inner being. My heart is completely broken. Lord, I beg of you, tell me that my dream was all a mental hallucination, with no reality in it.

JESUS   Did you see anything more?

MAGDALENE   Yes, I saw something more. I saw something unbelievable. Three days after your death you appeared before me. I saw you vividly. I ran to tell Peter and your other disciples. Everybody believed me except one disciple.

JESUS   Who was it? Who did not believe you?

MAGDALENE   It was that unfortunate Thomas.

(Enter Thomas.)

THOMAS   Magdalene, I overheard your conversation with the Lord. I, too, had a similar dream. In my dream I saw something more. The Lord, out of his infinite bounty, made me believe him unmistakably and said, "You believe me because you see me. Happy and fortunate are those who believe me without seeing me."

(Thomas sings.)

With doubt my mind began,
With fear my heart began,
With clay my life began,
All in this shortest span.

JESUS   Excellent, excellent, I never knew that you had such a sweet voice. Thomas, your dream has reality in it in great measure. Magdalene, your dream will soon be transformed into reality. Magdalene, please sing me a song. You have not sung for me for a long time.

(Magdalene sings.)

There was a time when I stumbled and stumbled,
But now I only climb and climb beyond
And far beyond my Goal's endless Beyond,
And yet my Captain commands: "Go on, go on!"

JESUS   Magdalene, I am well pleased with you. What the Father needs is a heart of purity and you have it in ample measure. A pure heart is a peerless treasure. You heard me saying a few months ago that the pure in heart are blessed, for they will see God. You will see God in me.

MAGDALENE   Lord, I have already seen God in you. Something more, I see you only as God. You are none other than your Heavenly Father. You do everything. But you give Him all the credit. Such is your heart's magnanimity.

JESUS   Dear Magdalene, you are wrong. My Heavenly Father is the only doer. I am a mere instrument of His.

Nimitta matram
nimitta matram
nimitta matram
nimitta matram

(I am a mere instrument.)

THE SON

TS 20. SCENE 19

(Heaven. Krishna is playing on his divine flute.)

KRISHNA Ah, Jesus is singing my favourite song on earth. How soulfully he is offering the wealth of my song to mankind. No, I must be totally frank. That song is not mine. I did not compose that song. It was our Father Supreme who composed that song. He taught me that song and I sang it on earth. He taught Jesus the same song and now he is singing it on earth so soulfully and so fruitfully.

Ah, today our Jesus is coming back home. How hard he has worked, especially his last three years on earth. He needs and deserves some rest here in Heaven. *(Shouting aloud.)* Rama, Buddha, where are you? Come here please. *(Enter Rama and Buddha.)* Our brother Jesus is coming back today. Father gave me the message this morning.

RAMA AND BUDDHA Father always tells you everything first. You are His most favourite son.

KRISHNA Not at all. We all are His most favourite sons. What can poor Father do? Rama, last night you had to put up a brave fight against Satan and the forces of ignorance. Therefore, in the morning you were dead tired. Naturally you had to sleep far into the morning. Father did not want to disturb your sound sleep.

Buddha, you got up very early in the morning and started meditating. You went into your deepest trance. When Father saw you in your usual trance, He did not want to disturb you either. And what was I doing in the morning? I was playing on my flute and reminiscing about my Brindavan *lila* on earth with my divine Radha and my divine gopis, my totally devoted and completely surrendered devotees. Since

I was neither sleeping nor meditating, Father came to me and gave me the message of Jesus' arrival today.

RAMA AND BUDDHA   Krishna, you are sweetness and concern to all your devotees. To us, your brothers, you are all cleverness and all wisdom. No wonder the world, especially India, has such love for you.

KRISHNA   Brother Rama, Brother Buddha, let us not waste time. Our brother Jesus will soon arrive. His crucifixion has shattered me totally.

BUDDHA   I was simply horrified when I heard about it from Father the other day.

RAMA   When Father told me about Jesus' crucifixion, I was simply mortified. He has done so much for earth and, in return, earth offers him crucifixion. Earth is not ready for us.

BUDDHA   It seems that earth will never be ready.

KRISHNA   For my sake, for Father's sake, let us be ready to receive Jesus. Let us make a most beautiful throne for him.

(They make a golden throne. Jesus ascends and appears. They greet him most enthusiastically and place him on the throne. Enter Father.)

FATHER   *(blessing and embracing Jesus)* Jesus, my Jesus.

> *I saw your suffering face.*
>   *I cried and cried.*
> *I felt your forgiving heart.*
>   *I smiled and smiled.*
> *I clasped your illumining soul.*
>   *I danced and danced.*

PART V

LORD GAURANGA:
LOVE INCARNATE

FRIENDSHIP KNOWS NO EQUAL

SRI CHINMOY

LG I. DRAMATIS PERSONÆ

CHAITANYA
RAGHUNATH (HIS FRIEND)

LORD GAURANGA: LOVE INCARNATE

LG 2. SCENE I

(Chaitanya and Raghunath are in a boat crossing the Ganges, on their way to school.)

RAGHUNATH   I see a book in your hand, a special book. May I know what it is?
CHAITANYA   Oh, it is nothing. It is something silly.
RAGHUNATH   What is silly about it? Let me see.
CHAITANYA   *(hesitates)* You won't like it. If you want, I can read out a few pages to you.
RAGHUNATH   No, no. Please allow me to read it myself.

(Chaitanya hands him the book. Raghunath scans a few pages, then closes his eyes.)

CHAITANYA   Raghunath, what is the matter? Why have you closed your eyes? Is anything wrong with you? *(Raghunath starts to cry.)* Why are you weeping? Why are you weeping, my friend?
RAGHUNATH   Indeed, I am your friend. I am your friend, alas.
CHAITANYA   What is wrong with you? Please tell me. What have I done? Did you find some mistakes in the book? I am willing to correct them. Tell me. You know I care for perfection.
RAGHUNATH   Mistakes? No mistakes, but perfect Perfection. Alas, I also wrote a book on logic, and I thought that it would bring me immortal name and fame. And now I see your book. When people read your book, my book will pale into insignificance. Nobody will even touch it.

CHAITANYA   Ohhhhhh, is that why you are weeping? Is that why you feel miserable, my friend? Is this book of mine causing such suffering for you?

(Chaitanya grabs the book from Raghunath and throws it into the Ganges.)

RAGHUNATH   What have you done? What have you done? Such a precious and valuable book you have thrown into the Ganges?

CHAITANYA   Friendship comes first. I value my friendship with you infinitely more than I value my book. Raghunath, you need name and fame. God will give it to you. I need only one thing: the presence of Lord Krishna in my heart. I need only his presence, his feet in my heart.

(Chaitanya sings.)

*Se je-gan geye jai gan geye jai amar hriday dhware
dake amar ashar prane premer parabare
se je-gan geye jai gan geye jai amar hriday dhware
bhuban amar raibe na ar moher karagare*

(Ah, there He goes, singing around my heart's door.
He calls my heart of hope to enter into His Ocean
   of Love.
Ah, there He goes, singing around my heart's door.
My world will no longer remain in the prison-cell
   of attachment and self-delusion.
Ah, there He goes, singing around my heart's
   door.)

LORD GAURANGA: LOVE INCARNATE

CHAITANYA Lord Krishna, Lord Krishna! My life can remain on earth without everything except Sri Krishna.

RAGHUNATH But the world will curse me! You have made such a tremendous sacrifice for me.

CHAITANYA No sacrifice. It is my love for you. My love for you has played its role. If God feels it necessary, He will make me known. If He wants me to be His instrument, He will make me His instrument and thus give me the opportunity to serve Him. With your book you will serve, you will illumine mankind. And with my love of God, I will illumine mankind.

RAGHUNATH You see everything according to your inner Light, according to your own realisation. There is a vast difference between you and me. I am an insignificant creature. But you are the chosen instrument of God. In you I see God's infinite Love, God's infinite Compassion. In you I see God's Message of highest Truth. A day will come when the entire world will appreciate you. The entire world will appreciate the knowledge of your mind, admire the love of your heart and adore your ecstatic oneness with God, with Lord Krishna.

O WORLD-RENOUNCER, BE CAREFUL!

SRI CHINMOY

LG 3. DRAMATIS PERSONÆ

CHAITANYA
A GROUP OF HIS DISCIPLES
THE YOUNGER HARIDAS (A DISCIPLE)
GOVINDA (A DISCIPLE)

LORD GAURANGA: LOVE INCARNATE

LG 4. SCENE I

(Chaitanya and a group of disciples. Enter the younger Haridas.)

CHAITANYA   Haridas, I understand that you have brought rice from Madhavi?
HARIDAS   Yes, my Lord.
CHAITANYA   You have brought rice to me from a woman?
HARIDAS   Yes, my Lord.
CHAITANYA   From a beautiful woman?
HARIDAS   Yes, my Lord.
CHAITANYA   You have drunk her beauty?
HARIDAS   *(embarrassed)* Yes, my Lord.
CHAITANYA   I shall never see your face again! Never! You have renounced the world, but you have looked at her face. How many times have I told you not to look at women's faces, but to look at their feet? I told you to bring food for me. But you didn't have to bring food from a beautiful woman. You have looked at her face and drunk her beauty to your heart's content. Haridas, you have betrayed your spiritual life. I can't have you with me any more.

(Haridas touches the Master's feet, weeping bitterly.)

CHAITANYA   Haridas, enough. In this life I shall not see your face any more. *(Calls.)* Govinda, Govinda! Take him away! Take Haridas away.

(Enter Govinda.)

GOVINDA   *(quietly to Haridas)* Haridas, Haridas, don't worry. Lord Chaitanya will forgive you one day. Right now he is just punishing you, but you know that his love is for everyone. His love is boundless, and it is for everybody.

(Exeunt Haridas and Govinda. A few minutes later, enter Haridas crying and touches Chaitanya's feet. When Chaitanya ignores him he starts singing, imploringly.)

> *Khama karo khama karo ei sheshbar*
> *samarpiba jaya malya charane tomar*
> *ami taba asimer mauna barabhay*
> *tumi sindhu ami bindhu mor parichai*
>
> (Forgive me, forgive me, this is the last time, forgive me.
> I shall offer to You at Your Feet the garland of Victory.
> I am the silent compassion of Your Infinity.
> You are the Ocean, I am the tiniest drop.
> This is my only identification.)

CHAITANYA   No, Haridas, no more. I won't look at your face. You deserve this punishment. You should know not to look even at a wooden statue of a woman. Even the sages are tempted by women. Your renunciation was no renunciation. It was all a show — a farce! You deserve your punishment. In this lifetime I shall not see you any more. Do whatever you want with your life.

HARIDAS   Lord, I shall wait and see for a few months. If you do not accept me again, then I shall commit suicide. I shall cast this body, this life, into the Ganges.

CHAITANYA   Don't threaten me, Haridas. Do anything you want with your life. Die today if you want to. I don't need you. You have cast a slur on the life of renunciation. Householders can do anything. My householder disciples have received instructions from me about how they can lead a regulated vital life, about how they can control their vital life. In your case, you accepted the life of renunciation. After that, how can you enter into the world of mental and vital enjoyment, Haridas? I am ashamed of you. A world-renouncer does not behave as you have behaved. Leave the path of the *sannyasin*. Who asked you to offer your life entirely? Who asked you to pretend? Who asked you to deceive the world? Leave this place for good.

HARIDAS   Lord, since you will not see me any more, my life is useless. I shall enter into the other world. From there I shall serve you. This life without you is death, and I embrace death in order to offer you my dedicated service from Heaven. In Heaven also you have your divine existence. You have appreciated my voice many times, my singing capacity and my chanting. From Heaven, I shall sing through my soul and please you here, my Lord.

CHAITANYA   Haridas, leave me.

(Haridas touches the feet of his Master for the last time and leaves.)

CHAITANYA   *(to the others)* I know he will take his life. But I have to show the world that the life of renunciation is not a joke. He who accepts the life of renunciation must not mix with women, wealth or worldly possessions. This path is arduous. This life is most difficult. Its goal is the Goal of Goals. I tell you, to commit suicide is the worst possible sin. But if one gets the inner assurance from his spiritual Master that the Master approves, the Master can compassionately relieve him of the sin of committing suicide. Then he will not suffer from it. Haridas is getting my inner assurance. I shall permit him to commit suicide, and I shall free him from that sin. He will be able to serve me in Heaven. From Heaven he will be able to sing inwardly, and please me with his divine voice. But I wish to warn you people, only on very rare occasions do spiritual Masters tolerate suicide. In his case, I shall tolerate it and forgive him. But this is an exception. Don't commit suicide, thinking that you will be able to come down into the world again and make better progress. On the contrary, when you commit suicide, you take a wrong turn and go backwards. Not only do you lose your potentialities and destroy all your possibilities, but you start your spiritual journey over again from the very beginning. You are lost, totally lost. You delay your progress immeasurably. So, my children, never commit suicide. Be brave. Fight the world. Face your inner weaknesses and conquer them. Strengthen your inner life; strengthen your outer life. Act like a hero. Be the master of yourself. God has to be pleased in this world. Temptation has to be conquered; illumination has to take place on earth, in you, in each individual in the entire world.

DAMODAR, I AM FAR ABOVE MORALITY

SRI CHINMOY

LG 5. DRAMATIS PERSONÆ

DAMODAR (AN ELDERLY ADVANCED DISCIPLE OF CHAITANYA)
A BEAUTIFUL YOUNG BOY DISCIPLE
CHAITANYA

LORD GAURANGA: LOVE INCARNATE

LG 6. SCENE I

(Damodar is in the garden. Enter a young beautiful boy.)

DAMODAR   Are you here again? How many times have I to tell you not to come here? If you come here any more I shall punish you. I don't want you to see our Lord.

BOY   It is our Lord who asks me to come here every day. He loves me and I love him. And I shall come here in spite of you.

DAMODAR   I shall punish you if you come again. What right have you to come here? You are a little boy. You don't know how to pray or meditate. This place is for grown-ups like me, who know how to meditate and pray.

BOY   Yes, but our Lord is teaching me how to pray and meditate. He is all love for me, and I am all love for him.

DAMODAR   This is my last warning. If I see you here tomorrow, I shall thrash you.

(Enter Chaitanya. The boy bursts into tears.)

BOY   *(to Chaitanya)* This man is scolding and insulting me. He says I must not come here any more or he will beat me.

CHAITANYA   *(to Damodar)* What right have you to say that to this little boy? Damodar, this is my place. I want him to come every day. He is most devoted to me. He is all love for me. I want him. I need him. You have no right to prevent him from coming here. *(To the boy.)* Today I wish to teach you a special song. This is a song that I have sung millions of times in my life. I have travelled hundreds and hundreds of miles while singing this particular song. I want you to learn it.

Jagannatha swami nayana pathagami bhavatu me

(O Lord of the Universe, do appear before my eyes.)

(The boy sings. Chaitanya corrects him. He sings it again. They practise. Finally, Chaitanya is very pleased.)

CHAITANYA   You have a wonderful voice. I am so happy, so pleased with you. Come here every day.
Damodar, go and bring some food for him.

(Damodar goes out and returns with food. He is in a sulking mood.)

CHAITANYA   My child, sing the song again. That particular song pleases me most. *(The boy sings the song most soulfully.)* Tomorrow come here again. This is your home. Come every day. And give your mother my divine love and divine blessings.

(The boy bows to Chaitanya with deepest joy and pride. Exit boy.)

DAMODAR   Lord Chaitanya, you are a rogue, or else you are a fool!
CHAITANYA   I am a fool? I am a rogue? Damodar, why do you call me these things?
DAMODAR   You are a rogue because you are not practising what you are preaching. You are asking us to lead a spiritual life, a life of morality, a life of celibacy. But what are you doing?
CHAITANYA   What kind of immoral life have I led?
DAMODAR   You are associating with this boy outwardly, but inwardly you are establishing a vital connection with his mo-

ther. Just because of your affection and love for his mother you are showing this boy affection. I know it!

CHAITANYA Stop, Damodar! Enough of your nonsense! You know very well that I am not doing anything of the kind. Now why do you say that I am a fool? I want to know why you called me a fool?

DAMODAR Even if you are sincere, even if, as you say, you have nothing to do with his mother, still you are a fool. Why should the world believe you? The world has every right to suspect you. You know that this boy has no father. You know that his mother is young and very beautiful. People will say that just because of his mother you are showing him all affection and love. They will say that you actually care nothing for the boy and that you give him all this attention in order to get his mother in the future.

CHAITANYA Damodar, the world is full of corruption and vital impurity. The world is very likely to misunderstand me. But I know that I have realised God. I have established my oneness with my Lord Krishna. Lord Krishna was misunderstood when he used to offer his divine love to the Gopis, especially to Radha. He was misunderstood by many, if not all. If people think that I have some bad motive when I show affection to this boy, then let them think it. I cannot satisfy the world. I have to please my inner life, my own soul. I know his mother is extremely devoted to God, extremely sincere in her inner life. I am proud of her spiritual life. I know that one day she will become my disciple. One day she will follow my path. But if the world does not believe me, it is the fault of the world. Damodar, each individual sees others according to his own light. Human beings see me through the darkness of their own impurity. Their minds are full of impure thoughts and impure ideas, which they project into me. But I wish to say that I am millions of miles away from this impurity. My entire being is flooded with purity. When I see the world according to my own Light, I see purity in all of you; I see Light in all of you. A real spiritual Master of my height is infinitely higher than the bonds of morality. The life of morality and vital purification is for you and not for me, Damodar. So do not worry about my life. Think of your own life. I have come into the world to perfect the world, to liberate the world from temptation. I will not be caught by the temptation of the world. A day will come when you will also transcend the barriers of morality and enter into my realm, which is divine, perfect spirituality, the life of oneness, constant oneness with my beloved Krishna. I shall allow this boy to come here every day. He will be very devoted to me. I shall teach him songs; I shall teach him to pray; I shall teach him how to meditate. In him you will find a special gift of my Lord Krishna.

KRISHNA, I SHALL DIE IN YOUR ABSENCE

SRI CHINMOY

LG 7. DRAMATIS PERSONÆ

CHAITANYA
SRIBAS, GADADHAR (CLOSE DISCIPLES OF CHAITANYA)
OTHER DISCIPLES
SHACHI (MOTHER OF CHAITANYA)

LORD GAURANGA: LOVE INCARNATE

LG 8. SCENE I

(Chaitanya is alone.)

CHAITANYA   Krishna, where are you? Where are you? I can no longer bear your absence. I want only a glimpse of your smile, O my beloved Krishna, O my All. Show yourself to me. If not, to death this body of mine I shall give.

(Enter Sribas, Gadadhar and some of Chaitanya's other close disciples, who sit near the Master's feet.)

CHAITANYA   I am glad to see you all. I wish to tell you something quite important. I shall leave you soon. With an unparalleled devotion you all have served me. I offer to each of you my heart's ceaseless gratitude. But I must go. I must go and find my beloved Krishna. Once I find him, I shall be back.

SRIBAS   Lord, your cruel announcement falls on us like a thunderbolt. Perhaps others can survive being separated from you, but I shall never survive it.

GADADHAR   I have lost all faith in God. Our Lord wants to see Krishna, and for that he is leaving us all. He is forsaking even his old mother. God's ways are not mysterious at all. They are just cruel, unbearably and unpardonably cruel.

CHAITANYA   Gadadhar, for God's sake, aim not your venomous arrow at my heart. My Lord Krishna is all Love, all Compassion, all Perfection. Indeed, my greatest difficulty lies in leaving my old mother. I must overcome the problem. With Krishna my life is my heart's delight. Without Krishna my life is the torture of hell. Meaningless and fruitless is my life without him. I need only Krishna.

(Enter Shachi, Chaitanya's mother.)

SHACHI   Nimai, I have just come to learn that you are leaving me. My son, that can never be done. Impossible! Your elder brother took to *sannyasa*. He renounced the world. I shall not allow you to follow in his footsteps. Time and again you promised me that you would not desert me like your brother. Tell me frankly, are you determined to leave me, my son? Don't you know that I cannot bear your absence even for a fleeting second?

CHAITANYA   O Mother of my heart and soul, Krishna is calling me. Mother, please, please allow me to go. I want to go to a sacred place. I feel that then I shall be able to meet my Krishna. Mother, without your full permission I shall not go. But if you allow me to go and find my Krishna, I promise you, Mother, I shall be back.

SHACHI   *(blessing Chaitanya)* My heart's pride, my life's only joy, you have my sanction. You go in search of your beloved Krishna. After you have found him, come back without fail. I shall be counting the moments until your safe return. *(With folded hands and closed eyes she prays.)* O Lord Krishna, show yourself to my Nimai. You are his All. And he is my All.

(Chaitanya touches his mother's feet and goes away. Shachi opens her eyes.)

SHACHI   Nimai, Nimai!
ECHO   *Nai, nai ....* [nowhere, nowhere]

SRIBAS

SRI CHINMOY

LG 9. DRAMATIS PERSONÆ

CHAITANYA
SRIBAS (A DEAR DISCIPLE OF CHAITANYA)
A FOLLOWER OF CHAITANYA
OTHER FOLLOWERS OF CHAITANYA
WIFE OF SRIBAS
RELATIVES OF SRIBAS
SON OF SRIBAS

LORD GAURANGA: LOVE INCARNATE

LG 10. SCENE 1

(Left stage: courtyard of Sribas' house; right stage: room adjoining the courtyard. Chaitanya is singing Hari Bol, Hari Bol *and dancing in ecstasy with his followers in the courtyard of Sribas, a dear disciple of his. All of a sudden from inside the house is heard wailing and screaming. Sribas leaves the party and runs into the house. His wife is in tears; other relatives are also weeping.)*

WIFE   Our only son! Our only son is lost forever! What can I do? What can I do?

SRIBAS   Why are you crying? Why are you weeping? What is there to cry about? His time has come. That is why he has gone to the other world. Today the Lord is dancing in our courtyard. Even the worst possible sinner will go directly to Heaven if he dies here. Since our son left the world from here, he will undoubtedly be happy. If you really love your son, then be happy, be delighted. Join us in our singing and dancing, for here, today, the Lord is with us.

WIFE   This is not the time to listen to your philosophy. We have lost our only son. I have love for our Master, Sri Chaitanya. But when one's only son dies, it is impossible to maintain the same love for the Master and the same faith in the Master.

SRIBAS   You are crying, and our relatives are crying. But our Lord is dancing in ecstasy. He is in a divine consciousness. If he hears your crying and wailing, and comes back to his normal consciousness because of it, then I shall throw myself into the Ganges. If you put an end to his ecstatic dance, then I shall put an end to my life!

(The wife calms down. Other relatives are still crying.)

SRIBAS *(to the others)* We have lost our dearest; we have lost our only son. But my wife and I are not crying. If you have to cry, then leave our house. It is we who have suffered the loss. But to us it is no loss; it is a real gain, a real reward, because today my Lord has come to my house. Now it is not my responsibility to think of my son. My only responsibility is to think of my Master. My Master will take care of my son. So if you want to cry and weep, then all of you leave this house. This is not the place for you.

(Sribas goes back to the garden and starts singing and dancing with the others. All of a sudden, Sri Chaitanya stops singing and dancing.)

CHAITANYA I do not know what, but something has gone wrong with me. Has anything happened at Sribas' house? *(To Sribas.)* Has any calamity taken place in your house?

SRIBAS Lord, on the day that you have blessed my home with your divine presence, how can there be any calamity here?

ANOTHER FOLLOWER Lord, something *has* happened.

CHAITANYA What has happened?

FOLLOWER Something serious has happened.

CHAITANYA What is it?

FOLLOWER Sribas' son has died.

CHAITANYA When? When?

FOLLOWER An hour ago.

CHAITANYA Now why didn't you tell me?

FOLLOWER You were communing with Lord Krishna, my Lord. We didn't want to put an end to your ecstatic dance. We didn't dare to do it. And why should we have done it? To us your dance is infinitely more important than this death.

SRIBAS To me your ecstatic dance is all-important. The death of my son is of no importance in comparison.

CHAITANYA *(starts crying)* He who can forget the loss of his only son in my presence — how can I forget his sacrifice? How can I appreciate his heart enough? How can I admire his heart enough? Sribas, you are really a man of divine sacrifice. I have never seen a man like you. Whose sacrifice can equal yours?

SRIBAS Lord, there is no sacrifice on my part. For me there is only you. You have come to my home. Today is the happiest day of my life, the greatest day of my life.

CHAITANYA Sribas, please go and bring the child. Let me see him.

(Exit Sribas. He returns carrying his son and followed by his wife. He places the child in front of the Master. Chaitanya looks at the child and concentrates on him.)

CHILD Lord, it was Your wish that I should die. Who can violate Your law?

(Everyone is astonished to hear the dead child talking.)

CHILD You brought me, Lord, into this world of Yours, and it is You who are sending me to the other world, which is equally Yours. Who is my father, who is my mother, if not You? You are the eternal Father; You are the eternal Mother. I bow to You, O Lord. I am going to Your other home.

CHAITANYA Sribas, now your child's soul has left the body. He has gone to my other world. I have a place ready for him in Heaven. I will take care of him there as I am taking care of you, your wife and all your spiritual sisters and brothers here. Sribas, you had only one son. Now you have two sons. I am your son and my dearest disciple, Nityananda, is your son. One son has gone to the other world; two sons will take his place here.

(Sribas touches the feet of Chaitanya then dances with joy.)

WIFE *(touching Chaitanya's feet)* Lord, in You I see my child. In You I see the Heavens. In You I see the entire universe. Today I see not only Your physical presence, but Your universal Reality as well.

CHAITANYA Today you have proved to be the real counterpart of Sribas. His aspiration and your aspiration have become totally one today. I shall carry both of you deep inside my heart and lead you to the abode of Hari.

(Chaitanya blesses Sribas' wife with joy and pride.)

MOTHER TOUCHES THE SON'S FEET

SRI CHINMOY

LG II. DRAMATIS PERSONÆ

CHAITANYA
SRIBAS (A DEVOTED DISCIPLE OF CHAITANYA)
SHACHI (MOTHER OF CHAITANYA)

LORD GAURANGA: LOVE INCARNATE

LG 12. SCENE 1

(Chaitanya is in Krishna consciousness.)

CHAITANYA Sribas, Sribas! Where is my flute? Where is my flute? Give me my flute.
SRIBAS My Lord, the Gopis have stolen your flute.
CHAITANYA The Gopis? Where are they? Where are my Gopis? Where is my Radha? Where is she? Where is she?

(Enter Shachi, Chaitanya's mother. Seeing his divine consciousness, she immediately bows down and touches his feet.)

SHACHI O my son, O Nimai, you are no longer Nimai. You are no longer my son, Nimai. You are Lord Krishna, Lord Krishna Himself.

(Shachi sings.)

Jibana nadi tire dhire dhire
oi ase mor priyatama
benu hate madhur prate oi ase
praner jata asha
jata bhalobasa
ranga oi sri charane
sapi aji tomai nami

(Behold, with His Flute in His Hand,
My Beloved slowly is coming
to the bank of my life-river
In today's morning sweet.
All my life's hope,
All my life's love,
To Your Power-red Feet divine I offer,
And to You I bow and bow.)

CHAITANYA   Mother, I am so proud of you. This is the first time that you have touched my feet on your own. Previously I used to ask you to come and touch my feet when I was in Krishna consciousness. But today you have come and touched my feet spontaneously. Mother, I am so proud of you. You have seen me in my highest consciousness, and you know what I am.

SHACHI   My son, I know, I know what you are. You are God. But still I will never forget even for a moment that you are also my son, my darling. You have blessed me by coming into my family, and immortalised me by being my son. I know that one day you will leave me. You will renounce the world. You will take to *sannyasa*. You will follow the path of renunciation. I tell you, my son, the human in me will miss you and suffer, but the divine in me will be proud of you, knowing that you are liberating mankind from ignorance and giving men a new life. You are putting an end to their life of suffering and granting them the life of Bliss.

CHAITANYA   Mother, the human in you will not miss me either, because I will transform the human in you into the divine. Wherever I am, Mother, your physical consciousness will feel my presence. I shall eternally remain within you and around you. You will feel my physical presence too, Mother.

My subtle physical presence will be around you all the time, I assure you.

SHACHI   My son, I know you are God. You can do everything and you will do everything, not only for me but for all of humanity. You are not only *my* joy and my pride; you are also the joy and pride of the entire universe. You and your creation are inseparable. When I look at your creation I see how great you are. And when I look at you yourself, I see how compassionate you are. In your creation I see the miracle of your indomitable power. In you I see the endless flood of compassion.

O CHAITANYA, I NEED YOUR LOVE

SRI CHINMOY

LG 13. DRAMATIS PERSONÆ

AKBAR (THE MOGUL EMPEROR)
EMPRESS

LORD GAURANGA: LOVE INCARNATE

LG 14. SCENE 1

(The palace of the Mogul Emperor Akbar.)

EMPRESS   Akbar, may I know in what you are so deeply absorbed?

AKBAR   I am absorbed in the thought of Chaitanya.

EMPRESS   Very often I see that you think of him and meditate on him. Have you forgotten that he is a Hindu? What will people think of you? What will your subjects think of you when they come to know that you meditate on a Hindu so deeply and so often?

AKBAR   Let them think whatever they want of me, but I can't live without loving Chaitanya. His divine love has conquered my heart. His divine mystic dance has illumined my heart. He is the Lord of my aspiring heart. The depth of his love I can never express. I beg of him only to give me a drop from the sea of his nectar-love. He has already achieved by his boundless love what I am trying to do so desperately. In his heart Hindus and Muslims have become one. He has realised Allah; he has realised the highest Truth.

EMPRESS   You are great. Everybody admires you. I don't think you have to be an admirer of Chaitanya.

AKBAR   They admire me, but their admiration of me is not as sincere as my admiration of Chaitanya. They admire my outer power. I admire Chaitanya's inner power. My power destroys everything. Chaitanya's power loves everything, loves everyone, fulfils everyone. This is the difference between Chaitanya's power and my power. My power wants to destroy the world. My power wants to lord it over the world. My power wants name and fame. His power wants to love the world, become the world and fulfil the world. O

Empress, I shall tell you what I feel about Sri Chaitanya. He is not an ordinary mortal like us. He is the son of Truth. He is Truth Itself. And this Truth is Love. This Truth is oneness with Allah and His Creation. This Love my heart constantly needs. Only the dust of Chaitanya's feet can transform my life into the Kingdom of Heaven.

(Akbar sings.)

Kemane tomare pujibo bidhata kemane
kemane tomar charane bandhibo kemane
kemane tomar nayane heribo kemane
kemane basibo tomar tarite kemane
kemane tomar banshari bajabo kemane
kemane tomare debo ei hiya kemane
rupantarer alor gitika kemane
kemane gahibo dibase nishithe kemane

(How can I worship You, My Lord?
How can I bind Your Feet?
How can I see Your Eye?
How can I sail in Your Boat?
How can I play Your Flute?
How can I offer You my heart?
How can I sing day and night the
Song of Light for my transformation?)

MY LAST DESIRE IS TO PLACE
YOUR FEET ON MY HEART

SRI CHINMOY

LG 15. DRAMATIS PERSONÆ

THE ELDER HARIDAS
GOVINDA (AN ATTENDANT OF CHAITANYA)
CHAITANYA
TEN DISCIPLES OF CHAITANYA

LORD GAURANGA: LOVE INCARNATE

LG 16. SCENE I

(The elder Haridas is extremely sick. He is lying down. Enter Govinda with some prasad [sacred food] sanctified by Chaitanya.)

GOVINDA I have brought your food. Here is *prasad* for you. *(Haridas gives him a thankful smile.)* Don't worry, you will be all right. Eat the prasad.
HARIDAS I can't eat my prasad yet.
GOVINDA Why not?
HARIDAS Because I have not yet finished my *japa* [repetition of a sacred name]. Today is the first day I have ever done my japa lying down. Today I am unable to get up from my bed, so I am doing my japa lying down, and it is not at all intense.
GOVINDA You are sick. How can you expect your japa to be intense, Haridas? First you have to get well. As soon as you become strong, your intensity will return.
HARIDAS No, I can't eat the food. Oh, but I have to eat the prasad of my Lord Chaitanya, or it will be an insult to him. At the same time, if I eat it before finishing my japa, then also it will be an insult to him. In that case I shall eat a little, very little of his prasad, and then continue doing my japa. In that way I will not insult my Lord by rejecting his sanctified food and, at the same time, I will not insult him by eating his food without earning it by doing my spiritual disciplines. *(Takes a small mouthful of prasad. Enter Chaitanya.)*
CHAITANYA How are you today, Haridas?
HARIDAS Lord, physically I am worse, but spiritually I am better. Spiritually I feel I have more love for you, I have more faith in you. But forgive me, my Lord, today for the

first time in my life I have not been able to complete my japa. I am unable to get up from bed.

CHAITANYA Don't worry, Haridas. Countless times you have done japa. Lord Krishna is most pleased with you and I am most pleased with you. You have already achieved perfection in your spiritual life. Now you don't have to do japa at all. You don't need any meditation. This is the time for you to take rest and wait for the call from the Beyond, from the other world.

HARIDAS My Lord, I am ready for your call from the other world. But you have to fulfil a desire of mine. Will you not fulfil my last desire? You have always pleased me; you have always spoken highly of me, although I don't deserve your praise at all. I came of a very low family. I was an untouchable. Everybody hated me. But you lifted me up. You gave me status. You gave me name and fame. You made me very close to you. My Lord, this life of mine is only a life of gratitude to you. You have made me what I am. What I was is unthinkable. What I have become is all through your compassion.

CHAITANYA Your power of receptivity has deeply pleased my heart of love and compassion. Now tell me, please. I want to know your last desire.

HARIDAS My last desire is that you should place your feet on my heart before I die. You are my whole world. When you place your feet on my heart, I will get infinite Joy, Peace and Bliss. You have been telling us for the past few months that you will soon leave the world. But my only desire is for you to place your feet on my heart and let me die before you, my Lord. That is my last desire.

(Chaitanya embraces Haridas.)

LORD GAURANGA: LOVE INCARNATE

CHAITANYA Govinda, go and bring a few disciples of mine. Let us sing *Hari Bol*. Let us sing our *kirtan* [religious song in honour of Sri Krishna].

(Exit Govinda. Re-enter with ten disciples. They start singing Hari Bol, Hari Bol. Chaitanya places his foot on Haridas' heart.)

HARIDAS My Lord, you are my world. You are my light. You are my heart's breath. You are my soul's delight.

(Haridas dies. Chaitanya lifts up Haridas' body and begins to dance, singing Hari Bol, Hari Bol.)

CHAITANYA He has gone to my other home. I have two homes: one on earth and one in Heaven. He has gone to my Heavenly home. He will make everything ready for my arrival. In the spiritual life there is no caste; there is no rank. He came of a low family, but in God's Eye we are all one. Truth is not the monopoly of the Brahmins. Truth is everybody's property. He who realises the Truth is above all others. Haridas has realised the Truth. He is above everything, above everybody. To have a disciple like Haridas is something. To fulfil his last desire is something. To be with him in the other world is something. Something good. Something divine. Something immortal.

LORD GAURANGA: LOVE INCARNATE

SRI CHINMOY

LG 17. DRAMATIS PERSONÆ

CHAITANYA — LORD GAURANGA
NITYANANDA (HIS BELOVED COMPEER)
JAGAI, MADHAI (TWO BROTHERS, HOOLIGANS)

LORD GAURANGA: LOVE INCARNATE

LG 18. SCENE 1

(Chaitanya and Nityananda are walking along the street singing Hari Bol *with utmost joy.)*

NITYANANDA   O Lord Gauranga, your rise in the firmament of Bengal at this time, a time when our province is shrouded in a mist of superstition, ignorance and pessimism, is a supreme blessing from Providence. The supernal Light that you are throwing on our slumbering and downtrodden country is stirring its children to a new life. Your work and your miracles are not done to arrest the attention of people, but to bestow your love, your compassion on poor suffering humanity. To you a sinner is not an object of ire or contempt, but an object of compassion and love.

CHAITANYA   In my philosophy, Nityananda, we need not extinguish the senses. We should keep the senses intact. But also, we should never forget that we have to keep them under proper control.

NITYANANDA   Ah! Here come those two fiends in human shape, the brothers Jagai and Madhai.

(Madhai, the younger and fiercer of the two, is holding an earthen jar. Suddenly he flings the jar at Nityananda, striking and wounding him on the forehead.)

NITYANANDA   You have struck me. My forehead is wounded and bleeding from the blow of this jar. But even so I am beside myself with joy, because finally Lord Gauranga's attention will be drawn to you two, the worst possible sinners, and his redeeming Grace will at last be showered on you. His mere touch or look performs the miracle of miracles.

CHAITANYA   *(flying into a rage, to Madhai)* How dare you strike my Nityananda? I shall invoke my *chakra* to punish you, Madhai, for I will not tolerate the suffering of my true disciple, who is dearer to me than my own life!

NITYANANDA   My Lord, I do not want salvation just now. First save the greatest sinners in the world, and then you can take my case into consideration.

CHAITANYA   Nityananda, indeed you are forgiveness incarnate. But my rage is not pacified. I am bent on punishing Madhai.

(Chaitanya turns toward Madhai. Madhai stares at him for a long time as if spellbound. Silence falls on the group.)

MADHAI   *(aside)* At the mere sight of Chaitanya, I feel a great change coming over me. My inside is being clawed as earth is clawed by a cat. His silent influence is changing my life. *(To Chaitanya.)* O Chaitanya, my Lord, I don't ask forgiveness of you, nor am I afraid of punishment. Let it come, and I shall welcome it. Only tell me, is there any way, any penance, by which I can, at any future period, attain to your lotus feet? Only tell me the way, if there be any, and then cast me off.

CHAITANYA   Madhai, your prayer is at once striking and significant. *(Blesses Madhai and Jagai.)* Both you and your brother, Jagai, will be transformed into the holiest of holy souls. There can be no shadow of a doubt that this miracle that I am envisioning will soon become the most evident Truth.

MADHAI   O Lord Chaitanya, a life replete with miracles is yours; and ours is a life filled with gratitude to you, O Love Incarnate.

(Madhai sings.)

LORD GAURANGA: LOVE INCARNATE

He jogiraj dikkha amai dao go aji dikkha
rupantarer amar bani pabo aji shikkha
ghurbona ar dure dure
nachbo shudhu hriday pure
gaibo giti premer sure
dekhbo amai pran mukure
nirabatar lagi ami magi aji bhikkha

(O Yogi of the highest magnitude, initiate me.
Today offer me Your initiation.
Today I shall learn the immortal message of transformation from You.
I shall not wander any more in the farthest corners of the world.
I shall only dance in the city of my heart.
Inside the city of my heart I shall sing songs of Love Divine.
And I shall see myself in the mirror of my sanctified heart.
Today I beg of You to offer me only one thing: silence, silence.
O Yogi of the highest magnitude, initiate me today.)

PART VI

DRINK, DRINK
MY MOTHER'S NECTAR

THERE IS NO GOD

SRI CHINMOY

DD I. DRAMATIS PERSONÆ

NAREN
BHAVANANDA
BHUPEN (YOUNGER BROTHER OF NAREN)

DRINK, DRINK MY MOTHER'S NECTAR

DD 2. SCENE I

(Naren is meditating in his room. Enter Bhavananda.)

NAREN *(stands up)* Come in. Come in, please. I am so glad to see you. I have not seen you for a long time. I have many things to discuss with you. The first thing I would like to ask you is this: does God exist, brother? It seems to me that there is no God. And even if He exists, it makes no difference to me. He never hears, He never feels the excruciating pangs of the poor. He never feels the suffering of bleeding humanity. The God who cannot feed the hungry with a piece of bread is an indifferent God, a cruel God. Who can believe he will have all happiness, all satisfaction in the other world from that kind of God?

BHAVANANDA Naren, have you gone crazy? What is wrong with you? What nonsense are you speaking? Why do you talk like this?

NAREN Why not? Why not? Do you know, brother, what happened this morning? Early in the morning as I got up I was uttering the name of God most soulfully. My mother said to me, "Shut up. Since your childhood you have been praying to God and meditating on God. And now look what God has done to us. Your father has left this world, and misery, suffering and poverty have embraced us. We have no food, no money, no means of supporting the family. My heart is breaking into pieces. I cannot even feed my little children, my sweet children. I will have nothing to do with a God who cannot take away our sufferings." Now tell me, brother, what am I supposed to say to my mother?

BHAVANANDA   Naren, let us not find fault with God. If you find fault with God, then some serious calamity will take place in your family. I am warning you.

NAREN   I am not afraid of anything. Let the worst possible calamity take place. I don't give a damn. I don't care.

BHAVANANDA   Naren, please go to Thakur from time to time. Thakur will be so sad to hear what is happening in your life. He is the only one who will be able to console you.

(Enter Bhupen.)

BHUPEN   Brother, please bring me some candy today. I am so fond of candy. Please don't forget.

NAREN   Please, Bhupen, do not bother me. We are having a very serious conversation. Please, please go away, Bhupen. Don't bother us right now.

BHUPEN   I will go away, but first you have to promise to bring candy for me. You have to bring candy without fail.

(Exit Bhupen.)

NAREN   So, brother, you see? I am his elder brother, and I will not be able to fulfil his loving demand. I have no money at all, not even enough to buy a piece of candy for him. He who cannot fulfil such a simple desire of a younger brother is not worthy of being called an elder brother. His life is a real disgrace. So why should I care for God? No! We Hindus worship stone gods, so our God has become stone-hearted.

BHAVANANDA   Don't say so, Naren. God is all Compassion. I see that what I have been hearing from people is true: you have become an atheist.

DRINK, DRINK MY MOTHER'S NECTAR

(Exit Bhavananda.)

NAREN A real friend, indeed! He came here to test me. He came here not to show his concern, but to know what kind of life I am leading. He came not as a friend, but as a critic, as a rogue, as a detective. No, I shall not go to Thakur any more. *(Pauses.)* But alas, what am I doing? What am I doing? Is not God-realisation the sole object of my life? To earn money, to feed a family, can never be the aim of my life. I must renounce the world. There is no other way. I must renounce the world and search for God. There can be no other way.

(Naren sings.)

Tamasa rate nayan pate
herile jadi amar pane
apan kare amai laho
he dayamoy karuna dane
tomar ami abodh shishu
ekla chali gahan pathe
duhate more jariye dharo
bhasiye jena na jai srote

(In the dark and dense night,
You cast Your benign Eyes upon me.
Take me and make me Your very own, offering
 Your Compassion.
I am Your innocent child. Alone do I walk on a
 thick, dense path.
With Your two Arms, embrace me.
Allow me not to be drowned and washed away by
 the turbulent currents of life.)

MY NAREN CAN NEVER BE AN ATHEIST

SRI CHINMOY

DD 3. DRAMATIS PERSONÆ

SRI RAMAKRISHNA
RAKHAL
BHAVANANDA
TARAK
JOGIN
OTHER DISCIPLES
NAREN

DRINK, DRINK MY MOTHER'S NECTAR

DD 4. SCENE 1

(Sri Ramakrishna with his disciples at Dakshineshwar.)

RAKHAL   Have you heard about our Naren recently? Everybody is speaking ill of him. Everybody says that he has become an atheist. But I don't believe it.

BHAVANANDA   You don't believe it? I suspect him. This morning I was at his house. He speaks like a real atheist.

SRI RAMAKRISHNA   Shut up! Shut up! My Mother Kali has told me that this can never be so. My Naren can never be an atheist. If I hear once more from you people that my Naren has become an atheist, I shall never again see your faces! Never!

TARAK   Our Naren can never be an atheist. I know him.

JOGIN   Impossible! Our Naren can never be an atheist. Even if I see any defect in Naren, I will not believe it. I will think it is the fault of my own eyes. If I hear anything bad about Naren, I shall think it is the fault of my own ears. Our Naren can never do anything wrong.

TARAK   Certainly, certainly. That should be our attitude. He is our real friend. Our Naren is pure. It is very rare to have a God-like character like Naren's.

SRI RAMAKRISHNA   Excellent, excellent. *(Pointing to his own body.)* It is for Naren that I have come here into the world. You try to recognize Naren. One day he will conquer the whole world. I see in the spiritual Master Keshab Sen only one knowledge-sun. But in my Naren I see eighteen knowledge-suns.

(Enter Naren. He prostrates himself before Ramakrishna. Ramakrishna places his hand on Naren's head.)

SRI RAMAKRISHNA   May Mother bless you.

NAREN   Today I have a special request.

SRI RAMAKRISHNA   Is there any request of yours that I will not fulfil?

NAREN   Then please fulfil this request. My mother and my little sisters and brothers are practically starving. We have become absolutely poverty-stricken. After the death of my father, all our relatives turned against us. Now my family has no means of support. I am the eldest member in my family and I can do nothing for them. If you make a special request to the Mother to save me from this financial difficulty, she will listen to you. I am sure that if you ask the Mother, she will definitely listen to your request.

SRI RAMAKRISHNA   Naren, I am ready to beg from door to door for you. Do you think that I have not yet asked my Mother about you? But what can I do? You do not believe in her; that is why she does not pay any attention to my request. All right. I have an excellent idea. It is Tuesday. Go to the Temple of Mother Kali today and invoke her. Pray to the Mother. Whatever you want, I assure you, she will grant to you.

NAREN   All right. Today I shall test your stone-hearted Mother, Thakur.

SRI RAMAKRISHNA   My child, don't say that. She is not stone-hearted. She is all love. She is all compassion.

MOTHER, GIVE ME
THE LIGHT OF KNOWLEDGE,
THE LIGHT OF DISCRIMINATION
AND THE LIGHT OF RENUNCIATION

SRI CHINMOY

DD 5. DRAMATIS PERSONÆ

NAREN — VIVEKANANDA
SRI RAMAKRISHNA
DISCIPLES OF SRI RAMAKRISHNA

DRINK, DRINK MY MOTHER'S NECTAR

DD 6. SCENE I

(It is night. Inside the Kali Temple, Naren is meditating. After a while, he prostrates himself before the statue of Mother Kali.)

NAREN   *Jnana viveka vairagya de ma.* Mother, give me the Light of Knowledge, the Light of Discrimination and the Light of Renunciation, so that I can always see you.

(Enter Sri Ramakrishna hurriedly.)

SRI RAMAKRISHNA   Naren, have you asked Mother Kali for money for your family? What have you been doing?
NAREN   What a surprise! I forgot all about it.
SRI RAMAKRISHNA   No harm. I shall give you another chance. Ask her for money, for material wealth. Mother will give it to you.

(Naren turns to the statue and begins meditating again.)

NAREN   Mother, give me the Light of Knowledge, the Light of Discrimination and the Light of Renunciation. Mother, Mother of mine, Mother of my heart and soul.
SRI RAMAKRISHNA   Again the same thing? Why do you forget that your mother and brothers and sisters are all starving? Ask the Mother to save your family from poverty. This is the only time that you can ask the Mother for that. I will not be able to give you the same opportunity every day. I am ready to give it to you any time. But Mother will not allow it. Today I have promised you because Mother has told me that she will fulfil your prayers today, no matter what you ask of her. Now you have lost your second chance.

But I wish to give you another chance. Please, my son, this time don't forget. Remember, you must ask the Mother for material wealth. That is what you need. Right now you don't need spiritual wealth.

NAREN   No, I won't take any more chances. I do not need material wealth. I want nectar from the Mother, and not anything else. For gourds and pumpkins I will not ask. I can ask only for the nectar-fruit.

SRI RAMAKRISHNA   Since you cannot ask the Mother for material wealth and prosperity, then I wish to say that you will never have a comfortable life. But from now on you will be able to manage. You and your family will not starve. You will be able to live at least from hand to mouth. Mother will do that much for you. *(He shouts.)* Come, all those who are here! No matter where you are! Come! All my disciples, come!

(Enter disciples.)

SRI RAMAKRISHNA   You people have told me that my Naren has become an atheist. Look! He could not ask for material wealth from my Mother. Do you know that he starves? His mother and his sisters and brothers have no food at home. Yet he could not ask Mother Kali for material wealth. Nowhere on earth will you find anyone who can equal my Naren. He is your leader. He will lead and guide you. He will preserve you. This body of mine is completing its role. Soon I will belong to the other world. *(To Vivekananda.)* Naren, my child, sing a song. I shall meditate while you sing.

(Naren sings. Sri Ramakrishna meditates in deep trance.)

DRINK, DRINK MY MOTHER'S NECTAR

Sundara hate sundara tumi
nandana bana majhe
nishidin jena antare mor
tomari murati raje
tumi chhara mor nayan andhar
sakali mithya sakali asar
chaudike mor bishwa bhubane
bedanar sur baje
pabo kigo dekha nimesher tare
ei jibaner majhe

(You are beautiful, more beautiful, most beautiful,
Beauty unparalleled in the garden of Eden.
Day and night may Thy image abide in the very
 depths of my heart.
Without You my eyes have no vision,
Everything is an illusion, everything is barren.
All around me, within and without,
The melody of tenebrous pangs I hear.
My world is filled with excruciating pangs.
O Lord, O my beautiful Lord,
O my Lord of beauty, in this lifetime, even for a
 fleeting second,
May I be blessed with the boon to see Thy Face.)

ASK HIM IF HE SERVES ME OR CONTROLS ME

SRI CHINMOY

DD 7. DRAMATIS PERSONÆ

VIDYASAGAR (A SCHOLAR AND SAGE)
VAISHNAB CHARAN PUNDIT (A FRIEND OF VIDYASAGAR)
HRIDAY (NEPHEW AND ATTENDANT OF SRI RAMAKRISHNA)
SRI RAMAKRISHNA

DRINK, DRINK MY MOTHER'S NECTAR

DD 8. SCENE 1

(Vidyasagar's house in Calcutta. Vidyasagar is studying most attentively in his room. Enter Vaishnab Charan Pundit. They bow to each other and exchange greetings.)

PUNDIT   I have been here in Calcutta for a few days. I am sorry that I was not able to come and pay my respectful homage to you earlier.

VIDYASAGAR   *(smiling)* I am so glad, so proud, that you have come to my home at last. Is everything going well with you? Please have a seat.

PUNDIT   *(taking a seat)* Everything is fine, by God's Grace. How is your health, Vidyasagar?

VIDYASAGAR   Not good. My body is not functioning well. I am old. Now I am preparing myself for the other world.

PUNDIT   Don't say that, Vidyasagar. Don't you know that in your absence thousands and thousands of people will be fatherless? This health, this body you have to maintain for at least one hundred years.

VIDYASAGAR   Don't curse me, brother, don't curse me. Already things have started to go wrong in my family. My son has become disobedient. He has cast a slur on our family. I do not know how much more suffering is in store for me.

PUNDIT   Ungratefulness is the order of the day. Bengalis have become an object of pity just because they have become totally ungrateful. The other day we had a special meeting of Pundits, and at that meeting the Pundit Panchanan said that you have ruined the Hindu religion. He said that with the help of a number of Hindu youths you are destroying the whole country. He said that there is nothing divine in your activities, no true feeling or self-sacrifice in your selfless service for Bengal. He feels it is all for name and fame. I am so sorry to tell you this. You have no idea how I suffered, and how I have been suffering for the past few days, since I heard Panchanan, of all people, speaking against you.

VIDYASAGAR   There is nothing to feel sorry about. Everything is God's game. I do nothing, my friend. It is God who works in and through me. I am just an instrument: *Nimitta matram.* But I feel that you have made a mistake. I feel that you have heard something wrong. *(Pauses.)* I have never done any service for that Pundit. How is it that he speaks ill of me? I have come to the conclusion that only those whom I have helped in some way will criticise me. Those whom I have not helped in any way will never criticise me. And I clearly remember that I have not helped Panchanan in any way. I am sure he was speaking of somebody else.

(Enter Hriday.)

HRIDAY   O sage, my maternal uncle is constantly praying to God and meditating on God. By thinking and praying all the time he has become insane. Today he feels like seeing you, Vidyasagar.

PUNDIT   Your uncle? The Thakur of Dakshineshwar?

HRIDAY   Yes, he is outside.

PUNDIT   Outside! Why didn't you bring him in? *(Vaishnab Charan Pundit goes out and brings Ramakrishna in. He then speaks to Vidyasagar.)* Today Paramahansa, the great liberated soul, the realised soul, has come to you. You can be extremely proud that he has come to you.

(Sri Ramakrishna bows to Vidyasagar. Vidyasagar in turn bows and offers Ramakrishna a seat.)

DRINK, DRINK MY MOTHER'S NECTAR

SRI RAMAKRISHNA For so long I have been living in a small pond. Today I have come to the ocean.

VIDYASAGAR Since you have come to the ocean, please accept some saline water. It is all I can offer you.

SRI RAMAKRISHNA Vidyasagar, you are doing well. It is good to show love and compassion. But attachment is very bad. When someone loves only the members of his own family it is attachment. One has to see God in everyone. When a person sees the presence of God in everyone, that is called compassion. I have come to visit you because I see that you serve God in everyone. I have come to appreciate your divine wisdom. Do you think that you have grown horns, and that that is why I have come to see you?

VIDYASAGAR Today any home has been sanctified by your feet. Today my home becomes a place of pilgrimage.

PUNDIT *(to Vidyasagar)* He is all divine Love. His madness is the intoxication of divine Love. Like Sri Chaitanya, he enters into the great *samadhi*, the transcendental trance.

VIDYASAGAR Yes, I know it. I can see it. I can feel it. *(To Ramakrishna.)* This boy, does he serve you? *(Indicating Hriday.)*

SRI RAMAKRISHNA Ask him if he serves me or controls me. I am terribly afraid of him.

HRIDAY Uncle, it is very bad on your part to say so. Have I ever disobeyed you? Have I ever governed you? Do you ever listen to me? You do not pay any attention to the outer world. You forget about the weather; you forget about food. That is why I take care of you. Sometimes I kindly command you to do a few things, but it is only for your health. Don't make me feel ashamed whenever we go places, or I shall go away. I do not have to help you, and if you don't care for my services I shall not remain with you any longer. *(He begins to leave.)*

SRI RAMAKRISHNA   Oh, don't go, don't go, Hriday. Don't leave me alone. *(To Vidyasagar and Pundit.)* My nephew is so nice. He loves me day and night. If he had not been with me, who would have taken care of me? I even forget to put on my clothes. If he did not control me, then how could he show his face in respectable society? I would shame him and all my family. *(Hriday comes back and sits down, appeased.)* Vidyasagar, again I wish to tell you that you are doing the right thing. You are serving God in humanity. You are serving God with utmost Love. That is why God is pleased with you. Your life of sacrifice will be remembered by the world forever.

(Ramakrishna rises. Vidyasagar and Pundit both rise and bow to Ramakrishna. Ramakrishna bows to them. Exeunt Ramakrishna and Hriday.)

PUNDIT   He is really a great spiritual Master. I have heard much about him, and I inwardly feel what he is.

VIDYASAGAR   I also feel what he is. He is really great. He is not only the pride of Bengal and India, but the pride of the entire world. *(Pauses.)* Work, work, work! Alas, my days are numbered. Yet I have not been able to serve God devotedly and soulfully. I am unable to think of my Inner Pilot because I am constantly thinking of other people and helping others. And people don't even speak well of me. They don't even appreciate me. If I do not bring my Inner Pilot into my life, my service to mankind will be of no use.

PUNDIT   Vidyasagar, you are really great. Your sincerity has touched the very depths of my heart. You are playing your role most devotedly, most soulfully. The creator in you is truly great, but unfortunately the critic in you is creating problems. Do not be the critic, but be the lover of humanity.

You are the creator, creating love in mankind. Perfection you want, and perfection God will give you. It is the constant dedicated service you are doing for Him and for humanity that will give you perfection. You act. In your action self-perfection will dawn. Self-criticism will never give you perfection. Vidyasagar, I am advising you, but it is you who should advise *me* every second of my life.

VIDYASAGAR No, God is speaking in and through you. I am so grateful to you, Pundit. From now on, now that I have seen Ramakrishna, I will pay more attention to my spiritual life. My spiritual life and my life of dedication to mankind will go together. My life of realisation and my life of dedication, which is the manifestation of Love and Light on earth, will go together from now on.

PUNDIT Vidyasagar, a man like you is very rare. Bengal is blessed because she can claim you as her own. Mother Earth is blessed because she has you as her chosen son.

THE SYNTHESIS OF ALL RELIGIONS

SRI CHINMOY

DD 9. DRAMATIS PERSONÆ

SRI RAMAKRISHNA — THAKUR
HRIDAY (NEPHEW AND PERSONAL ATTENDANT OF THAKUR)
NAREN, RAKHAL, BABURAM, TARUP (DISCIPLES OF THAKUR)

DRINK, DRINK MY MOTHER'S NECTAR

DD 10. SCENE 1

(Night. Thakur is walking in the Panchavati grove under the trees in a contemplative mood. Enter Hriday.)

HRIDAY Uncle, let us go home. It is cold, and the wind is blowing very hard. I see fog being formed. You are not taking care of yourself.

THAKUR You go. I am coming.

(Exit Hriday. Thakur meditates. Re-enter Hriday.)

HRIDAY Don't delay, Uncle, don't be late. You forget everything, and then it is I who suffer afterwards.

THAKUR What can I do? My Mother has called me here. The moment she asks me to go home, I will go. Do you think that I don't suffer when I make you suffer for me?

HRIDAY I am going, but don't be late.

(Exit Hriday.)

THAKUR *(to himself)* The synthesis of all religions, the union of East and West, self-dedication, self-sacrifice: these are all big, big words, big theories, big ideas, big ideals. But where are they, Mother? Mother, you are talking to me about all these things. These are such high ideals. But where are your dedicated soldiers? Mother, you never tell me lies. Where are they? Where are your chosen children? O chosen children of my Mother Kali, my heart is crying for you. Come. Come. Do Mother's work. You have to fulfil the Mother. You have to manifest the Mother on earth.

(Enter Naren.)

THAKUR *(with all affection and love)* Ah, Naren, you have come. You have come to me after such a long time. I have been talking to worldly people for so long. I have become practically deaf from hearing the complaints and unaspiring chatter of ordinary people. People are throwing all their worldly desires into me. Now I have nobody I can speak to about my inner life. I have nobody to tell what is going on in my heart. Naren, tell me, when are you going to come again?

NAREN The moment I get an opportunity I will be back again. Why do you think of me so much? Why do you speak to others all the time about Naren, Naren, Naren? Don't you know the story in the *Puranas* about King Bharata who always thought of his deer? Then, in the following incarnation, he became a deer.

THAKUR You are right. But what can I do? I can't keep my mind away from you. All the time I think of you. When I don't see you I feel miserable. *(Closes his eyes and speaks to Mother Kali.)* Mother, listen to what Naren is telling me. *(After a few moments he opens his eyes and speaks to Naren.)* I will not listen to you. You are not saying the right thing. Mother says that I see you as Narayan, I see you as the incarnation of God. The day I don't see you as the incarnation of God, I will not even look at your face.

NAREN If that is true, then why have you ignored me for such a long time? I have come to you and you have avoided me, ignored me mercilessly. You have shown me such contempt the past few times.

THAKUR Mother, Mother, listen to this fellow! *(To Naren.)* Can I avoid you? Can I ignore you? Can I show contempt to you? Impossible! You do not know; you cannot fathom my inner workings. Naren, tell me one thing. Granted, I have not been nice to you. I have been very unkind, very rude to you. So why do you keep coming to me?

NAREN I come here to listen to you. I adore you. I worship you. I want to see you, Thakur, even if you are unkind to me. I love your presence. I love your meditative mood. I love your trance. I love everything you do because I love you.

THAKUR My son, I have been testing you. I wanted to see what would happen if I didn't show you affection and love — whether you would stay with me or not. It is only you who can bear such indifference and contempt from me. Had it been somebody else, he would not have come to my place any more. Nobody else would have stayed with me. Whoever got that kind of treatment from me would have hated me to the end of his life.

NAREN It is all due to your compassion, to your love, that I stayed. You know that my anger is of the quickest. But you gave me shelter in your heart. You brought me into your soul and made me your true son.

THAKUR *(smiling)* Naren, I have occult powers, abundant occult powers, all occult powers. But what do I do with them? I don't even wear clothes. Who is going to use these powers? I am thinking of telling Mother that I would like to give you everything, all my occult powers. You have to do much work for the Mother. If I give you these powers you will be able to work most effectively for the world. What do you think of this idea?

NAREN Please tell me, will these occult powers help me in realising God?

THAKUR No, they can't help you in realising God. But when you start working for God, they will be of great help to you.

NAREN   Then I don't want them. I want God first. After God-realisation it is up to you and God to give me occult powers.

THAKUR   Excellent, excellent. Oh, my Naren, who else is like you? Who is free from greed, but you? Most seekers cry for occult power, but I am eager to give you my occult power and you do not want it. You want God, my son, not occult power, and God is the only thing that we all need.

(Enter Rakhal, Baburam and Tarup. They bow to Thakur.)

THAKUR   One has to be a hundred per cent devoted to God like Naren. Only then can one realise God.

RAKHAL   I know that. His sincerity has impressed me greatly. My brother is all love for you, all love for God. May I ask you a question today?

THAKUR   Of course, of course. If I don't answer your question, then whose question shall I answer?

RAKHAL   Please tell me the essence of the *Vaisnava* philosophy.

THAKUR   The *Vaisnava* philosophy is very simple. Love humanity and serve humanity: this is the philosophy.

RAKHAL   Please explain it to me further. It is not clear to me.

THAKUR   Remember the name of God. The Truth and the possessor of the Truth are one. Lord Krishna and his true devotee are one. The devotee's whole world is nothing but Lord Krishna. It is Krishna who has become everything for him. This is what a real *Vaisnava* thinks and believes, and it is absolutely true. We have to show compassion to all human beings. *(Pauses.)* No, I am wrong. Who are we to show compassion to all human beings? We are feebler than ants. What right, what capacity do we have to help mankind? We have to serve all human beings and know that we are then serving God, for they are all manifestations of God. This is the right attitude. We have to serve all human beings, knowing and feeling that they are all manifestations of God.

TARUP Please tell me how I can have purity.

THAKUR Love mankind and serve mankind as devotedly as possible. Then automatically you will have purity. You have to see God in every human being. Only then will you have devotion. And when you have devotion, real devotion for God, then your heart will be pure.

NAREN If ever God gives me the opportunity and capacity, I shall preach before the whole world. I shall speak to the whole world; the rich and the poor, the *Brahmins* and the *Chandalas* will hear your message from me. I wish to offer your message to the entire world. Please bless me so that my desire will be fulfilled.

THAKUR My blessing is already there. It is for you, for all of you. It has been raining down on you for the last few years. The Mother is playing her own game in and through you all. You are all just instruments of the Mother.

(Enter Hriday.)

HRIDAY Uncle, I can't bear you any longer. I can't. You have really become insane. Now I know you will suffer from this cold and I will suffer even more.

THAKUR Oh, I had forgotten. Hriday, forgive me, forgive me. Come, come, all of you, come.

(Exeunt all except Naren, who sits down on the ground and sings with folded hands.)

Jago amar swapan sathi
jago amar praner pran
jago amar chokher jyoti
rishi kabi murtiman
jago, jago, jago
jago amar bishwal hiya
byapta jaha bishwamoy
jago amar sei chetana
bishwatite shesh ja noy
jago, jago, jago
jago amar dhyani-swarup
jago amar baddhwa jib
sarba jiber tandra tuti
jago amar mukta shib
jago, jago, jago

(Arise, awake, O Friend of my dream.
Arise, awake, O Breath of my life.
Arise, awake, O Light of my eyes.
O Seer-Poet in me,
Do manifest Yourself in me and through me.
Arise, awake, O vast heart within me.
Arise, awake, O consciousness of mine,
Which is always transcending the universe
And its own life of the Beyond.
Arise, awake, O Form of my meditation transcen-
    dental.
Arise, awake, O bound divinity in humanity.
Arise, awake, O my heart's Liberator, Shiva,
And free mankind from its ignorance-sleep.)

DRINK, DRINK MY MOTHER'S NECTAR

SRI CHINMOY

DD II. DRAMATIS PERSONÆ

SRI RAMAKRISHNA
DISCIPLES
CAPTAIN (A DISCIPLE)
A DEVOTEE

DRINK, DRINK MY MOTHER'S NECTAR

DD 12. SCENE I

(Ramakrishna with his disciples. Enter Captain.)

RAMAKRISHNA   Come in, Captain. *(Captain bows to Ramakrishna.)* I know you have read the *Bhagavad Gita* many, many times. I wish to hear from you about the *Gopis*.

CAPTAIN   When Krishna was at Vrindavana he had no wealth, but the Gopis loved him more dearly than they loved their own lives. Their love for Sri Krishna was so pure, so genuine, so divine. They gave him their vital desires and their psychic aspiration. They gave him their all.

RAMAKRISHNA   Krishna, Krishna .... *(Enters into trance.)* Captain, tell me more.

CAPTAIN   Not to speak of ordinary yogis, even the great yogis cannot have free access to Krishna's heart. But because of their devoted love and unconditional surrender to him, the Gopis always had free access to Krishna's heart.

A DEVOTEE   Thakur, our greatest novelist, Bankim Chandra, recently wrote an excellent book on Krishna.

RAMAKRISHNA   I see. Do you know that Bankim does not believe in Radha? He believes only in Krishna.

CAPTAIN   That means he does not believe in Krishna's divine *lila*.

RAMAKRISHNA   But Bankim also says that sex life is necessary.

CAPTAIN   It is very strange that on the one hand he thinks and feels that sex life is necessary, while on the other hand he does not believe in the divine lila, the divine game. I see in him nothing but contradictions.

RAMAKRISHNA   You call it contradiction and I call it lack of realisation. Mere book learning and God-realisation are never, never the same thing. For God-realisation you have to pray, you have to meditate. You have to cry like a child. A child cries for his mother and he gets her. If you cry for the Divine Mother's Nectar, you will get it without fail. Drink, drink my Mother Kali's Nectar as much as you want to. Be immortal, my sweet children.

THIS BODY WILL NOT LAST VERY LONG

SRI CHINMOY

DD 13. DRAMATIS PERSONÆ

SRI RAMAKRISHNA
RAKHAL
NAREN
OTHER SELECTED DISCIPLES

DRINK, DRINK MY MOTHER'S NECTAR

DD 14. SCENE I

(Sri Ramakrishna with some of his selected disciples.)

RAMAKRISHNA My health is failing very rapidly.

RAKHAL Please tell us how we can restore your health.

RAMAKRISHNA That depends on the Will of God.

NAREN I know your will has become inseparably one with God's Will.

RAMAKRISHNA In this body two persons live: God in the form of an Avatar, and God in the form of a devotee. An Avatar's devotees come with him and go away with him.

RAKHAL So you must not go away alone, leaving us behind.

RAMAKRISHNA The religious mendicants appear quite unexpectedly out of the blue. They sing and dance, and again they disappear quite unexpectedly. Hardly anyone recognises their aspiration. Similarly, spiritual Masters appear and disappear without being recognised. *(Ramakrishna closes his eyes for a minute.)* I tell you all that a life without renunciation is no life at all. Renounce your ignorance. Renounce your knowledge. Renounce what you have and what you are.

NAREN When I talk of renunciation some people get terribly annoyed with me.

RAMAKRISHNA Naren, don't be afraid of them. Say what you must say. It is through renunciation that you can and you will realise God. *(Caresses Naren.)* Much.

NAREN *(with a smile)* What do you mean by "much"?

RAMAKRISHNA Much renunciation has been accomplished by you. Naren, I have told you many times that you have come into the world for me.

NAREN   I don't quite understand what you say. Please explain it to me.

RAMAKRISHNA   You are here on earth to manifest me. I have already given you all that I have. I have nothing left.

NAREN   Do you mean that I have to believe all that you say to me?

RAMAKRISHNA   You will not only believe me but make all of humanity believe who I am.

NAREN   You talk. I listen.

RAMAKRISHNA   True. But in the near future you are going to act.

NAREN   From the very dust of your feet you can give birth to millions of Narens like me.

RAMAKRISHNA   Stop, stop. From the very Heart of God, from the very Breath of God you have come. Naren, my Naren, with you I am complete.

NAREN   Thakur, in your heart I am fulfilled. At your feet I am perfect. *(Prostrates himself at Ramakrishna's feet.)*

SRI RAMAKRISHNA'S PASSING

SRI CHINMOY

DD 15. DRAMATIS PERSONÆ

SRI RAMAKRISHNA
SARADA DEVI
FIRST DISCIPLE
SECOND DISCIPLE
THIRD DISCIPLE
OTHER DISCIPLES
NAREN

DRINK, DRINK MY MOTHER'S NECTAR

DD 16. SCENE I

(The day of Sri Ramakrishna's passing. His disciples and consort, Sarada Devi, are standing by his bedside. Three disciples are standing a little apart from the others.)

FIRST DISCIPLE   It pains me to see our Master like this. His frail frame seems less dependable than a storm-tossed raft.

SECOND DISCIPLE   By going deep within, still one can discover his true divine personality. Even now one can never doubt his greatness. In his teachings abides a colossal Will that can shake the world.

THIRD DISCIPLE   No Indian youth of the rising generation can dream of escaping the subtle influence of Sri Ramakrishna Paramahansa.

FIRST DISCIPLE   Ramakrishna will appear to one person as a man of overflowing emotion, to a second as an ardent aspirant, to a third as a man of philosophical wisdom, to a fourth as a man of unique sincerity.

SECOND DISCIPLE   It is inevitable that different persons should hold different opinions regarding his personality. For in a matter like this, a flawless intellectual analysis is impossible, and all our human judgement will sadly fail to yield any useful answer.

THIRD DISCIPLE   But nobody will ever hesitate to call him the most beloved child of the Divine Mother Kali. His sole aim in life was to have nothing save and except a constant union with Mother Kali. This aim he fulfilled. In one word we can sum up the message of his life: Mother.

FIRST DISCIPLE   It is Ramakrishna, too, who has shown the greatest reverence for women that the world has ever known. He feels that women are the embodiment of the Divine

Mother and he treats them as divinities. His own consort, Sarada Devi, he worships as the Divine Mother Herself.

SECOND DISCIPLE   The higher consciousness that constantly floods the mind and heart of Sri Ramakrishna exerts a unique influence not only on us, his disciples, but also on all persons around him. It lifts everyone above the ordinary plane to partake of the divine sweetness of Heaven. His very life is in itself the most effective refutation of the half-believer and the unbeliever in the Divine.

THIRD DISCIPLE   Here is a man whose authoritative voice declared that he had not only seen the Omnipotent, but could show Him to his beloved disciple, Naren.

(Hearing Naren's name mentioned, Ramakrishna opens his eyes.)

RAMAKRISHNA   *(pathetically)* Naren.... Naren, why are you silent? You look confused, almost baffled. I have read your mind. Still you doubt me, Naren?

(Naren comes closer to his Master, but remains silent.)

RAMAKRISHNA   He who is Rama, He who is Krishna, in one form is Ramakrishna.

(Shedding tears, Naren bows to Sri Ramakrishna and touches his feet.)

NAREN   I shall not doubt you any more, Thakur. In your presence, I have found that man can be perfect even in this body. The descent of Avatars like you, O Master, is for the purpose of uplifting and furthering the progress of mankind in the evolutionary process. You go on doing good for mankind in your earthly body as long as it serves the interest of humanity. You are free from the results of your actions, good or bad, big or small.

SARADA DEVI   Now that my Kali — Ramakrishna — is about to pass behind the curtain of Eternity, an excruciating pain is torturing my heart.

(She begins to cry bitterly. To everyone's surprise, Ramakrishna raises himself slightly.)

RAMAKRISHNA   Why do you weep so bitterly? I leave your Naren with you.

SARADA DEVI   Yes, my Divine Lord, it is true. You are the seed sown in the world-soil, and our Naren is the bumper crop which humanity shall reap. Thakur is the Inspiration, his Naren is its Expression. So humanity will have both Inspiration and Expression as its peerless possessions. *(She bows down to Ramakrishna.)* Glory to you, O Thakur. In you we find a triumphant living example of the truths that you preach. To you we offer our deepest homage. Our hearts feel that what you possess is the Infinite, and that the Infinite is your heart's Eternal Home.

(Sri Ramakrishna leaves the body.)

VIVEKANANDA WAITS
FOR THE INNER MESSAGE

SRI CHINMOY

DD 17. DRAMATIS PERSONÆ

VIVEKANANDA
A PEON

DRINK, DRINK MY MOTHER'S NECTAR

DD 18. SCENE 1

(Madras. Vivekananda is in his room.)

VIVEKANANDA   *(to himself)* Not to satisfy my mental curiosity have I decided to sail for America. No, not to make a noise in the world. My Master's silent blessing has kindled the inspiration-fire in me to share his light with the soil and soul of America. No country is superior in all spheres of life. As regards spirituality, the Americans are far inferior to us, but their society is far superior to ours. The East has become lost by moving away from materialism; the West, by keeping clear of spirituality. I deeply feel that a happy marriage of the two is the supreme need of the world. Life without spirituality is as poor as life without material power. Hence the East must be surcharged with the dynamism of the West, and the West must be inspired with the ancient wisdom of the East. We will teach them our spirituality and assimilate what is best in their society. Sri Ramakrishna has synthesised most of the major world religions by his direct and immediate realisation of the Truth in each of them. He has pierced the core of each religion, extracted its essence and become the perfect embodiment of that particular path to the Supreme. His precepts are couched in the simplest language, in words that fly straight into the hearts of the people. The blessings that not only India but the entire world has received and will receive from him, from his unique universal sympathy, stand matchless. I look upon the world as my dear Motherland, and upon mankind as my true brothers and sisters. Come what may, to serve them with my Master's soul-stirring message is my cherished religion.

But now, on the eve of my departure for America, I have decided that I will cross the seas only after receiving some concrete indication from my Master. I am sure my Thakur would sanction my going to America were he still alive. But let me wait for a sign from him.

DD 19. SCENE 2

(A week later.)

VIVEKANANDA For the past week I have waited and waited for some concrete sign from my Master, but all in vain. *(Pauses.)* Since my spiritual Mother and my Master are one and the same, I shall seek her permission to go abroad. I shall write a letter to Sri Sarada Devi from here in Madras.

(He sits and begins writing the letter.)

DD 20. SCENE 3

(A few weeks later. Naren sings:)

Ore mor kheya ore mor neye
ore ananda bani
niye jao mor trishita kshudhita
supta chitta khani

(O my boat, O my Boatman,
O Message of Transcendental Delight,
Carry me. My heart is thirsty and hungry,
And it is fast asleep at the same time.
Carry my heart to the other shore.)

VIVEKANANDA   Still I have not received a reply from my divine Mother. But just last night I had a most significant dream in which I saw Sri Ramakrishna proceeding to the West over the waves and waters. This I have taken as approval of my plan.

(Enter a peon. He hands Vivekananda a letter.)

VIVEKANANDA   Thank you.

(Exit the peon.)

VIVEKANANDA   Ah! From my divine Mother! *(Reads the letter.)* I have received wholehearted permission from my spiritual Mother. Now with redoubled faith I am able to undertake the voyage to America. A spiritual force of Sri Ramakrishna's power will forever retain its dynamism. It will spread

DRINK, DRINK MY MOTHER'S NECTAR

beyond the narrow limits of one little province, of one country, of one continent. The renown of my Master's spiritual teachings shall travel far and wide, touching the heart of the world and awakening its slumbering soul.

NAREN, YOU ARE THAKUR'S PROMISE

SRI CHINMOY

DD 21. DRAMATIS PERSONÆ

NAREN
RAKHAL
A FEW BROTHER DISCIPLES

DRINK, DRINK MY MOTHER'S NECTAR

DD 22. SCENE I

(Naren has just arrived at the railway station. He has come back from a triumphant visit to the West. Rakhal has come to meet him with a few brother disciples. They are all extolling Naren to the skies. Rakhal and brother disciples sing:)

*Deshe deshe ghure berai deshe deshe
premer shikha bahan kare hese hese
sakal desher gopan katha
sakal praner byakulata
ek halo aj asim pathe
alinganer alor brate
hiya tarir majhi tomai bhalobese*

(From country to country we roam,
Carrying the flame of Love Divine,
Smiling and smiling.
The secret thought of each country
And the yearning of each life
Here become one.
On the road of Infinity,
In the embrace of the covenant
Of the Light Supreme,
O Boatman of our Heart-Boat,
By loving You, we do all this.)

(Rakhal offers Naren a garland.)

NAREN Rakhal, it is you who deserve this garland. You are the son of Thakur. Thakur has called only you his son. *Guruvat guru putreshu.* [The son of a Guru is like the Guru himself.] So it is you who deserve this garland.

RAKHAL *Jaishtha vrata sama pita.* [An elder brother is like one's own father.] You are older than I. You are like my father. It is you who deserve this garland, and I shall put it on you.

NAREN No, Rakhal. Thakur used to say that you had the highest experiences. Your experiences have surpassed all our experiences. You are the *Raja,* the King. I am so proud of you, of your spiritual attainments.

RAKHAL Naren, Thakur told us that you would be our leader. We shall always look upon you as our dearest leader. We shall always be at your command. To serve you, to please you, to listen to you will be the one thing that will give us joy.

NAREN Rakhal, with your soul's height and with my soul's dynamism we shall manifest our Lord, Sri Ramakrishna, in every corner of India. And not only in India, but over the length and breadth of the world. In you is Thakur's poise and peace.

RAKHAL In you is Thakur's pride and fulfilment. You are Thakur's promise.

NAREN, YOU ARE MY JOY;
YOU ARE MY PRIDE

SRI CHINMOY

DD 23. DRAMATIS PERSONÆ

SARADA DEVI
FIRST DISCIPLE
A FEW OTHER CLOSE DISCIPLES
NAREN

DRINK, DRINK MY MOTHER'S NECTAR

DD 24. SCENE 1

(Sarada Devi with some of her close disciples.)

SARADA DEVI I am so anxious to see my Naren. I am told that he will be here soon. You know how hard he has worked for Thakur in America. Because of him Thakur will be well known all over the world. I am so proud of my Naren.

FIRST DISCIPLE Mother, it is all your Grace, all Thakur's Grace. Because of your Grace, Naren has succeeded in America, in the West. He was nothing, absolutely nothing before he came into your life.

SARADA DEVI No, he was everything. Thakur brought him from the highest world. Thakur gave him everything before he came into this world. And Thakur's name is known throughout the length and breadth of the world only because of my Naren's ceaseless dedication and aspiration.

(Enter Naren.)

NAREN Mother, I have come. *(He prostrates himself before Sarada Devi's feet.)* Mother, I shall not touch your feet, and I shall not allow anybody else to touch your feet from now on. We touched Thakur's feet and gave him all our impurities and all our vital desires. He accepted our impurities and ignorance unconditionally and he died from them. Now I don't want to touch your feet, and I don't want anybody else to touch your feet. If we touch your feet I know that you will immediately take away all our sins, as Thakur did. And if you take away all our sins, then we shall lose you soon. Mother, I don't want to lose you.

SARADA DEVI   *(blessing Naren)* You are Thakur's dearest son. You will forever remain his dearest son.

NAREN   Mother, many, many times I have doubted Thakur. Even the day he left the earth-scene I doubted him. But out of his infinite bounty he convinced me, on his deathbed, of who he is. Mother, I am the tiniest drop of the infinite sea of compassion which is Sri Ramakrishna. Mother, I am so proud that I have never doubted you or your realisation, even for a second. Mother, Mother, in this lifetime it is you who will be the sole object of my adoration. Only your devotees, your disciples, your children, shall be the chosen instruments of God. I feel in you the living presence of Mother Kali. I see you as the Mother of the Universe. I see you as the Goddess Supreme. I see you as our Thakur. You carry the banner of Thakur's Light. Mother, you have kept yourself hidden. But how can you hide yourself from all your loving children? You cannot. In you is the purest and most perfect manifestation of God. In you, Mother, is my realisation.

SARADA DEVI   Naren, Thakur gave you his infinite love and infinite concern. He gave you his All. I give you, my Naren, my infinite joy and my infinite pride. I give you my All.

(Naren sings.)

DRINK, DRINK MY MOTHER'S NECTAR

He karuna sindhu
ami taba bindu
charan tale thai
nitya jena pai
jani janani jani
tomai ami hani
ananda indu

(O Ocean of Compassion,
I am Your tiniest drop.
At Your Feet my haven I always seek.
I know, Mother, I know,
You I strike, You I hurt,
O my Moon of Light-Delight.)

TWO MOTHERS AND A SON

SRI CHINMOY

DD 25. DRAMATIS PERSONÆ

SARADA DEVI (DIVINE CONSORT OF SRI RAMAKRISHNA AND
  SPIRITUAL MOTHER OF VIVEKANANDA)
VIVEKANANDA
BHUVANESHWARI (PHYSICAL MOTHER OF VIVEKANANDA)
A FRIEND OF BHUVANESHWARI

DRINK, DRINK MY MOTHER'S NECTAR

DD 26. SCENE I

(Sarada Devi and Vivekananda are outdoors at Belur Math.)

SARADA DEVI Naren, tell me something about your mother.

VIVEKANANDA Mother Divine, your infinite compassion is illumining my life of ignorance. You want me to speak of my physical mother. In my childhood I found my confidante in nobody but my mother. I disclosed everything to her. Only on rare occasions, in very trying times, did she lose her patience and faith. I have often exploited her kindness and sweetness as I now exploit your compassion and forgiveness.

SARADA DEVI Naren, sweeter than the sweetest is the smile of our physical mother. Deeper than the deepest is her affection. Mightier than the mightiest is the power of her blessing. Vaster than the vastest is her hope for her children. From your physical mother you inherited not only moral purity and an aesthetic sense, but also many intellectual faculties and a unique memory. Her influence moulded your life considerably, and your influence is shaking the world.

VIVEKANANDA Mother, my dearest spiritual Mother, Mother of my soul and eternal Life, however great the earthly mother may be, her love is no match for the disinterested love of the spiritual Mother. It is absolutely necessary to feel that our spiritual Mother is our real Mother and that we are her real children and divine warriors.

(Enter Bhuvaneshwari and one of her friends. They stroll towards Vivekananda and Sarada Devi, but do not notice them.)

BHUVANESHWARI   I am glad you have come with me to Belur Math to see my son Naren's work, his great accomplishments.

FRIEND   Yes, all these newly constructed buildings, and such beautiful surroundings.

BHUVANESHWARI   My Naren has done all this.

(Vivekananda overhears his mother and immediately turns to her.)

VIVEKANANDA   Mother, I must correct you. Not your Naren, but hers. *(Points to Sarada Devi, who is meditating.)* Your Naren is by no means capable of such achievements. I am seated between two extremes: an utmost incapacity and an omnipotent power. Your Naren is all incapacity. He could not even support his mother and the younger members of his family after his father's death. My divine Mother's Naren is all capacity. It is her unconditional blessing alone that has made me what I am now. My real source is her heart. My only goal is her feet.

(Naren sings.)

DRINK, DRINK MY MOTHER'S NECTAR

Ekla ami tomar kachhe jabona ma jabona
ekla ami tomai kabhu bandhbona ma bandhbona
tomar hiyar mauna bhasha
ei dharanir dipta asha
tomar praner premer dhara
moder lagi bandhan hara
ekla ami tomar kachhe jabona ma jabona
sabar sathe tomai pabo ei shudhu mor sadhana

(Alone I shall not go to You, Mother,
I shall not go.
Alone I shall not bind You,
I shall not bind You.
Your Heart's silence-language
and the illumined hope of this world,
and Your Heart's nectar-flow,
Are always boundless for us.
Alone I shall not go to You, Mother,
I shall not go.
With all I shall get You:
this is my life's only aspiration,
only meditation, only Goal.)

PART VII

THE DESCENT OF THE BLUE

THE DESCENT OF THE BLUE

SRI CHINMOY

DB I. DRAMATIS PERSONAE

[The first edition of *The Descent of the Blue* presented no *dramatis personæ*.]

THE DESCENT OF THE BLUE

DB 2. ACT I, SCENE I

(The Abode of Existence-Consciousness-Bliss. Mind has not been born there. The One without a second and the Mother of the Trinity are rapt in trance in the holy Fire. The teeming Gods go round the Infinite and the Mother of the Golden All, singing anthems to them.)

FIRST BAND OF THE GODS   The face of Truth is covered with a brilliant lid; that do thou remove, O Fosterer, for the law of the Truth, for sight.

SECOND BAND

> *From the non-being to true being,*
> *From the darkness to the Light,*
> *From death to Immortality.*
> *OM. Peace! Peace! Peace!*
> *So be it.*

(Their creation has compelled the primaeval parents to descend upon earth for the Divine Play and thus to terminate the earth's ceaseless pangs.)

BRAHMA   It is I who create. None save I is the Infinite's creative Power. Therefore, no equal have I.

VISHNU   It is I who uphold. I am His preserving Power. Hence, matchless am I.

SIVA   I am Rudra. I am His force of Destruction. Boundless also is my Compassion for the doleful earth. It is I who lead the earth and her children towards a new creation. Therefore, unique am I.

BRAHMA   Earth sows, Heaven reaps. Our supremacy amongst each other can be proved only on the earth, and there alone shall we be able to find which of our devotees are truly superior.

VISHNU   I am one with you in that.

SIVA   Needless to say, I shall accompany you. We are but the triune limbs of the Supreme. We exist simply because we must needs help Him in his Divine Play.

BRAHMA   Has the earth invoked our presence there? Without their mounting cry how can we descend?

VISHNU   I shall sow the seed of yearning in the heart of the mortals. With a heart full of devotion they will pray to us.

SIVA   Remember, the Asura with his hosts will not remain asleep. How can the earth hail our advent, she who has been under the octopus tentacles of the brooding Giant of Evil?

BRAHMA   We are fully aware. Mahadeva, you will be our Captain! It is you who will ruthlessly destroy the Adversary and found our victory on the aspiring soil.

(Behind the curtain a tremendous call and yearning.)

O, save the earth! O, save the creation! Do flood the earth with the sanctified waters of the Truth and cast the Falsehood down into the Chasm of Nothingness. Set the earth-life free from the roaring den of Death. Brahma, Vishnu, Siva! deign to alight on this orphan earth where Ignorance reigns supreme. We yearn to see your divine Play on the sorrowful dust.

OM anandamayi chaitanyamayi satyamayi parame
OM anandamayi chaitanyamayi satyamayi parame
OM anandamayi chaitanyamayi satyamayi parame

THE DESCENT OF THE BLUE

THE MOTHER   Alas, the earth is inundated with ceaseless sorrows and pangs. Her throbbing heart compels my descent. I am the Mother. Who but I can save my children?

THE INFINITE   I, too, on earth shall descend. My advent the East shall acclaim, thine the West.

THE MOTHER   My Grace shall give Immortality to earth. With me will I carry the flame of fire-pure Transformation.

THE INFINITE   I will found thy supernal Kingdom on the neglected earth.

DB 3. ACT I, SCENE 2

(The residence of Dr. K.D. Ghosh. A smiling garden in front. Swarnalata, his wife, plucks flowers and sings.)

What shall we mortals do? O, ours to meet
With worshipping brow the flowers of His feet!

(Enter K.D. Ghosh.)

KRISHNA DHAN   I cannot believe my ears! You sing surprisingly sweetly. They say you are "the Rose of Rangpur" and I know you to be a matchless woman. But I have never heard you sing.

SWARNALATA   Truth to tell, I am not inclined to music; at least, music is not my forte.

K.D.   Who was it singing then like an angel?

SWARNA   Ah! don't you know that alone anybody can sing?

K.D.   Not always. The singer in me, if any, wouldn't sing, even if alone.

SWARNA   I believe you, too, would sing if you dreamt my dream.

K.D.   Dream! Do open your heart. Am I not your husband?

SWARNA   True, you are my confidant. But it's not the proper moment to give away the secret. Let me see if my dream comes true.

K.D.   Swarna, you too! — you appear to be my eighth wonder.

SWARNA   That is a long story. It would be a *Mahabharata* if I told it. To be brief, I had a toy Krishna when I was a child. As I grew up, I was wont to pray to Sri Krishna in the evening when the earth sank into silence. My sole desire was to be the mother of the embodied Divine.

K.D. We are too human for a divine dream. Kausalya, Devaki, Sachi — was there anyone on earth who suffered more than they? What a fanciful desire, indeed! What a lofty dream!

SWARNA But you have not yet heard me out.

K.D. Do say your say. I will keep it to myself. I give you my word of honour.

SWARNA But do you know yourself? You are an atheist.

K.D. Atheist! My father was a Hindu, so am I. I am a worshipper of Kali. My father's mother is at Varanashi. A devotee of Lord Siva is she. Am I an atheist because I move in European society?

SWARNA Let it be. My dream demands your heart's encouraging, your true sympathy!

K.D. Swarna, I empty my heart to you.

SWARNA My prayer shall bear fruit before long. He, the Light of the world, is within me. *(A bashful smile.)*

K.D. Is He? *(A broad smile.)*

(Enter a poor Muslim in hot haste.)

ABDUL Babu, Babu! cholera has broken out in our village. I am very, very poor. Two of my sons were snatched away to the other world last week. My youngest, my dearest, my last son threatens to go. I pray, do call at my hut. Your very presence shall cure my dying son.

K.D. I shall try my best. My life on earth has no other aim but to protect the weak and help the needy. Those who wallow in wealth can call in eminent doctors. But my hand and bottle are for those whose friend is poverty itself. My work is to have money from the haves and contribute to the funds of the have-nots.

ABDUL Babu, Babu! I can pay the flood of your sympathy only with my tears of delight.

(Exeunt K.D. Ghosh and Abdul.)

SWARNA   *(with tears streaming)* Alas! him to call an atheist whose heart is a surge of sympathy — the living image of philanthropy? O Merciful! O Light of the blind! your pardon, your high pardon my sharp tongue desires.

THE DESCENT OF THE BLUE

DB 4. ACT I, SCENE 3

(The Himalayas. A galaxy of Kuthumis. The ingress and egress of the aspirant souls.)

FIRST KUTHUMI   The largesse of the mind is almost come to an end. Mind is the fount of problems. A permanent solution is not to be had there.

SECOND KUTHUMI   True, mind is unable to solve all problems. Dangers weave their meshes around the human souls. But who or what can make the impossible possible?

THIRD KUTHUMI   I know, I know. It is the pinnacled light of the Supermind which is utterly empty of all problems. It is a fount of harmony, of unity-in-multiplicity.

FOURTH KUTHUMI   The endless urge of the Supermind is to descend upon the earth and change her consciousness.

FIRST KUTHUMI   To serve the purpose God's human birth is the supreme need.

SECOND KUTHUMI   Many a time He has descended on the earth across the centuries. But earth seems to have made no satisfactory progress. He comes and goes at His chosen times. Each and every time His Mission appears to be thwarted by the wilful ignorance of the earth. The wide hunger of Time devours all the spiritual wealth that He brings down. A ruthless oblivion lords it over the mortals.

THIRD KUTHUMI   It is victory and not defeat that is the first and last word of God. Soon the Infinite shall alight on the throbbing heart of the soil.

FOURTH KUTHUMI   When, why, how, where?

THIRD KUTHUMI   It is in India, it is in the land of the sages and the spiritual giants that He will see the light of day.

SECOND KUTHUMI   And what is expected from us?

FIRST KUTHUMI   Ours is to be a flower-offering to Him, to His Mission.

THE DESCENT OF THE BLUE

DB 5. ACT I, SCENE 4

(The residence of Rishi Rajnarayan Bose. He adores the formless Aspect of the Brahman.)

RISHI   Swarna, Swarna! Take your seat right beside me. Swarna, I had a dream last night. To me that dream seems more vivid than reality itself.

SWARNA   Father, may I have a share?

RISHI   Certainly, my dream concerns you much. You all know that I have been a votary of the Nirakara Brahman for a couple of decades. But now no more. I saw Him.... It is beyond my power of expression. My eyes swam in light and delight.

SWARNA   Who was it, Father?

RISHI   The Light of the world, Sri Krishna.

SWARNA   Where?

RISHI   My daughter, in you, in you and nowhere else. Since the small hours of the morning I have been a torrent of ecstasy. I have also seen the Gods bow down on their knees before Him, your coming son. Swarna, you are my matchless jewel.

SWARNA   Father, you are my greatest pride. You stand very high in the estimation of all. You are the polestar of the Nation. Your voice has rung out the inmost voice of India. Now it is my hope that God will make me worthy of your prophetic vision.

SRI CHINMOY

DB 6. ACT I, SCENE 5

(The abode of Manomohan Ghosh, a Barrister and close friend of Dr. K.D. Ghosh. Behind the screen.)

The Birth of the Infinite
(5 a.m., 15 August 1872)

The golden dawn of the cosmos rapt in trance,
Awaits the birth of the All.
The seven worlds' bliss converges in her heart
With august and sun-vast call.
Slowly the Peak unmeasured of rapture-fire
Climbs down to our human cry.
His diamond vision's deathless Will leans low
Our mortal yearnings nigh.
Suddenly life's giant somnolence is stirred.
His all-embracing Wing
Declares, "I come to end your eyeless fear:
To me alone now cling!
"No fleeting dreams your teeming births do trace:
Now own my infinite bloom.
In me the flood of Immortality!
Nowhere shall be your doom."

MANOMOHAN My joy knows no bounds that your son takes birth in my house.

K.D. No doubt, it will be a matter of great rejoicing if the dream of my wife comes true.

MANOMOHAN How does her dream run?

K.D. Friend, to me it is just a dream, a chimera's mist, but to her it is a blazing truth.

MANOMOHAN   Krishnadhan, I wish to hear her dream and not your comment on it.
K.D.   Well, during her confinement she dreamt that it was Sri Krishna who would take human birth through her.
MANOMOHAN   I see nothing wrong in her dream. You are a pessimist from head to foot. Come, let us hurry to the child. Who knows, we may find the Marvellous One?

SRI CHINMOY

DB 7. ACT I, SCENE 6

(The child is in the lap of his mother. She is fondling him.)

SWARNA   My child, are you the Lord of my dream? I have seen you time and again. Today my dream has donned the cloak of reality.

(Enter her father, Rishi Rajnarayan)

RISHI   Swarna, I have come to see my Beloved, the Lord of the Gods.

SWARNA   There you are, Father. *(Swarnalata places the child on her father's lap.)*

RISHI   *(with a broad smile he lifts the child onto his head.)* Ah! It is Aurobindo, it is a lotus, still in the bud.

SWARNA   Father, I see no wonder in his face. In my dream he was the Wonder of Wonders.

RISHI   My daughter, do not look at him with your earthly eyes. To me he remains the same as in my vision when I saw him as the Light of the world. Never forget that God is the Thaumaturge of thaumaturges. Therefore, his appearance has put a mask on his real nature. Swarna, what a pride now tingles through my blood! My heart is swayed by a riot of joy. Krishna, Krishna is come. Dark clouds of doubt must not blight your vision. He is our Aurobindo. He is the Divine Lotus. Petal by petal He will bloom to a perfect perfection.

DB 8. ACT I, SCENE 7

(The parlour of Dr. K.D. Ghosh. Evening sets in.)

K.D. I have a fine proposal, Swarna. I would like to call in an Englishman.

SWARNA What for?

K.D. To tutor Benoy and Mano in English.

SWARNA And then....

K.D. For Auro an English governess.

SWARNA If my approval has any value then you have it hundred per cent.

K.D. Something more....

SWARNA What is it?

K.D. Starting from to-day, indeed from to-day on, Bengali is not to be spoken in our house. English, only English. How I wish my children could speak in English, write in English, think in English and even dream in English! They must be Englishmen to the core. I shall soon send them to Darjeeling and place them in a convent school. A few years later, I shall take them to London. My sons must be among the brightest jewels in India's crown.

SWARNA An exquisite plan, indeed. But before that why not say that you want to send me to the land of Death? How dare you think that I can endure the absence of my sweet children? I will go mad.

K.D. I knew it well that the mother in your heart is too strong. You are a typical Bengali woman. You want your sons to be helpless, mere babes in arms. Your pale, pathetic look pierces my heart. Swarna, your skin must not lose its colour because of worry. Do not be upset.

SWARNA   I am sorry. It is not in me to cross you. But you have given me a great shock.

THE DESCENT OF THE BLUE

DB 9. ACT I, SCENE 8

(Darjeeling. Benoy, Mano and Auro are returning from school. On the way they happen to meet a sannyasin. Many people have gathered about him. He smokes profusely.)

A VILLAGER   Sadhuji, please give me some religious knowledge.

SANNYASIN   All I can give you is a bit of advice. I am afraid, although my advice will reach your sceptic ears, you will never apply it in the practical field. *(Some of the villagers burst into a peal of laughter.)* My advice, you know? The world is an illusion. Have no link with it!

A MERCHANT   Be pleased to read my palm.

SANNYASIN   You, you wallow in the pleasure of wealth. Am I right?

MERCHANT   Absolutely perfect. But, Sadhuji, I have not seen the face of peace even for a fleeting second.

SANNYASIN   Ah, peace! peace is not to take birth here in this world. It is the offspring of another world. This world is made of din, dust and dizzying demonstrations.

MANOMOHAN   Please run your eyes over my palm, and drop a few hints about my years to come.

SANNYASIN   Ah, a poet, a fine poet. This is what your future says.

MANOMOHAN   *(pointing at Auro)* And how does the fate of my younger brother run?

SANNYASIN   *(looking ahead he meets Aurobindo's curious eyes; but in the twinkling of an eye Auro, frightened, sprints off.)* His future is at his command.

   Now you are afraid of me, but a day will come when you will become a great Yogi.

MANOMOHAN   Only a few days back Auro composed a beautiful poem on Kanchanjunga. The teachers have appreciated it greatly.

SANNYASIN   No wonder, he is not a common boy. He will be a great Yogi who has to play a great part on the world scene! Brahman! Brahman! O Lord of my breath, Thou art verily Thy unfathomable mystery.

THE DESCENT OF THE BLUE

DB 10. ACT II, SCENE I

(London. K.D. Ghosh, with his wife, sons and daughter, arrives at the residence of Mr. Drewett. Benoy, Mano and Auro will live there.)

MR. DREWETT   Good morning, Mr. Ghosh. Come, come, my young friends! *(Looking at Mrs. Drewett)* You were praying for a child. Now God brings you three in a row.

MRS. DREWETT   Thank God. Mr. Ghosh, I shall love them as if they were my own children. *(Caressing Auro)* I shall teach you English myself. I will not let you go to school at this tender age.

MR. DREWETT   I shall teach you Latin. I shall help you in every way. My young friend, I can brook no delay. Come, let us start our Latin lesson. Just repeat what I say.
>   Father - *Pater*
>   Mother - *Mater*
>   Brother - *Frater*
>   Sister - *Soror*
>   Son - *Filius*
>   Daughter - *Filia*
>   And now please repeat all the words by yourself.

(Auro's answers are perfect.)

Wonderful, your memory is wonderful.

AURO   Sir, what is the Latin for "God" and "Goddess"?

MR. DREWETT   Well, *Deus* and *Dea*. What made you ask this, my boy?

DB II. ACT II, SCENE 2

(St. Paul's School)

HEADMASTER   A brilliant lad, this Indian! He is by far and away the best student in almost every subject. He is at home in English, French, Latin and Greek.

THE ENGLISH TEACHER   Our boys are hopelessly beaten by Aurobindo, an Indian. I have never come across such a student.

HEADMASTER   I am proud of him, for he belongs to our school. And he is so loving, so polite.

THE DESCENT OF THE BLUE

DB 12. ACT II, SCENE 3

(Benoy, Mano and Auro in straitened circumstances.)

BENOY   At last I have secured a job in a club. Our starvation may end here.

MANO   Fortune dawns on us at last. But what is wrong with father? Why has he stopped sending money?

BENOY   My feeling is that father is not keeping in sound health. Alas, the moment I think of Auro my heart aches. He is only just out of his childhood.

MANO   Poor Auro, he has to learn the meaning of poverty at the very start of his life.

BENOY   For the last three months we have been unable to have a full meal. God knows how many days more we are to go on thus.

MANO   My poems bring in cheers, praises, appreciations but not a single penny. Such is my fate!

(Enter Auro.)

AURO   Here, a hundred shillings!

(Benoy and Mano jump up with astonishment.)

BENOY AND MANO   Where on earth did you get it?

AURO   An article of mine has been published, and they have given me this. Now, I would like to tell you something. You two always think of my suffering and poverty. But why do you forget the truth that there are millions on the earth whose condition is infinitely worse than ours? Our present condition makes us better able to fathom their sorrow. With a cheerful face let us brave the future.

THE DESCENT OF THE BLUE

DB 13. ACT II, SCENE 4

(Home. Mano reads out to Benoy, his eldest brother, a poem composed by himself.)

MANO

> Augustest! dearest! whom no thought can trace,
> Name murmuring out of birth's infinity,
> Mother! like Heaven's great face is thy sweet face,
> Stupendous with the mystery of me.

(Enter Auro.)

AURO There is a letter from father. He gives a brief account of the atrocities of British rule in India. He has also sent a few cuttings from the *Bengalee*.

(Mano snatches away the letter and begins to read it aloud.)

AURO We must pay the British back in their own coin.
MANO Yes, by all means.
BENOY What are you up to?
AURO Freedom, freedom of India by hook or by crook. We must dedicate ourselves to set India at large. Almost all the civilised nations on the earth are free. Utterly meaningless will be our lives if we fail to make our Motherland free.

DB 14. ACT II, SCENE 5

(At Cambridge. The Principal had sent for Aurobindo. Aurobindo was very bashful. It was not in his nature to come to the fore. Enter Aurobindo.)

AUROBINDO   Good morning, Sir.

PRINCIPAL   Ah, at last you have come. Better late than never. I have sent for you three times.

AUROBINDO   Sorry, Sir, please excuse me.

PRINCIPAL   My dear boy, nothing wrong with you, I suppose? Now, I come to the point: your essay on Milton. I have never seen such a wonderful piece by an undergrad since I came over here. You have headed the list.

AUROBINDO   *(bashfully smiling)* Thank you, Sir, it is so kind of you. If there was any inspiration, it must have been from the great subject of the essay himself.

THE DESCENT OF THE BLUE

DB 15. ACT II, SCENE 6

(Indian Majlis. Aurobindo and a dozen Indian students.)

AUROBINDO   The British must no longer lord it over India. Come, let us mobilise ourselves to uproot their rule from the soil of our Motherland.

FIRST MEMBER   I have crossed seven seas and thirteen rivers just to appear in the I.C.S. If I listen to you I shall soon run into difficulties with the authorities, and, worse still, my life may be ruined.

AUROBINDO   I, too, shall sit for the I.C.S. But I shan't serve the British Government.

SECOND MEMBER   To be sure, the freedom of India can never be won by us, for we are unimaginably weak. And if not, show us the way.

AUROBINDO   At the very outset we must make the people of India feel the unavoidable necessity of being a free country.

THIRD MEMBER   You mean revolution? Be sure, I affiliate myself with no such thing! You may call me a poltroon, if you like. I am not at all prepared to risk my life. *(Places his hands on his chest.)* It is the only one I have.

FOURTH MEMBER   I am absolutely at one with you. Who does not know the supreme truth that Non-violence is the greatest of all virtues? Circumstances will lead our dear Mother India to freedom if so is the Will of God. We are not to sacrifice our valuable lives, and again we are not to commit the ghastly sin of putting an end to English lives.

AUROBINDO   *(after heaving a sigh)* Mine is a road absolutely different from yours. God guides my life to another goal.

FIFTH MEMBER   Where do you get so much inspiration from?

AUROBINDO   I do not really know. Just last night I had a terrible dream. I saw a demon drinking the blood from the very breast of an old woman. We all went in hot haste to her rescue. To our joy we saved her life. But some of us were removed to the other world by that demon. I was just pondering who that woman was. Soon I heard a voice, so vivid, so pathetic! "I am your Bharatmata." And there ends my dream. From to-day the sole aim of my life is to make India as free as a bird in the sky.

SIXTH MEMBER   There is a secret society here at Cambridge named "Lotus and Dagger." Would you like to be a member of it?

AUROBINDO   Certainly, most gladly. With all my heart I shall serve the society.

SIXTH MEMBER   Then one day I shall take you there.

AUROBINDO   Thanks in advance, dear friend. Let that day come soon!

THE DESCENT OF THE BLUE

DB 16. ACT II, SCENE 7

(The momentous year 1893. Swami Vivekananda goes to America with the message of India. Aurobindo returns to India to make her free. The residence of the Gaekwar of Baroda at London. Enter James Cotton and Aurobindo.)

JAMES COTTON   Good morning, Sir. Here is my young friend Mr. Ghosh. A brilliant student from Cambridge.

AUROBINDO   Good morning, Sir.

GAEKWAR   Good morning. I have heard much about you from Mr. Cotton. I would be highly pleased if you accompanied me to India. I am sure you will stand very high in the estimation of our countrymen.

AUROBINDO   Thank you, Sir. I was just waiting for an opportunity to go to India, my Motherland.

DB 17. ACT II, SCENE 8

(Aurobindo is asleep. It is far into the night. It is the eve of his departure. Enter Bharatmata. Hair dishevelled, face overwhelmed with sorrow, old sari with many holes.)

BHARATMATA   My son, I am come at last. India demands your express arrival. For you will awake the slumbering nation. Darkness has begun to thicken in front of me. It will serve no use to lengthen my story by fruitless emotional gestures. Make me free, make me free, my son.

AUROBINDO   Mother, I offer my heart and soul to abide by your high command. No more shall you utter the wail of misery. I shall turn the wind of *Swadesh* into a gigantic tornado.

BHARATMATA   I am so happy, I am so happy, my son, for your face shows a thunder-willed determination.

(Enter the presiding deity of Britain.)

DEITY   My son, I have brought you up for the last fourteen years with kindly love and affection. Have I no claim?

AUROBINDO   Certainly, you do have. But our India must have freedom to save all humanity from peril. In the years to come, India and Britain will cherish a unique amity. No futile wrangling — the flood of peace shall inundate both countries.

DEITY   My sole request to you is that you will not do away with my language and literature. Nothing more, nothing less I ask of you.

AUROBINDO   To you I am immensely indebted. My pen shall ever serve your language and thus I shall as well serve you.

THE DESCENT OF THE BLUE

(Enter the World-Mother on tip-toe. She looks intently into his face.)

MOTHER Do you recognise me?
AUROBINDO I have seen you time and again in the world of dream. But shall we ever meet in the physical world?
MOTHER Why not, why not? At the divine hour I shall go and stand beside you in India. Down to earth we shall carry our highest Truth. You and I shall be the harbingers of a new humanity. I know, but you do not yet know that you are the new Sri Krishna of India. You are my Lord.

SRI CHINMOY

DB 18. ACT III, SCENE I

(Khulna. A religious mendicant sings while passing by the residence of Dr. K.D. Ghosh.)

MENDICANT

>*Mother, Mother, Mother Kali!*
>*Knowledge of earth is strange to me.*
>*I know not how to sing of Thee.*
>*My feeble mind is a fruitless tree.*
>*Thine Eyes are fire, Thy Heart is love.*
>*My bosom pines to be thy dove.*

K.D.   Ah, what moving and melting music! Mother Kali to my rescue! Who else can cool my racking pain? Worried thoughts about my son Auro are eating into my heart.

(Enter a messenger with a telegram)

MESSENGER   Sir, a wire for you.
K.D.   At last! Maybe it's from Auro.

(On opening the message he falls to the ground. His soul turns the keen vibration of its pain to an inner music.)

THE DESCENT OF THE BLUE

My Auro! Auro! all world-pain in flood
Within my finite breast.
My pride, my country's pride, O earth's hope-noon,
The all-transforming Crest!
Alas! to feed my longings high, no more
Shall I see my Auro, my son.
The sombre night envelops my mortal sheath.
To-day my heart is undone.
Now cruel fate has torn my vision's Rose.
Auro, I shut my eyes
To see your golden face, to be with you
In the blue-white climbing skies.

(K.D.Ghosh had almost intuitive high hopes that his Auro was to brighten the face of the mother country. The ship which was to carry Auro sank on the way. But Auro boarded a second ship. On the assumption that his son must have perished with the lost ship his father died of a broken heart.)

DB 19. ACT III, SCENE 2

(Deoghar. The abode of Rishi Rajnarayan Bose. The Rishi is chanting a Vedic hymn.)

THE RISHI   I set in front Fire, the messenger, and speak to the carrier of the offerings; may he bring to their session here the gods.

(Enter Auro and his maternal uncle Jogendra.)

JOGENDRA   Father, look, here is Auro.

(The Rishi springs to his feet and hugs Auro warmly to his breast before the grandson can bend his head down. The Rishi knew well that his Auro was no ordinary human being but Sri Krishna in human form. A deep silence seems to vibrate with their hearts' exchanges.)

THE RISHI   Jogen, call Swarna quick. Where is she? Swarna, Swarna! *(Half-choked in joy he calls out to his daughter at the top of his voice.)* Auro, my child, do you find your country, your Motherland, familiar?

AURO   Dadu, I'm afraid I can recall nothing that I had seen and heard before I left India. Things now appear to be refreshing, inspiring, enlightening. As I stepped on India's soil, at Apollo Bunder, Bombay, I felt drowned as if in a sea of peace.

THE RISHI   Oh, it's significant, deeply significant. It is a signal. Mother India wants you to be her own, for her work, for her soul's work. It was her soul's embrace to her chosen child.

THE DESCENT OF THE BLUE

(Enter Swarnalata with two of her women friends.)

SWARNA   *(after scanning Auro's face for a few seconds)* No, Father, not at all. This youth doesn't take after my child Auro. In England I left him quite young on earth. How could he grow such a big moustache! My son can never grow so big. No, you can never be my son. He had more grace in his face. Impossible, impossible. Father, I'm not such a fool as you take me to be. Oh, now, now!

(Exit Swarnalata in utter delusion. A chorus of laughter by Jogendra and the two women. Silent, amazed, Auro looks on.)

THE RISHI   Auro, your mother is off her head and so am I. Like father like daughter.

AURO   If my mother is queer in her brain then I, too.... There's no other possibility.

(Enter Swarnalata.)

SWARNA   I remember well that my Auro had a cut on one of his fingers. Let me see if you have the mark.

AURO   *(shooting a glance half-afraid at his mother's face and showing his finger)* Here it is, mother, here's the mark.

SWARNA   My Auro, my Auro! You are my son Auro. Father, he is my son Auro. Truly, he is the Krishna of my dream. *(Overwhelmed with joy she places her right palm on her son's devoted head.)* Now I am more than right that you are my son Auro.

AURO   Dadu, goodness gracious! At last my mother has to say, "Eureka, Eureka!"

DB 20. ACT III, SCENE 3

(Baroda. Aurobindo's own chamber. He is rapt in his studies. His room is a treasure-house of the Goddess of Learning. Suddenly he closes his book.)

AURO   I simply don't know how man can go on doing anything against his inner preference for long. My nature revolts at the Administrative Service. The work I am doing is not at all congenial to me. I shall ask the Gaekwar to shift me to his College.

(Enter a peon and hands Aurobindo a letter.)

PEON   Sir, His Highness the Gaekwar requests the favour of your company at lunch and he seeks for your advice to settle a serious matter.

AURO   I see. Thank you.

(Enter Dinendra Kumar Roy.)

AURO   Dinen Babu, His Highness has asked me to lunch. So I have to miss your company to-day.

DINENDRA   It is so kind of the Gaekwar. But isn't it time for you to be there?

AURO   *(looking at his watch)* Yes, it is. I'm off.

DB 21. ACT III, SCENE 4

(Baroda. Aurobindo's room. Absorbed in studies. Enter Dinendra Kumar.)

DINENDRA   A telegram for you.

AUROBINDO   *(after reading it)* Ramesh Babu — Ramesh Chandra Dutta — arrives to-morrow from Bengal. We must make all necessary arrangements for him.

DINENDRA   Keshta! Keshta!

(Enter Keshta.)

KESHTA   Babu, Babu.

DINENDRA   To-morrow a very, very great man comes from Bengal. So your cooking must be especially fine.

KESHTA   Easily done, Sir. But one thing. We have run short of spices and ghee.

DINENDRA   *(handing the servant a five-rupee note)* Buy spices and ghee from the market, and don't forget to get potatoes, cauliflowers and green mangoes.

DB 22. ACT III, SCENE 5

(Baroda College. Aurobindo is now Professor of English. He declares a prize....)

AUROBINDO   I declare a prize in an Essay-cum-Debate Competition on "Japan and the Japanese."

(K.M. Munshi, a student, stands up.)

MUNSHI   Sir, how can nationalism be developed?

AUROBINDO   *(pointing to a wall-map of India)* Look at that map. Learn to find in it the portrait of Bharatmata. The cities, mountains, rivers and forests are the materials which go to make up Her body. The people inhabiting the country are the cells which go to make up Her living tissues. Our literature is Her memory and speech. The spirit of Her culture is Her soul. The happiness and freedom of Her children is Her salvation. Behold Bharat as a living Mother, meditate upon Her and worship Her in the nine-fold way of *bhakti*.

MUNSHI   Sir, how can I meditate upon the Mother?

AUROBINDO   Just go through the works of Swami Vivekananda, and you will be able to meditate upon the Mother.

THE DESCENT OF THE BLUE

DB 23. ACT III, SCENE 6

(Lunch. Aurobindo, Ramesh Dutta and Dinendra Kumar. Keshta serves them.)

RAMESH   Mr. Ghosh, does your cook serve you with such dishes daily?

AUROBINDO   No, no. These are special dishes for you.

DINENDRA   Good Heavens! special dishes, indeed! *(Looks daggers at Keshta.)* Keshta, how incorrigible you are! You have spoilt everything. Your very sight is repugnant to me. Barmecide covers were better far than your concoction. What a burning sensation from mouth to gullet!

KESHTA   Sir, excuse me this time. I am extremely sorry. I shall be very, very careful next time.

DINENDRA   And where is your ghee? You have given us so much water for our bath, you fool!

AUROBINDO   How is it that I was quite unaware of all this? I wonder how I could eat without feeling anything!

(Dinendra and Ramesh burst into laughter.)

DINENDRA   Aurobindo, my young friend, you do not belong to this earth. You remain in your own world.

KESHTA   *(looking at Dinendra Kumar)* Sir, next time I shall prepare a grand dish.

AUROBINDO   *(with a compassionate look)* Keshta, it will be quite nice of you if you can.

KESHTA   Sir, I promise, I shall be no fool again.

DB 24. ACT III, SCENE 7

(Baroda. Charu Dutta's bungalow. Aurobindo spends a short holiday there. Charu Dutta, Lilavati and Subodh.)

CHARU   Chief, to our great good luck we have you with us to-day. This time I have something to confide to you. I have read your *Bhavani Mandir*. It has moved me to my depths. I have decided to give myself to the service of your great Ideal.

AURO   Very glad, godspeed.

SUBODH   We intend to open a National College in Bengal with you as the Head.

AURO   Believe me, I must go to Bengal if you sincerely want me there.

SUBODH   We hesitate to offer you a remuneration far beneath your notice. Still, poor Bengal would have a princely youth like you for the post.

AURO   My friend, to be able to serve the Mother is itself a high honour for any one.

SUBODH   Your sacrifice has ennobled your country. Your sacrifice will win her freedom.

LILAVATI   Ah, stop, Subodh. *(Turning to Aurobindo and handing him a little saloon rifle.)* Come, Ghosh Saheb, take a hand.

AURO   *(hesitatingly)* Sorry, Lilavati. I have never touched a gun. I know nothing about shooting.

(At repeated requests of Lilavati, Charu and Subodh, he takes the rifle. Charu explains to him the technique of aiming over a V-sight.)

AURO   No, Charu is too hasty. Lilavati, you stand by me.

(Aurobindo starts firing at the head of a match stick about twelve feet away from him. He repeats it several times, every time with success.)

LILAVATI   Ghosh Saheb, wonderful, unbelievable. You have mastered the art of shooting in a trice.
CHARU   If realisation in Yoga does not come to such a man, will it come to bunglers like you and me?

DB 25. ACT IV, SCENE I

(A trip to Kashmir. The Maharaja of Baroda and Aurobindo on Shankaracharya Hill.)

MAHARAJA Arvind Babu, now we are on the top of the hill. We have ascended a thousand feet above the level of the valley of Kashmir. As we climbed higher and higher I felt as if a screen were slowly lifting up and revealing the splendid beauty of Kashmir. It seems you, too, are thrilled all over by the scenery of this place.

AURO My feeling is at once overwhelming and inexpressible.

MAHARAJA What is it? I must hear it from you, I must. *(He comes closer to Aurobindo.)*

AURO I made no effort, yet I have had an experience of something so vivid, so astonishing.

MAHARAJA Do confide it to me, my young friend!

AURO It is the vacant Infinite! It cannot be described in words. I am sure this experience will leave an abiding impression upon my mind.

MAHARAJA How wonderful you are! You have spiritual experiences while I merely enjoy the beauty of the scenery. By the bye, do you know the funny story about the Hill?

AURO No. I would like to hear it.

MAHARAJA The story is that during his itinerant life the great Vedantin, Shankaracharya, with some of his disciples paid a visit to Kashmir. For some time they made their stay on this hill, and it was at this instance that this temple of Shiva was first set up. Hence this hill has been known as Shankaracharya Hill.

AURO Now what about the funny portion?

MAHARAJA   Ah, have patience, I am coming to the point. I have told you that Shankara came over here with his disciples. Soon they ran short of provisions. But nobody from the neighbouring villages turned up to offer hospitality to them. It was after some days that a few pundits came to meet them. The disciples of Shankara flew into a rage. They said to the pundits: "Are you not ashamed of your indifference? Are you so ignorant of the *Shastric* injunctions on hospitality to guests? Did you care to know that we have been without food for some days?" The pundits did not hesitate to defend themselves and asked: "How on earth could you expect us to know this?" Then they turned to Shankara and said that if he had any spiritual power he could have easily fed his disciples. Thereupon Shankara said: "I don't believe in Shakti. The world is an Illusion." The pundits cried out: "No, never, the world is real. It is Reality itself. The world is neither illusion nor hallucination."

AURO   The pundits are right, absolutely right.

MAHARAJA   Ah, but let me complete the story. I have come to the end. The miracle begins. One of the pundits invoked a goddess by chanting some mantras and placed his right palm on the ground. Lo, jets of water began springing up from below the very spot. Poor Shankara had to admit the existence of Shakti.

AURO   I fully believe in the power of such mantras.

MAHARAJA   So do I.

SRI CHINMOY

DB 26. ACT IV, SCENE 2

(Calcutta. Grey Street House. Mrinalini Devi reads out a letter which she has just received from Aurobindo.)

Dearest Mrinalini,

[....] You have, perhaps, by now discovered that the one with whose fate yours is linked is a very strange kind of person. Mine is not the mental outlook, the aim of life and the domain of action which the generality of people in this country have at present. It is quite different in all respects, it is uncommon. Perhaps, you know by what name the generality of people call extraordinary ideas, uncommon actions, unusually high aspirations. They label all these things a madness, but if the mad man succeeds in the field of action then instead of calling him a lunatic they call him a great man, a man of genius.

MRINALINI   *(saying to herself)* I fully agree with you, my Lord. I am sure your efforts will be crowned with success.

(She continues reading.)

.... it is my firm faith that whatever virtue, talent, higher education and knowledge and wealth which God has given me belongs to Him.

THE DESCENT OF THE BLUE

MRINALINI   O Merciful God, Thy Grace knows no bounds. I bow to Thee with all my heart and soul for giving me a husband who has no equal on earth.

(She continues reading.)

.... I know I have the strength to uplift this fallen race; it is not physical strength, I am not going to fight with the sword or with the gun, but with the power of knowledge. The power of the warrior is not the only kind of force, there is also the power of the Brahman which is founded on knowledge. This is not a new feeling within me, it is not of a recent origin, I was born with it, it is in my marrow, God sent me to the earth to accomplish this great mission.

(She is thrilled with joy and jumps up.)

MRINALINI   I know, I know, you are not an ordinary human being. You are a Godlike man. Your great mission must succeed.

(She goes on.)

.... You should always offer to Him this prayer: "May I not come in the way of my husband's life and his ideals and his path to God-realisation; may I become his helper and his instrument." Will you do it?

MRINALINI   My Lord, I fail to believe my eyes. How could you imagine that I might come in the way of your life and your ideals and your path to God-realisation? I have no existence without you. I am entirely yours, within and without.

THE DESCENT OF THE BLUE

DB 27. ACT IV, SCENE 3

(Baroda. The Maharaja and Sister Nivedita.)

NIVEDITA   Maharaja, I am driven by necessity to ask for your help.

MAHARAJA   Yes, I am at your service, if possible.

NIVEDITA   I strongly feel that the revolutionary movement will be considerably more effective if you lend your powerful active support to it.

MAHARAJA   My help! Good Heavens! I am sure I am of no use to the movement. The spirit of Revolution is lacking in me. But that does not mean that I don't want freedom. Nivedita, you are the spiritual daughter of Swami Vivekananda. You are surcharged with his indomitable Will. India is proud to have you.

NIVEDITA   I pray, Maharaja, do not laud me to the skies. It is my Master's Will that has brought me to India, the country of my heart and soul. What I have done for India is nothing and what I may do may count for nothing. That I have been able to dedicate my life, my everything, to serve our Bharatmata is a source of great joy to me.

MAHARAJA   Nivedita, Swamiji's Nivedita! Truly you are Nivedita, the offering, to the whole country. Now, you want my help in your revolutionary work. Please give me some time to make up my mind. I should like to discuss the matter with Arvind Babu.

NIVEDITA   You mean Aurobindo. I am sure he will press you to join and help the revolutionary movement. He himself will plunge before long into the vortex of the Indian National Independence Movement and stand in the forefront of the struggle.

MAHARAJA   My Arvind! He will leave me! I was quite in the dark about it all. Alas, he will come to unnecessary grief. I must meet him at once.

DB 28. ACT IV, SCENE 4

(Baroda. Sri Aurobindo's residence. Morning. Sri Aurobindo still in bed. Enter Barin in soiled and ragged clothes.)

AURO Who is there?
BARIN Sejda, it's I, Barin.
AURO O my goodness, how is it that you are in this state? Go into the bathroom and wash up.
BARIN Sejda, I have come....
AURO Ah, you are so impossible. Go straight into the bathroom. I shall listen to you afterwards.

(Exit Barin. Sri Aurobindo sits up on the cot. Enter Sarojini, his sister.)

SARO Sejda, Bari is come. Has he met you? Where is he gone?
AURO He is in the bathroom.
SARO Bari is very spirited. I am sure he will do much for the country. But, Sejda, he is not at all sweet towards me in his conduct.
AURO But I am sweet to you. Am I not?
SARO I know, it is useless to tell you anything against anybody. You simply take it very lightly. And you never realise your indifference cuts me to the quick.

(Enter Barin, clean and tidy.)

AURO Bari, Saro has a severe complaint against you.
BARIN Didi's complaint! Has she anyone on earth whom she loves more than me?

SARO   Very clever you are. Truth to tell, I hate you for your rude behaviour.

BARIN   Didi, you may hate Sj. Barinda Kumar Ghosh. But to hate your youngest brother Bari is beyond you. Sejda, do you believe that she looks down upon me?

AURO   I can't think so. Saro, I am sorry that you have lost to Bari. And, I believe your surrender will be complete if you give him a cup of tea and a hot cake.

(Enter Mrinalini Devi with tea and sweets.)

SARO   *(in excitement)* Ah, Baudi, you have come to my rescue. These two brothers are simply torturing me.

(Mrinalini Devi gives a smile.)

BARIN   Now, Didi, allow me to have a serious talk with Sejda.

SARO   Who forbids you? But, mind you, neither Baudi nor I am going to leave the room.

BARIN   No harm. Sejda, it is you who have infused into me the revolutionary spirit. Now you must tell me how to begin the revolutionary work. I can brook no delay.

AURO   You need not. That auspicious moment is well-nigh come.

THE DESCENT OF THE BLUE

DB 29. ACT IV, SCENE 5

(Evening. Barin, with some of his friends, experiments with a Planchette. Aurobindo keenly observes it. They invoke the spirit of Ramakrishna. The Planchette moves.)

BARIN Thakur, Thakur, through your infinite kindness you have appeared before us. Please tell us whether our freedom movement will be a success or not.

(The spirit of Ramakrishna remains silent.)

BARIN Thakur, pray give us your advice. We shall obey you.

(Ramakrishna continues silent.)

BARIN It seems you are displeased with us. We are helpless, blind human beings. Show us the way to fulfil our ideal.

(The Planchette writes out the sentence: Mandir gado, mandir gado *[Make temples, make temples]. The spirit disappears.)*

BARIN Sejda, Ramakrishna has at last said, *Mandir gado, mandir gado*. What does it signify?
AURO I believe Ramakrishna Paramahansa wishes us to establish temples in our hearts.
BARIN What for?
AURO Barin have faith in Ramakrishna, He was the dearest child of Mahakali. He was God manifest in a human being. We shall in the years to come realise the significance of making temples in the inmost recesses of our hearts.

DB 30. ACT IV, SCENE 6

(Sri Aurobindo's chamber. Sri Aurobindo and Barin.)

BARIN   Sejda, to-day you must tell me when I should begin my revolutionary work.

AURO   Bari, to-morrow you may start for Calcutta. You will help Jatin Banerjee there in his work. I have asked him to work among the grown-ups and the educated. You and Abinash Bhattacharya will work amongst students.

BARIN   Sejda, if there be any disagreement between Jatin and me....

AURO   No, Bari, you must never think of that disheartening thing. I am there behind you all. Don't fear. I, too, will be coming to join you all.

BARIN   Sejda, there is only one leader in India to whom I can bow. You know who he is. It is you who are at once my guide and India's only hope.

THE DESCENT OF THE BLUE

DB 31. ACT IV, SCENE 7

(Patkar and one of his friends. Both are Aurobindo's students.)

FRIEND Patkar, at times I see you visit our Professor Arvind Ghosh's place. I take it he has great affection for you.

PATKAR As if he only has affection for me and I have none for him!

FRIEND Who says that you have none? Affection you have; in addition, you have great admiration for him.

PATKAR My dear friend, you are right. I am all admiration for him!

FRIEND Patkar, pray tell me something about the Professor.

PATKAR It does my heart good to tell people about his high qualities. I will tell you of an incident that actually took place yesterday. I was at his place. He was deeply absorbed in his studies. A large sum of money was kept in a tray on his table. So I could not help asking him why he had kept his money like that. The Professor said, "Well, it is a proof that we are living in the midst of honest and good people." "But you never keep an account which may testify to the honesty of the people around you?" I asked him. With a smiling face he said, "It is God who keeps account for me. He gives me as much as I want and keeps the rest to Himself. At any rate He does not keep me in want, then why should I worry?" Could you conceive such living faith in God and in His constant presence? To my sorrow, he leaves for Bengal shortly, and is not expected to return.

FRIEND Really?

PATKAR Now that the Partition of Bengal has taken place he feels her call and goes to her rescue. He will certainly light a fire in the minds of the youths of Bengal and change the situation. We have seen the stuff he is made of, a hidden fire! Don't you think so?

FRIEND   I quite agree with you. I feel his fire will spread beyond Bengal to every part of his beloved land.

THE DESCENT OF THE BLUE

DB 32. ACT V, SCENE I

(Aurobindo comes to a Bengal partitioned and distressed. Aurobindo and Mother Bengal.)

MOTHER BENGAL   My child, you come to me in my moment of utter distress. Look at my state. How long will you suffer me in this way to grovel in the dust?

AURO   Mother, look into my bleeding heart. The stab in your heart is a stab in the heart of every one of us, your children. We are determined to let you, our mighty Mother, no longer lie prostrate and dismembered. Our first task will be to restore you to your full stature, whole and strong, and at the same time to launch a supreme effort to free you for ever from your thraldom. The fire that we shall kindle here will spread all over the world. For the moment our love for you will be the love of fire; there will be a fire everywhere till the black forces ranged against our Bharat Mata are a heap of ashes, and her benign face shines with the light of liberty. We stand vowed to do or be vanquished. If our efforts are crowned with success, then only shall we begin our second task — the task of the spiritual liberation of our sisters and brothers at home and abroad. Rest assured, we shall look to your great need first. Nothing will see us swerve an inch from our path. Bless us, O Mother.

MOTHER BENGAL   Your words are worthy of the great soul in you that speaks them. Your Mother will be with you at all times. Mother India expects her children in Bengal to rise and join hands with her children everywhere from North to South, from East to West. Godspeed to you and your sisters and brothers in the vast sacrifice you have undertaken.

DB 33. ACT V, SCENE 2

(The residence of P. Mitter, Bar-at-law. Aurobindo and Barin. Jatin Banerjee, whom Aurobindo had helped to get into the Baroda army for military training.)

P. MITTER   Aurobindo Babu, Barin and Jatin did their best to organise the youths. But of late there has been a sharp difference of opinion between them. Barin differs from Jatin's principle of military discipline with regard to the youths who, he says, will do better through love and sympathy than under subjection to a military regime. He fears that strict discipline may scare away the tender ones. Jatin insists on military discipline as essential to an effective basis for our organisation. Until the two views are harmonised, there will be no progress in the work. It is now yours to do the needful.

AURO   Both of them are right, each from his own point of view. *(Looking at Jatin)* You and Barin have sacrificed so much for the Mother. The spirit of sacrifice and self-accommodation must govern your actions. First of all, let there be love and sympathy in dealing with the new recruits. Then let them be inspired by love of the country to sacrifice their life. Once this love has taken firm root in their youthful hearts you have to introduce military training and discipline to make of them strong, obedient instruments. Jatin, certainly you can co-operate with Barin and Barin with you through the next necessary stages. Don't you agree to this?

BARIN AND JATIN   *(in one voice)* Certainly that is the best course.

THE DESCENT OF THE BLUE

DB 34. ACT V, SCENE 3

(Bengal National College. Principal Aurobindo Ghosh's English class. The class begins with the recital of "Bande Mataram" in chorus. Among the authorities Rash Behari Ghosh, Sir Gurudas Banerjee and Nagendra Nath Guha happen to overhear it from afar. Recitation over, all take their seats; one of the students stands up.)

STUDENT Sir, may I ask you a question not relevant to our lesson?

AURO Yes, you may. No harm.

STUDENT Sir, we feel inspired when you speak of India's renaissance. But when we turn to her drawbacks our whole outlook is obscured by doubt.

AURO Well, my boy, do you believe with me that the spirit of nationalism that is now stirring the hearts and souls of our countrymen is a gift of the Divine? Do you believe that the Divine Himself is our Leader?

THE CLASS IN A BODY Yes, Sir, we do.

AURO Then take it from me that whatever drawbacks stand in India's way will be swept away by His Force. The Nation is rising and will go on rising, maybe at times through ups and downs, to the infinite heights. If she does not, she will be an ignominious failure, and ultimately become extinct. But have no such fear. India rises to do God's Will, to give His Message to the world, to help humanity out of its human darkness into its innate divinity. India's renaissance is as sure as God Himself. Cast doubt away. Be sincere in your unshakeable faith. It will carry you through.

DB 35. ACT V, SCENE 4

(Prof. Manomohan Ghosh in Dacca Government College. The Professor of English and his students. One of the students stands up.)

STUDENT Sir, to-day we would like to hear from you something about your younger brother Aurobindo.

MANO *(placing his right hand on his chest)* Alas, what about my poor self?

STUDENTS IN A CHORUS Aurobindo Ghosh's life is a life of stupendous sacrifice.

MANO As if mine were a life of sheer enjoyment! Do you ever care to know that once upon a time I walked in step with Laurence Binyon and Oscar Wilde? It will be a big surprise to you if I say that I was on the way to being a great poet. Now it is all a dream to me. I came over to India to offer my poetic inspiration to her. Strangely enough, she has not recognised it.

STUDENTS But we, your students, have recognised your poetic inspiration.

MANO Have you? Then I am prepared to say something about my younger brother Aurobindo! You know, he is fully responsible for the failure of my career. He is a bar to my success. The Government fail to swallow his fiery speeches. My only crime is that I, too, came of the same parents. They might be thinking that my room, too, is not free of bombs and ammunitions!

(The students burst into hilarious laughter.)

STUDENTS Sir, pray, tell us something in favour of Aurobindo Ghosh.

MANO Well, my boys, truth is a very sacred thing. I do not use it so often as you people do.
STUDENTS But why?
MANO The reason is so simple. The more you use it the sooner it gets spoilt.
STUDENTS For our sake, for your beloved students' sake use it at once.
MANO Listen, then. I do not care a straw for anybody's unwillingness to subscribe to my firm belief. There are only two and a half men in India: one is Aurobindo and the other Barin, and the half is Tilak!

DB 36. ACT V, SCENE 5

(Aurobindo, Rash Behari Ghosh, Sir Gurudas Banerjee and Nagendra Nath Guha.)

RASH BEHARI   Aurobindo Babu, please do not take me amiss. We admit that Nationalism is an invaluable thing. But to preach it in the College, we believe, is not advisable. You always insist on admitting the boys who have been rusticated from Government institutions on political grounds. You say that they are just the sort of stuff that you want for this College. Moreover, it is not safe at all. The Government have already started looking upon our College with an eye of suspicion.

AURO   *(after heaving a deep sigh)* I think our College must have an ideal of its own. Will you be pleased if it follows other Colleges *in toto?*

GURUDAS   Not at all. But the thing is, if the students pay more attention to politics and nationalism than to their studies, then their studies will go to the dogs.

AURO   I don't think politics and nationalism stand as a bar to their mental culture. One has to adore one's Motherland first. Mere mental information is of no use. I believe that one who has no love for his country is no better than a learned fool, although one may be rich in mental attainments.

GURUDAS   I must say, you are quite ahead of our age. Nationalism, politics and mental culture — these three cannot go together.

AURO   I am sorry, I fail to share your views. The name of our College is Bengal National College. Will it not be a negation of the *raison d'être* of the College if it keeps clear of Nationalism?

THE DESCENT OF THE BLUE

NAGENDRA Aurobindo Babu, you are always noted for your clarity of thought and expression, depth of understanding and the facility with which you make the abstruse intelligible. I am deeply convinced that your own lofty spirit of Nationalism will fill the country with a powerful idealism that will build up our Nation. But our College is a different matter....

SRI CHINMOY

DB 37. ACT V, SCENE 6

(22 August 1907. Bengal National College. The resignation of Aurobindo's Principalship of the College. His beloved pupils request of him a few words of advice. Their faces are overwhelmed with sorrow at his resignation. He has been profusely garlanded by these students.)

AUROBINDO   I have been told that you wish me to speak a few words of advice to you. But in these days I feel that young men can very often give better advice than we older people can give.

(One of the students stands up.)

STUDENT   Excuse me, Sir. If so, they speak of inspiration received from outstanding leaders like you. *(Cheers.)*

AURO   When we established this college and left other occupations, other chances of life, to devote our lives to this institution, we did so because we hoped to see in it the foundation, the nucleus of a nation, of the new India which is to begin its career after this night of sorrow and trouble, on that day of glory and greatness when India will work for the world. *(Thunderous applause)* .... When I come back I wish to see some of you becoming rich, rich not for yourselves but that you may enrich the Mother with your riches. I wish to see some of you becoming great, great not for your own sakes, not that you may satisfy your own vanity, but great for her, to make India great, to enable her to stand up with head erect among the nations of the earth, as she did in days of yore when the world looked up to her for light. Even those who will remain poor and obscure, I want to see their very poverty and obscurity devoted to the Motherland .... Work that she may prosper. Suffer that she may rejoice.

(Repeated cries of Bande Mataram. *In reply one of the students stands up.)*

STUDENT   *(with a choked voice)* Words cannot express our feelings. The brilliant future of our country you have called up before our minds has impressed itself upon our hearts. We feel, too, that it can be realised by us if we have a leader of your stature to guide us. We give you our soul's word that we will follow you, your noble ideal, your noble sacrifice.

(Loud cries of Bande Mataram.)

DB 38. ACT V, SCENE 7

(Bipin Pal and Aurobindo.)

PAL Aurobindo Babu, I have come to you with a special request. I know, you won't say nay, nor am I going to take nay from you. The *Bande Mataram* has now become much too big a burden for me to carry single-handed. I need your personal help as Assistant Editor. It must cope successfully with the rapid growth of the Nationalist movement. I could think of no better person to take up the job than you. Besides, I have every hope that from your powerful pen it will go on producing the needed type of food the country requires from day to day. Now tell me "yes".

AURO Thank you for your confidence in me, Mr. Pal. I agree to take up this work provided I have a free hand in the matter.

PAL Assuredly you will have everything entirely your own way. It's no business venture. There is no clash of ideals in the Party. So there is no question of interference with your work.

AURO Thanks again, Mr. Pal.

PAL Now that the *Bande Mataram* has your magic pen, I am sure India will no longer remain a slumbering Nation.

AURO And your trumpet voice will remain hushed? Your ceaseless stream of eloquence runs direct from your heart to inspire and conquer the hearts of our countrymen.

PAL Ah, pray, do not extol me to the skies. My voice, you may at best compare it with a sword. But who can ever deny that the pen is mightier than the sword?

AURO If I have extolled you to the skies, to what super-skiey ether would you be said to have extolled me?

PAL   Now, Aurobindo Babu, I expect you to join hands with me at once. The rising tide of Nationalism must suffer no stemming because of any failure on our part to rise to the situation as it develops, henceforth perhaps from moment to moment.
AURO   His work will be done by Him. We are mere instruments. But as instruments, we must be ready, too.
PAL   I fully agree. May Mother India bless you. Good-bye. Let us meet this evening at the *Bande Mataram* Office.
AURO   Very well.

(Exit Pal.)

DB 39. ACT V, SCENE 8

(Bhupendra Nath Dutt, brother of Swami Vivekananda, and Aurobindo.)

BHUPEN   You know I have been accused of sedition for two articles in the *Sandhya*. But I wish to offer defence in court.

AURO   Defence! You, Bhupendra Nath Dutt, brother of the indomitable Narendra Nath Dutt, will offer defence! No, never shall you do so.

BHUPEN   But why? May I know the cause of your objection?

AURO   It is very simple. Bhupen, it does not become you, a fiery revolutionary, to recognise an alien court. You must always be ready to meet prosecution with absolute indifference. You must accept all punishments in utter silence as a matter of course with erect head and dauntless heart. This is the spirit with which you must be surcharged to drive away the British from India.

BHUPEN   I am now convinced, Chief. And I consider myself to be a thing of some worth, for it is from you that I have taken oath of the revolutionary movement. I am ever at your service.

AURO   Bhupen, be sure, India cannot perish. Ours is a race that can by no means become extinct. In us is the abode of *Sanatana Dharma*, the Eternal Religion. A day shall come when this Religion of ours will be the future Religion of the entire world. Our high mission is to purge barbarism out of humanity and to Aryanise the world. To this end India must recognise herself first. This is the peerless work. To initiate this work Sri Ramakrishna came into the world. His dearest disciple, Naren, walked through fire and water to preach it all over the world.

BHUPEN   I needs must remain beholden to God at least for one thing.

AURO   *(bursting into laughter)* That's fine. You are not much indebted to God. Only for one thing.... And what is it?

BHUPEN   It is this, that God had not sent his representatives — Ramakrishna, Vivekananda and Aurobindo — at one and the same time. Ramakrishna played his divine role in secret and left the earth. Now, Chief, you have come on the scene. I am sure you, too, will meet with tremendous success. If God had sent all the three at a time, undoubtedly I would have been a terrible loser.

AURO   How do you mean?

BHUPEN   That I need not explain to you, for you have already read my mind and felt my heart.

DB 40. ACT VI, SCENE I

(Manicktolla Garden. The revolutionaries are engaged in a twofold activity: attending classes on the Gita, and preparing bombs and practising the use of firearms. Barin is their leader. Attired in ochre clothes like a regular sannyasin, Upen explains the Gita to them. It is no camouflage. They are as serious in their study of the Gita as in their revolutionary work.)

BARIN   Nolini, will you please go to Sejda's place to bring him here? He told me that he will come here to see our activities.
NOLINI   *(pride and delight brighten up his face.)* I, I to bring him?
BARIN   Yes, you go. You know, he is at the residence of Raja Subodh Chandra Mullick.
NOLINI   Yes, Barinda, I'm off.

(Exit Nolini.)

BARIN   *(turning to the revolutionaries)* So, Sejda is coming to-day. I hope he will be pleased with our revolutionary activities.
REVOLUTIONARIES   We hope so. Even if otherwise, we shall have his directions and guidance. Besides, his presence will be our inspiration.

THE DESCENT OF THE BLUE

DB 41. ACT VI, SCENE 2

(Nolini's first contact with Sri Aurobindo. He avails himself of a tramcar and arrives at Wellington Square. Raja Subodh Chandra Mullick's residence. On his arrival he asks the gate-keeper to inform Mr. Ghosh that he wants to see him. In those days he was not called Aurobindo, but Mr. Ghosh. It is 4 p.m.) Shortly after enter Mr. Ghosh.)

AUROBINDO   Who are you, please? Where do you come from?
NOLINI   Barinda has sent me to take you to our garden.
AUROBINDO   Tell Barin that I have not yet had my lunch. So it is not possible for me to go there to-day. I shall go some other day.

(With a respectful pranam Nolini takes leave of Aurobindo. Those few first words are still a cherished memory with him.)

DB 42. ACT VI, SCENE 3

(Bande Mataram Office. Shyam Sundar, Hemendra Prasad and Bijoy Chatterjee.)

SHYAM SUNDAR   It seems to me that the more the writings of Aurobindo Babu are coming out in the *Bande Mataram,* the faster is India progressing towards the goal of her freedom.
HEMENDRA PRASAD   My friend, it is a pity that only a limited circle knows who is behind the great ideal of the Boycott movement, Passive Resistance and National Education. Aurobindo doesn't care a straw for fame. He is all for action.

(A big procession passes by the side of the Bande Mataram Office. The self-dedicated volunteers send up to the skies their inspiring cry of Bande Mataram. *Song after song is sung, filling the atmosphere with fervent love of the country.)*

BIJOY   Our Jugantar Party will function no longer in secret. Look, look at the swelling stream of souls worshipping the country. Her awakening will be keener and deeper. Away from the rocks and shallows our ship is clearing towards the high seas.

THE DESCENT OF THE BLUE

DB 43. ACT VI, SCENE 4

(Surat Congress. The Moderates, the Nationalists, the Revolutionaries and the members of the different parties. Tilak, Lajpat Rai, Aurobindo, Rash Behari Ghosh, Surendranath Banerjee and many other leaders. A wild uproar arises over the Presidential election. At last they decide on their respective voting strength. Suren Banerjee, leader of the Moderate Party, stands up.)

SUREN BANERJEE   I propose Dr. Rash Behari Ghosh to the chair.
TILAK   *(getting up)* I propose Lala Lajpat Rai to the chair.
THE MODERATES   *(addressing Tilak)* Sit down, please sit down.
THE NATIONALISTS   How dare you, you fellows? One more shout at our Tilak Maharaj and you get the lesson of your life.
THE MODERATES   Don't yell. Your force is in your throat; ours in our arms.

(Chairs and tables are hurled about by the Moderates. The Nationalists, too, hit them back. Amid a great uproar there starts an exchange of blows.)

TILAK   I declare the Congress closed.
THE MODERATES   Shut up, you deliberate breaker of the Congress.

(One could read on the self-composed face of Sri Aurobindo his poignant thought.)

AUROBINDO   Alas, is this the India of my dream?

(The police come in to restore order. In silence Tilak, Aurobindo and some of the leaders leave the spot.)

THE DESCENT OF THE BLUE

DB 44. ACT VI, SCENE 5

(Tilak and Aurobindo with the Nationalists and the Revolutionaries.)

TILAK   So, Aurobindo Babu, they dub me the deliberate breaker of the Congress.

AUROBINDO   How could you expect anything better from such fools? Would they ever care to know that to no one else is the catastrophe so great a blow as to your patriotic heart? You are absolutely right in disliking the do-nothingness of that assembly. That you valued it both as a great national fact and for its unrealised possibilities and hoped to make of it a central organisation for practical work is a matter of great joy to me. I am sure you will be remembered by all "so long as our Motherland has pride in its past and hope for its future."

TILAK   Alas, it is my own countrymen who let loose the full flood of their abuse upon me. But to my joy your fate will be otherwise. All those who have true love of the country will come to love you, admire your great sacrifice and adore the Seer in you.

DB 45. ACT VI, SCENE 6

(Baroda. Sardar Majumdar's Wada. Aurobindo in a small room. Enter Lele Maharaj. With a bow Aurobindo motions him to a seat. Lele sits down and keeps his eyes fixed on Sri Aurobindo.)

AUROBINDO   I need your help in my sadhana.

LELE   I see in you a *jnani-bhakta* — a rare blessing. But why are you so weighted with thoughts?

AUROBINDO   Wave after wave of thought. How difficult it is to escape their onrush!

LELE   But I always take you to be an exception. Come, let us sit down on the floor.

(They sit down.)

LELE   Sit in meditation, but do not think, look only at your mind; you will see thoughts coming into it; before they can enter throw these away from your mind till your mind is capable of entire silence.

AUROBINDO   Let me try.

(He accepts Lele's statement with absolute faith and follows his instructions to the letter. He begins to meditate. After one day all thought ceases. Three days, during which a little food is taken mechanically from a plate, pass by. There is the full realisation of Nirvana. Lele communicates again with Aurobindo on the third day.)

LELE   Wonderful! What I wanted from you, you have done within three days. It took me six long years to still my mind. And, even so, what you have achieved seems something much vaster than I had expected. I cannot quite fathom that look on your face....

(Aurobindo is in deep silence.)

SRI CHINMOY

DB 46. ACT VI, SCENE 7

(Bombay. After his address at a meeting of the Bombay National Union, Aurobindo returns to the residence of a friend. Standing on a balcony he looks out on the city.)

AUROBINDO I see the whole busy movement of Bombay as a picture in a cinema-show, all unreal and shadowy. The entire material world is quite unsubstantial, void. Ever since I had the experience of the vacant state of Nirvana the silent Infinite alone has become real to me.

(Enter Lele.)

AUROBINDO *(with a bowed head)* Quite a success. I made a perfect void of my mind and followed your instructions to the letter after my *Namaskar* to the audience. Soon a voice from within me started speaking. Immediately there were thundering cheers.

LELE Arvind, I was fully aware of it. Your inner Guide spoke through you.

AUROBINDO Quite so, Lele Maharaj. Before I received your assurance I was in great anxiety. Not even one useful thought flashed across my mind. How could I constructively address a big gathering? But it all turned out wonderfully well. Lele Maharaj, you may read my heart and see how grateful I am to you.

LELE And in my heart I am profoundly proud of you.

THE DESCENT OF THE BLUE

DB 47. ACT VI, SCENE 8

(Calcutta. Aurobindo's residence. Aurobindo and Sudhir Sarkar, a young revolutionary and a great admirer of Aurobindo, living as a member of his family.)

AUROBINDO   Can you do one thing for me?
SUDHIR   Certainly. Please tell me what.
AUROBINDO   Take this note to Sundari Mohan Das. Just read it.
SUDHIR   *(reads aloud)* "The bearer is my friend, Sudhir. Kindly give him your opinion by word or in writing." *(Turning towards Aurobindo.)* I am not your equal. How on earth could I ever be called your friend? In learning, in intelligence and in age, in what respect am I your equal?
AUROBINDO   Why can't you be my friend? You love the country, so do I. Our ideal is one. So we are friends.

(Young Sudhir has the first taste of the humility of the great, and his admiration for Aurobindo grows a hundredfold.)

DB 48. ACT VI, SCENE 9

(Dighiriya Hill, Jesidih. Five crack revolutionaries: Barindra Kumar Ghosh, Ullaskar Dutt, Nolini Kanta Gupta, Prafulla Kumar Chakravarti and Bibhuti Bhusan Sarkar. Nolini Kanta, who has carried a live bomb all the way in a handkerchief, passes it to Prafulla. The latter takes his position behind a steep rock facing a slope. Ullaskar stands at his side. Barin and Bibhuti take their positions on two sides. Nolini is some way afar on a tree to command a full view. From Prafulla's hands the missile flies towards the slope. It was expected to explode after touching the ground. But its passage through the air causes a deafening explosion scattering splinters. A cheerful voice comes from the tree: "Successful! Successful!" Next moment there is sombre silence. The bright faces darken. All assemble round the prostrate figure of Prafulla. His skull is broken, issuing grey matter.)

BARIN   All's over. No hope left.

(Any form of cremation, burial or covering up the body is quite out of the question.)

BARIN   The first casualty in our first battle. Let it remain as it is. Our next step is our immediate return.

(Young Nolini's grief breaks the silence.)

NOLINI   Five we came. Four we go.
BARIN   *(snapping back at Nolini)* Nolini, no sentimentality, please.

THE DESCENT OF THE BLUE

DB 49. ACT VII, SCENE I

(4 May 1908. Aurobindo's residence — 48 Grey Street, Calcutta. Aurobindo is asleep. It is 5 a.m.) Sarojini rushes into Aurobindo's room.)

SAROJINI   *(waking up Aurobindo)* Sejda, Sejda! Police! Police!

(Aurobindo gets up. Enter Police Superintendent Creagan and party.)

CREAGAN   Are you Mr. Aurobindo Ghosh?
AUROBINDO   Yes.
CREAGAN   *(pointing to the police)* Handcuff and tie him up, ransack the whole house. *(Turning to Aurobindo.)* They say you are a B.A. Is it not beneath your dignity to sleep in such a small, unfurnished room?
AUROBINDO   I am poor, and live a poor life.
CREAGAN   *(at the top of his voice)* Then to become rich you have done all this? Now take the consequences. *(To the police.)* Wait, I'm coming back.

(Exit Creagan.)

AUROBINDO   *(to himself)* Poor obtuse Englishman, how can you appreciate the values of self-imposed poverty and of self-dedication to the cause of one's Motherland?

(Enter Krishna Kumar Mitra, Editor of Sanjibani, *uncle of Aurobindo, and solicitor Bhupen Bose. His uncle is unable to resist tears. Re-enter Creagan.)*

BHUPEN   *(addressing Creagan)* You are not entitled to treat Aurobindo like that. Take off the handcuffs and the rope.

(Creagan orders removal of the handcuffs and the cord.)

THE DESCENT OF THE BLUE

DB 50. ACT VII, SCENE 2

(Alipore Central Jail. A solitary cell 9′ x 5′ with a small courtyard in front. Aurobindo in contemplation. A column of blue Light from above descends and illumines his cell. A god-like figure emerges from the Light.)

FIGURE   How do you find your jail life here?
AUROBINDO   To me it's no jail. It is my *Yogashram*.
FIGURE   Yogashram?
AUROBINDO   Decidedly.
FIGURE   Your enemies have put you here.
AUROBINDO   I was striving hard to see Narayana within me as Friend, Master or Providence, but could not. Family ties, attachment to work and a number of other things stood like a wall between Him and me. Now those whom you call my enemies have peremptorily broken those attachments and whisked me away as if from my moorings and put me here in this splendid isolation where I can, quite undisturbed, dive into my depths and see my Lord, my Friend, my Guardian, my Guide, my All-in-all face-to-face. That is why I find in this solitary cell my precious seclusion for union with the Self of my self. He gave me an affectionate family, loving relations, friends, well-wishers, admirers countless in number but more than any one of them, more than all of them put together, my so-called enemies have done me the greatest good. They are no longer my enemies. They are the best of my friends. And this is not the only instance. It is one out of many. Hence, I say, enemies I have none.

DB 51. ACT VII, SCENE 3

(Statement of Barindra Kumar Ghosh before L. Birley, Magistrate of the first class at Alipore.)

BIRLEY   Do you wish to make a statement before me?
BARIN   Yes.
BIRLEY   Do you understand that your statement being made before a Magistrate will be admissible as evidence against you?
BARIN   Yes.
BIRLEY   Is your statement being made voluntarily or has any pressure been put upon you to make it?
BARIN   It is quite voluntary.
BIRLEY   Will you tell me what you have to say?
BARIN   Whatever I had to say I have said in a written statement.
BIRLEY   Have you any objection to making that statement to me here?
BARIN   Shall I begin at the very beginning?
BIRLEY   Yes.... When were you arrested?
BARIN   The day before yesterday, early in the morning.
BIRLEY   Where?
BARIN   At 32 Muraripukur Road.
BIRLEY   Who else was there?
BARIN   Ullaskar Dutt, Upendra Nath Banerji, Indra Bhusan Rai, Bibhuti Bhusan Sarkar, Paresh Chandra Mallick, Nolini Kanta Gupta, Kunja Lal Saha, Sachindra Nath Sen, Purna Chandra Sen, Hemendra Nath Ghosh, Sisir Kumar Ghosh, Bijoy Kanta Nag and others.
   Please take down my motive for disclosing these names. Our party was divided as to the propriety of disclosing these names. Some thought they would deny everything and take

the consequences but I persuaded them all to give written and oral statements to inspector Ramsaday Mukerji because I believe that, as the band was found out, it was best not to do any other work in the country, and because we ought to save the innocent.

SRI CHINMOY

DB 52. ACT VII, SCENE 4

(Sessions Court of Mr. Beachcroft. Prior to the identification parade Sudhir Sarkar, an accused, whispers to Nolini Kanta Gupta that during the parade he will be posing as one afraid of being identified, while Nolini, the real accused in connection with the Jesidih bomb affairs, should keep standing quite unconcerned. The accused are brought out into the open and made to stand in a line in front of the prosecution Counsel Mr. Eardley Norton. Prosecution witnesses are brought in one by one. Enter the first witness.)

NORTON *(asking the first witness)* Have you seen any of them?
FIRST WITNESS   Yes, I have.
NORTON *(cheerfully)* Point them out.

(The witness slowly passes along the line, points out one or two and then withdraws. Enter the second witness.)

NORTON *(To the second witness, the signal cabinman of Jesidih Railway Function who is expected to identify the persons involved in the local event)* Look at these men. Point out those you saw over the crossing on their way to Dighiriya Hill.

(The witness passes by the accused including Nolini. And, befooled by his cleverly studied movements, the witness fixes upon Sudhir as the culprit amidst a roar of laughter by the visitors and the accused. Enter the third witness.)

NORTON *(to the third witness)* Whom among these have you seen?

THE DESCENT OF THE BLUE

WITNESS   I know nothing, I know none of them. Neither do I know why the police have brought me here.

(Side-splitting laughter from the accused and the visitors.)

DB 53. ACT VII, SCENE 5

(Alipore Jail. Aurobindo in his cell.)

AUROBINDO Ten days' fast, with sleep once in three nights, has left me no whit weaker, rather I feel greater energy. Now it's time for *sirsasana*. *(He stands on his head. Enter Andrews Frazer, Lieutenant Governor, Bengal, with his aide-de-camp. He is surprised to see the Yogic posture of balancing the body on the head.)*

FRAZER What is all this, Mr. Ghosh? *(No answer.)*
FRAZER Mr. Ghosh! *(No answer.)*
AIDE-DE-CAMP He is practising Yoga.
FRAZER What is Yoga?
AIDE-DE-CAMP It is a process of seeing God.
FRAZER Queer! Sheer nonsense.

(Exeunt Frazer and his aide-de-camp. Aurobindo is sitting relaxed. Enter a Scotch sergeant.)

SERGEANT *(in a tone of bravado)* So, Arabinda, you are at last caught.
AUROBINDO Yet shall I escape.

(Enter the Jail doctor, Mr. Daly.)

DALY It pains me to see you confined to this solitary cell. The jail Superintendent has kindly listened to my request. He has allowed you to have a walk in the open courtyard.
AUROBINDO *(smiling)* I thank you both.

THE DESCENT OF THE BLUE

DB 54. ACT VII, SCENE 6

(Aurobindo in his cell. Early morning.)

AUROBINDO I wonder from where this fragrance is coming. There is no flower near by, nor even a gentle breeze.

(A voice breaks out in the silence.)

VOICE I am Vivekananda. I want to speak to you about the workings of the consciousness above the mind.
AUROBINDO Above the mind?
VOICE Yes. I myself had no idea of such workings while I was in the body. Now I have it and I will help you with it. For this I shall visit you every day for about two weeks.
AUROBINDO I believe these workings would lead towards some Supreme Dynamic Knowledge.
VOICE That is for you to discover. I can but show what I have found. The world's burden of progress rests upon your shoulders. It is a great happiness to find you ready to bear it. Godspeed.

(The spirit of Vivekananda disappears.)

SRI CHINMOY

DB 55. ACT VII, SCENE 7

(On reading Sarojini's appeal in the Bande Mataram *of 18 August 1908, for funds for the defence of Aurobindo, two patriots are walking to Sarojini's residence, at 6, College Square, Calcutta.)*

FIRST PATRIOT   We must not rest satisfied with our own contributions. The expenses are large and the whole country must meet them along with us.

SECOND PATRIOT   That is my feeling, too. We most work our hardest to collect funds from door to door.

FIRST PATRIOT   There is no other way of contacting the people face to face.

SECOND PATRIOT   We have to plan an organised effort.

(Enter the two patriots and greet Sarojini.)

PATRIOTS   We have brought in our humble mite. *(Each handing to Sarojini a hundred-rupee note.)* We are planning a door-to-door collection.

SAROJINI   That's all to the good. So far I have received less than half the sum required. Sixty thousand, that's the estimate of legal experts. The amount so far received is twenty-three thousand.

(Enter a Punjabi postman.)

POSTMAN   *(handing a ten-rupee note to Sarojini)* Mataji, please accept this poor man's offer. Aurobindo Babu is our god. We pray for his victory.

(Enter a bearded Muslim cabman.)

CABMAN   Baji [elder sister], Babuji has used my cab many, many times. I have received higher and higher Bakshis every time. I have wept and prayed to Allah for his release. Allah, Allah, help him out of the trouble! Kindly take this petty sum for his defence.

(Handing a five-rupee note to Sarojini, with a salaam he goes out. Enter a street coolie of Oriyan origin. Tears rolling down from his perspiring face.)

COOLIE   *(placing a half-rupee coin on Sarojini's table, with folded hands)* This wretched coolie has nothing more to give. Jagannath Prabho, save our country's jewel.

SRI CHINMOY

DB 56. ACT VII, SCENE 8

(Aurobindo's cell. Aurobindo in deep meditation. A blue Light fills the cell. Vasudeva appears in the midst of the Light.)

VASUDEVA   *(coming in front of Aurobindo)* Look at me, my child. I am He whom you have been seeking. I come to tell you that from now and for ever you will be finding me in you, with you, around you everywhere. The second thing is that your work for India in Bengal is now done. I have decreed India's independence. The rest of the work for it will be done by others yet to come. I sent you on earth to do my work for world-liberation and world-transformation. That will require a very long and intensive preparation on your part. Henceforth, concentrate on it according to my guidance. As regards your case here, it is my concern. Leave it all to me. I will instruct your counsel, speak through him and see you released. You will remain ever free from all their blind efforts afterwards to force you out of the sphere of your work — for the moment in India, then the world over.

(Aurobindo bows in silence. Vasudeva disappears.)

DB 57. ACT VII, SCENE 9

(C.P. Beachcroft, Additional Sessions Judge and Eardley Norton.)

BEACHCROFT   Mr. Norton, you know Arabindo Ghosh was a very brilliant scholar in England. He had no equal at St. Paul's. He won a scholarship at King's College, Cambridge. He was a contemporary of mine in the I.C.S. We both won honours at the University and, at the final examination of the Indian Civil Service, Arabindo the prisoner beat Beachcroft the Judge to second place in Greek and Latin. This is called the irony of Fate! Poor Arabindo!

NORTON   "To me it appears a matter for regret that a man of Arabindo's mental calibre should have been ejected from the Civil Service on the ground that he could not, or would not, ride a horse. Capacity such as his would have been a valuable asset to the State. Had room been found for him in the Educational Service of India I believe he would have gone far not merely in personal advancement but in welding more firmly the links which bind his countrymen to ours. The new era of reform, in spite of local and I believe temporary cleavage, illumines India's political sky and promises a future as much a matter of just pride to the Englishman as of hope and contentment and advance to the Indian."

DB 58. ACT VII, SCENE 10

(Alipore Court. Beachcroft, Additional Sessions Judge and the jury. Norton, C.R. Das and other lawyers. The day of Aurobindo's release. C.R. Das after summing up his whole case concludes his historic address.)

C.R. DAS ".... My appeal to you is this, that long after this turmoil, this agitation will have ceased, long after he is dead and gone, he will be looked upon as the poet of patriotism, as the prophet of nationalism and the lover of humanity. Long after he is dead and gone, his words will be echoed and re-echoed not only in India but across distant seas and lands,...."

(Beachcroft looks on, eyes indrawn. The prosecution counsel, Mr. Norton, who was listening spell-bound to the peroration, now looks at C.R. Das, relaxed and relieved of his year-long tension. Beachcroft starts addressing the jury. After his address to the jury the foreman takes leave of the court to retire for consultation with his colleagues. The jurors retire. The Court rises for lunch.)

THE DESCENT OF THE BLUE

DB 59. ACT VII, SCENE II

(After lunch.)

FOREMAN   *(turning to the Judge)* Your Honour, our fully considered verdict is unanimous so far as Aurobindo is concerned. We all are of the opinion that he is Not Guilty. As regards the others....

BEACHCROFT   I accept your verdict and acquit Arabindo of the charges brought against him. *(Turning towards C.R. Das.)* Mr. Das, I congratulate you on your laborious study, patience, endurance and your able conduct of the case concerning your client Arabindo.

C.R. DAS   I thank Your Honour for your kind appreciation of my personal efforts. I thank also the members of the jury for their unflagging patience and energy in following the case in detail from day to day and for giving their well-considered verdict.

NORTON   *(coming forward and shaking C.R. Das by the hand)* You have the reward of your labour. I congratulate you.

C.R. DAS   Thank you very much, my learned friend.

SRI CHINMOY

DB 60. ACT VIII, SCENE I

(Aurobindo, and the other released, in the dock along with those sentenced. Sudhir Sarkar, one of the latter, moves to Sri Aurobindo.)

SUDHIR   Government are holding out temptations before us. They promise to take us to Europe or America for our education, with the prospects of high posts afterwards. All this to have our secrets. What must we do?
AURO   Think of the Mother. Think of me. We will always be with you.

(The police take away the sentenced ones. C.R. Das takes Aurobindo and his released companions to his house. His carriages move slowly through surging crowds on both sides of the streets amidst deafening cheers of joy and cries of Bande Mataram. *The whole family of C.R. Das along with a body of nationalist leaders receive Aurobindo and his party with loud cries of* Bande Mataram *and repeated blowing of conch shells. Garlands, bouquets and flowers are showered upon the party from all sides.)*

After lunch and rest, while Aurobindo is sitting among others in a room, the younger ones of C.R. Das's house are peeping in. They retire after having a long look at Aurobindo from their unseen positions. One of them is accosted by a group of young men coming towards C.R. Das's house.)

YOUNG MEN   Sudhi, we are coming to see Aurobindo Babu. Certainly you have seen him?
SUDHI   Oh, yes, I have.
YOUNG MEN   Sudhi, Sudhi, tell us, how does he look?

SUDHI   Go in and see for yourselves, with your own eyes. His looks have to be seen and not described.

YOUNG MEN   We will. But you give us your own impression, Sudhi.

SUDHI   I found him sitting quiet and unperturbed amidst exuberant scenes of joy and happiness. He seems to be in his own atmosphere, among all yet isolated, in-drawn with a distant look, silence incarnate.

YOUNG MEN   *(silenced into surprise, in reverential tone)* We will simply see him and give him our pranams and withdraw without any demonstration.

SRI CHINMOY

DB 61. ACT VIII, SCENE 2

(Aurobindo's residence. Sarojini and Aurobindo.)

SAROJINI Sejda, oh that you were here to see how your countrymen, even of the lowest ranks, showed their heart's love for you by coming to me, singly or in groups, to make their offerings to your defence fund. Their love flowed in tears and in sacrifice of their day's earnings. The amounts were mostly poor, but immeasurably rich in their goodwill.

AUROBINDO Saro, I was, no doubt, not here to see the touching sight. But I could somehow sense it from the impact of their love upon me. Look at the heaps of telegrams and letters on my release. I repeat to you the concluding lines of what I have written to the Editor of the *Bengalee:* "If it is the love of my country which led me into danger, it is also the love of my countrymen which has brought me safe through it."

SAROJINI *(taking the letter from her Sejda's hand and reading aloud)*

To the Editor of the *Bengalee.*

Sir,

Will you kindly allow me to express through your columns my deep sense of gratitude to all who have helped me in my hour of trial? Of the innumerable friends known and unknown, who have contributed each his mite to swell my defence, it is impossible for me now even to learn the names, and I must ask them to accept this public expression of my feeling in place of private gratitude. Since my acquittal, many telegrams and letters have reached me and the love which my countrymen have heaped upon me in return for the little I have been able to do for them amply repays any apparent trouble or misfortune my public activity may have brought upon me. I attribute my escape to no human agency, but first of all to the protection of the Mother of us all who has never been absent from me but always held me in Her arms and shielded me from grief and disaster, and secondarily to the prayers of thousands which have been going up to Her on my behalf ever since I was arrested. If it is the love of my country which led me into danger, it is also the love of my countrymen which has brought me safe through it.

AUROBINDO GHOSH

6, College Square, 14 May 1909

SRI CHINMOY

DB 62. ACT VIII, SCENE 3

(30 May 1909. The memorable Uttarpara speech. A gathering of about ten thousand people. Aurobindo is profusely garlanded. Michhari Babu, son of Raja Piyari Mohan of Uttarpara, has specially got a garland prepared for Aurobindo, which reaches to the feet. The meeting is held under the auspices of the Dharma Rakshini Sabha, just after his acquittal from the Alipore Bomb Case.)

AUROBINDO   *(after triumphant cheers from the audience)* "When I was asked to speak to you at the annual meeting of your Sabha, it was my intention to say a few words about the subject chosen for to-day, the subject of the Hindu religion. I do not know whether I shall fulfil that intention; for as I sat here, there came into my mind a word that I have to speak to you, a word that I have to speak to the whole of the Indian Nation. It was spoken first to myself in jail and I have to speak it to my people.... I walked under the branches of the tree in front of my cell but it was not the tree, I knew it was Vasudeva, it was Sri Krishna whom I saw standing there and holding over me his shade. I looked at the bars of my cell, the very grating that did duty for a door and again I saw Vasudeva. It was Narayana who was guarding and standing sentry over me. Or I lay on the coarse blankets that were given me for a couch and felt the arms of Sri Krishna around me, the arms of my Friend and Lover. This was the first use of the deeper vision He gave me. I looked at the prisoners in the jail, the thieves, the murderers, the swindlers, and as I looked at them I saw Vasudeva, it was Narayana whom I found in these darkened souls and misused bodies.... Afterwards when the trial opened in the Sessions Court, I began to write many instructions for my

THE DESCENT OF THE BLUE

Counsel as to what was false evidence against me and on what points the witnesses might be cross-examined. Then something happened which I had not expected. The arrangements which had been made for my defence were suddenly changed and another Counsel stood there to defend me. He came unexpectedly — a friend of mine, but I did not know he was coming. You have all heard the name of the man who put away from him all other thoughts and abandoned all his practice, who sat up half the night day after day for months and broke his health to save me — Srijut Chittaranjan Das. When I saw him, I was satisfied, but I still thought it necessary to write instructions. Then all was put away from me and I had the message from within, 'This is the man who will save you from the snares put around your feet. Put aside those papers. It is not you who will instruct him. I will instruct him.' From that time I did not of myself speak a word to my Counsel about the case.... I had left it to him and he took it entirely into his hands, with what result you know.... Always I listened to the voice within: 'I am guiding, therefore, fear not. Turn to your own work for which I have brought you to jail and when you come out, remember never to fear, never to hesitate. Remember that it is I who am doing this, not you nor any other. Therefore, whatever clouds may come, whatever dangers and sufferings, whatever difficulties, whatever impossibilities, there is nothing impossible, nothing difficult. I am in the nation and its uprising and I am Vasudeva, I am Narayana, and what I will, shall be, not what others will. What I choose to bring about, no human power can stay.' ....I said, 'Give me Thy *Adesh*. I do not know what work to do or how to do it. Give me a message.' In the communion of Yoga two messages came. The first message said, 'I have given you a work and it is to help to uplift this nation. Before long the time will come when you will go out of jail; for it is not my will that this time either you should be convicted or that you should pass the time, as others have to do, in suffering for their country. I have called you to work, and that is the *Adesh* for which you have asked. I give you the *Adesh* to go forth and do my work.' The second message came and it said, 'Something has been shown to you in this year of seclusion, something about which you had your doubts and it is the truth of the Hindu religion. It is this religion that I am raising up before the world, it is this that I have perfected and developed through the Rishis, saints and Avatars, and now it is going forth to do my work among the nations. I am raising up this nation to send forth my word. This is the Sanatan Dharma, this is the eternal religion which you did not really know before, but which I have now revealed to you.... When you go forth, speak to your nation always this word, that it is for Sanatan Dharma that they arise, it is for the world and not for themselves that they arise. I am giving them freedom for the service of the world. When therefore it is said that India shall rise, it is the Sanatan Dharma that shall rise. When it is said that India shall be great, it is the Sanatan Dharma that shall be great. When it is said that India shall expand and extend herself, it is the Sanatan Dharma that shall expand and extend itself over the world. It is for the Dharma and by the Dharma that India exists'.... I say that it is the Sanatan Dharma which for us is nationalism. This Hindu Nation was born with the Sanatan Dharma, with it it moves and with it it grows. When the Sanatan Dharma declines, then the nation declines, and if the Sanatan Dharma were capable of perishing, with the Sanatan Dharma it would perish. The Sanatan Dharma, that is the Nationalism. This is the message that I have to speak to you."

THE DESCENT OF THE BLUE

(Exit Aurobindo. Some members of the Dharma Rakshini Sabha speak to one another.)

FIRST MEMBER   I have attended big political meetings addressed by veteran leaders. But this meeting, could I or anybody else foresee it? A set subject had been placed before him to speak on with sufficient time given him to think over it. But you see, how he soared unexpectedly higher over it to another subject of far-reaching scope and of deep significance.

SECOND MEMBER   Yes, he soared not only above the fixed subject but above the environment. He made us forget that we were at Uttarpara listening to one of our invited guests.

THIRD MEMBER   He spoke not in a human voice and I doubt whether it was he who spoke.

CHIEF ORGANISER   I agree with each of you. I feel strongly that Uttarpara will go down in history as an obscure point on India's map from which the whole of India and then the whole of the world listened to India's God-man, speaking to all humanity. The cadence of his sentences raised waves of power in my heart. What power is this? It looks as if he will leave the political field. But I feel assured that what India will lose in him as a political leader she will gain infinitely in having him as a dynamic force to create a superior India and a superior world.

SRI CHINMOY

DB 63. ACT VIII, SCENE 4

(Patriot Krishna Kumar Mitra's residence. Enter a friend of Mrs. Mitra.)

FRIEND   *(addressing Mrs. Mitra)* Sister, a thought has just occurred to me and I have come to tell it to you.

MRS. MITRA   Yes, I am all ears.

FRIEND   Aurobindo Babu is in your house. The Intelligence Department knows it. Krishna-da is in detention in Agra Jail. The I.B.'s report, that you are harbouring the terror of the British Government in your own house, will spell disaster. Who knows that your house will not be a centre of the watch-dogs? For your friends and relatives to visit your house will certainly be to risk their safety. You can never want your neighbours, friends and relatives to be the objects of the I.B.'s attentions. Harassment of innocents, I am sure, is the last thing you could think of. Over and above all this, there is the case of Krishna-da. If he is detained simply on suspicion, Aurobindo Babu's stay in your house will confirm it. All this will surely mean his indefinite detention.

MRS. MITRA   *(smiling)* Now....

FRIEND   Now for your safety and for the safety of all else concerned as well as for an early release of Krishna-da I should like you to request Aurobindo Babu to remove to some other place apart from his relatives.

MRS. MITRA   I appreciate your goodwill and your concern for our well-being. But, dear sister, to be on God's earth and at the same time to be in constant fear of danger to personal safety and personal interest, without believing in His Protection, is it not sacrilege? *(In a choking voice.)* Auro is more than my Auro. He is Mother India's chosen child.

If my friends and relatives dare not visit my house, I shall be sorry for them. Mother India needs her children to be of sterner stuff. If they cannot rise to the occasion, I repeat, I shall be sorry for them. But I cannot do otherwise. My heart revolts against the very idea of seeing Auro off from his beloved uncle's house. And what would your Dada think of me? I know him, perhaps, more intimately than anybody else. His love of truth, his love of country are the same in substance and in spirit as his love for Auro. So, my sister....

FRIEND   A true consort of a true leader. I feel ennobled by your lofty stand. I leave you and your darling Auro in the hands of Divine Providence in whom you have such flaming faith.

SRI CHINMOY

DB 64. ACT VIII, SCENE 5

(Dharma and the Karmayogin Office. Aurobindo and Nolini. Time: evening.)

AUROBINDO   Nolini, have you any desire to learn European languages, French, for instance, to start with?
NOLINI   *(taken aback)* If you are pleased to help me, most certainly.
AUROBINDO   The National College has a stock of my books, I have lent them to it. *(Handing him a short note.)* Take this to the College Library. They will give you a volume of Molière's works.

(Nolini goes out with the note and returns with the book.)

AUROBINDO   *(selecting "L'Avare")* Start here.
NOLINI   *(overwhelmed with surprise)* Such a big leap for a beginner!
AUROBINDO   *(smiling)* Shake off old ideas. Come along with me. Read as I do.

(Sri Aurobindo reads, Nolini follows — the former occasionally correcting the latter in pronunciation.)

Pronunciation well learnt, the thoughts and sentiments will present no difficulty. I will facilitate your understanding by writing the English meanings of difficult words in the margins.

THE DESCENT OF THE BLUE

DB 65. ACT VIII, SCENE 6

(Dharma and the Karmayogin Office. Aurobindo is occupied in writing for Dharma. Enter Nivedita.)

NIVEDITA   Excuse me, Mr. Ghosh, I have to interrupt you. I have just had it from an authentic source that the Government have completed a plan to deport you outright from India. They are going to execute it any moment.
AUROBINDO   Then?
NIVEDITA   I am come to ask you to leave British India forthwith.
AUROBINDO   I will foil their plan.
NIVEDITA   How?
AUROBINDO   I am going to publish, over my own signature, immediately in the *Karmayogin* "An Open Letter To My Countrymen" setting forth our policy and plan of work.
NIVEDITA   *(with a note of anxiety in her voice)* Will that suffice?
AUROBINDO   It will. And you will agree with me when you read it through.
NIVEDITA   I take you at your word, as always. I shall read it only to make my senses doubly sure. Nothing can give me greater delight than to find you safely at work, here in our midst, for your dear land.
AUROBINDO   Do I need your telling me that? I know your heart well enough.

DB 66. ACT VIII, SCENE 7

(Bagbazar. Nivedita's residence. She is poring over the latest issue of the Karmayogin. *Sudhira is standing by the table.)*

NIVEDITA   *(raising her head)* Listen, Sudhira, and tell me who could write like this? *(She reads out.)* "All great movements wait for their Godsent leader, the willing channel of His force, and only when he comes, move forward triumphantly to their fulfilment.... Our ideal of Swaraj involves no hatred of any other nation nor of the administration which is now established by law in this country. We find a bureaucratic administration, we wish to make it democratic; we find an alien government, we wish to make it indigenous; we find a foreign control, we wish to render it Indian. They lie who say that this aspiration necessitates hatred and violence. Our ideal of patriotism proceeds on the basis of love and brotherhood and it looks beyond the unity of the nation and envisages the ultimate unity of mankind...."

SUDHIRA   Who but Mr. Ghosh?

NIVEDITA   Right. These words will pass into history and materialise in the life of India. Mr. Ghosh is not simply India's glory. He is the glory of God in the world.

SUDHIRA   It is a thousand pities that the Government should think of him as a menace to their existence.

NIVEDITA   Menace, no doubt, to a ruthless engine of repression that the Government are. I am, however, strongly persuaded that Mr. Ghosh's present letter to his countrymen will do the job. It is as clear as it is outspoken and well within legal bounds. Aurobindo is the Truth that is India. And the Truth will triumph.

THE DESCENT OF THE BLUE

DB 67. ACT VIII, SCENE 8

(The Karmayogin Office. Aurobindo, Nolini, Suresh Chandra Chakravarty, Biren Ghosh and Bijoy Nag are trying automatic writing. Time: 8 p.m. Enter Ramchandra Majumdar.)

RAMCHANDRA   *(turning towards Aurobindo in a low voice)* I have just heard from Father that in a day or two the Government will forcibly enter our office and arrest you.

(Aurobindo in contemplation.)

SURESH   Is it actually true?
BIJOY   Authentic?
NOLINI   Is it possible? Have not the Government taken note of "An Open Letter to My Countrymen"?
RAMCHANDRA   They have. But they know their own way. They are led by secret reports.
AUROBINDO   *(abruptly)* Chandernagore.
SURESH   Chandernagore?
AUROBINDO   I am starting at once for Chandernagore. I am going by a back route to the bank of the Ganges.

(Aurobindo and party come to the Ghat. Aurobindo steps into a boat. Suresh and Biren follow him. The boat is rowed by two men.)

AUROBINDO   *(to Suresh and Biren)* Have no fear. I have heard the voice from Above.
SURESH   That sets our anxieties at rest.

DB 68. ACT VIII, SCENE 9

(Aurobindo's boat touches at Chandernagore.)

AUROBINDO Biren, go to Charu Chandra Roy and ask him if he agrees to my stay in his house.

(Exit Biren. Biren comes to the residence of Charu Bhandra Boy.)

CHARU Yes, please?
BIREN Aurobindo Babu wants to know if you can agree to his stay in your house without letting anybody know. He is at the Ghat, waiting in a boat for your word.
CHARU Please ask him to excuse my inability. With a heavy heart I tell you this. My connection with the Government you know....

(Biren comes out. Sisir Ghosh follows him.)

SISIR My young friend, do not lose heart. I shall take you to somebody who will gladly receive him.
BIREN *(delighted)* Who, who is he?
SISIR He is Motilal Roy.

(They now reach Motilal Roy's residence.)

SISIR Aurobindo Babu whom you regard so highly is at the Ghat. Can you arrange for his secret stay in our town?
MOTILAL Why this question of secrecy?
BIREN The Government were planning to arrest and deport him. A timely warning came and, after a little concentration,

he has got the command from Above to come here and remain in secret.

(Motilal hastens to the Ghat and asks the boatmen to take the boat near his house.)

DB 69. ACT VIII, SCENE 10

(Motilal Roy's residence. First floor. A furniture godown. Aurobindo in meditation with eyes open. Enter Motilal with a dish in hand.)

MOTILAL It seems you are in another world. You look absorbed in your depths. Will you tell me if I have a chance of taking to Yoga?
AUROBINDO Certainly you have.
MOTILAL My family tie....
AUROBINDO That's nothing.
MOTILAL Then, pray tell me how I can take up the spiritual life.
AUROBINDO Try to surrender everything to God.
MOTILAL Will it be possible for me?
AUROBINDO Why not? God is within and without us. He himself will do your Yoga.
MOTILAL Then please show me the easiest path.
AUROBINDO Surrender, that is the easiest. Try to surrender all you have and all you are.
MOTILAL *(bowing down to Aurobindo's feet)* Please give me your Blessing.
AUROBINDO *(Smiling and then placing his hand upon Motilal's head)* If you must have it, here it is.

THE DESCENT OF THE BLUE

DB 70. ACT IX, SCENE I

(Motilal Roy's residence. Aurobindo is in meditation in a small ill-lit room. Time: early in the morning. Suddenly there appears before him his familiar Figure of Vasudeva.)

VASUDEVA   I am glad that you have come over here as I wished. It is high time you plunged deeper into Yoga. You will feel more and more that it is I who am doing Yoga within you. Now I want that nothing may stand in your way. Hence, my chosen place for you is Pondicherry, South India. There your concentrated Tapasya will hasten the descent of a force which will facilitate the descent of a far higher Force to consummate your work.

(The Figure disappears. Enter Motilal Roy.)

AUROBINDO   Pondicherry, Pondicherry.
MOTILAL   What do you mean?
AUROBINDO   I am to start for Pondicherry. The sooner, the better.
MOTILAL   *(taken aback)* But why? Anything wrong?
AUROBINDO   Nothing at all. I have just got an *adesh* — a higher command to move straight to Pondicherry.
MOTILAL   Adesh! Then let me make the necessary arrangements.

DB 71. ACT IX, SCENE 2

(The steamer leaves Calcutta in the small hours of the morning of 1 April, 1910. Bijoy and Aurobindo.)

BIJOY   Now you are Jyotindranath Mitter, and I am Bankim Chandra Basak. Are we justified in passing ourselves off as other than we are?

AUROBINDO   No, not in the eyes of the moralists.

BIJOY   I am the last fellow to go in for morality. But why, of all places, Pondicherry?

AUROBINDO   It is His choice.

BIJOY   But how long will you be there?

AUROBINDO   As long as He wills.

BIJOY   What will be your plan of work there?

AUROBINDO   I will follow whatever plan He reveals to me.

BIJOY   I am afraid your work will be much more inward than now.

AUROBINDO   I feel so.

BIJOY   Then we have no place there.

AUROBINDO   How? My work will be for all, for all the world.

BIJOY   The purpose?

AUROBINDO   The Supreme Transformation of the world.

BIJOY   In what way can such a transformation come about?

AUROBINDO   By the ascent of man into the Spirit, the descent of the Spirit into man.

THE DESCENT OF THE BLUE

DB 72. ACT IX, SCENE 3

(31 March 1910. Srinivasachari's house, Pondicherry. Srinivasachari with his friend, Subramaniyam. Moni arrives from Calcutta. He presents an introductory note (2 x 2 inches) to Srinivasachari from Aurobindo.)

SRINIVASACHARI   *(reading the note most carefully)* My dear friend, I find it difficult to believe you. Aurobindo Ghosh has chosen Pondicherry for his stay!

SUBRAMANIYAM   Unbelievable, impossible.

MONI   I am shocked to see that you do not take this note to be genuine. It is in Aurobindo's own handwriting.

SRINIVASACHARI   Can anybody imagine that such a great national figure would come down to Pondicherry, a French pocket?

MONI   I give you my word of honour. If I am telling a lie, you may do anything with my life.

SRINIVASACHARI   You want simply a house for him?

MONI   Yes.

SRINIVASACHARI   Nothing further?

MONI   For the present, no.

SRINIVASACHARI   Then I, too, give you my word of honour that as soon as he arrives here I will arrange a house for him.

SUBRAMANIYAM   That's a fine idea.

MONI   *(turning towards Srinivasachari)* Well, Sir, I think it would be better if you kept it ready for him beforehand.

SRINIVASACHARI   When is he coming?

MONI   On April 4.

SUBRAMANIYAM   And if he doesn't turn up?

MONI   Then you may do with me anything you like.

SRINIVASACHARI   The time is so short. I am thinking of giving him a public reception.
MONI   I beg your pardon. He is coming over here *incognito*.
SRINIVASACHARI   Where have you yourself put up?
MONI   I am coming straight to you from the station. I don't know where to put up.
SRINIVASACHARI   Well, you will be in my house. *(He takes Moni into an adjacent room, and returns to his friend, Subramaniyam.)*
SUBRAMANIYAM   He may be a spy.
SRINIVASACHARI   I don't think so.
SUBRAMANIYAM   Anyhow, it is better to be on one's guard.
SRINIVASACHARI   I shall be on the alert. But I must find a suitable house for Aurobindo Ghosh. Pondicherry will be blessed by his presence, be it long or short. But in this dilapidated town can I find an accommodation suitable for him?
SUBRAMANIYAM   You can have a talk with Shanker Chetty. His house is three-storeyed. He can easily spare the needed accommodation.
SRINIVASACHARI   It is a good suggestion. I will act on it at once.

THE DESCENT OF THE BLUE

DB 73. ACT IX, SCENE 4

(4 April 1910. The Dupleix *touches at Pondicherry. Moni and Srinivasachari are moving towards the steamer in a small boat which sways from side to side amid high waves. Their eyes scan the places on the upper deck.)*

MONI *(pointing to two figures)* Oh, there, there!
SRINIVASACHARI Oh, yes, thank God. *(His face is lit up.)* I will take Aurobindo Babu to his appointed place. You come later with your friend and with the luggage. I shall give the coolie the necessary instructions.

DB 74. ACT IX, SCENE 5

BIJOY *(on the upper deck, pointing his finger towards Moni as the boat comes still nearer)* There he is! Moni is coming with a friend. Is he your friend?

AUROBINDO Yes. Moni has done the job.

THE DESCENT OF THE BLUE

DB 75. ACT IX, SCENE 6

(Time: 5 p.m. Tea is served in Aurobindo's cabin. Aurobindo and Bijoy come down to the lower deck, receive Srinivasachari and Moni and take them to the tea-table.)

SRINIVASACHARI   I am sorry I suspected your emissary. I have instructed him to come a little later with your companion and your luggage. You and I can proceed in a *pousse-pousse* waiting for us.
AUROBINDO   First have a cup of tea before we land.
SRINIVASACHARI   Thanks, Aurobindo Babu, thanks. The fish-shaped biscuits play upon my nerves.
AUROBINDO   Biscuits are biscuits. There is no fish in them. What is your objection then?
SRINIVASACHARI   My conscience would prick me all the same.

(Moni and Bijoy, amused, exchange glances, and smile. Then they both empty the dishes.)

SRINIVASACHARI   My heart is too full of joy at your arrival to say anything. One of my friends has suggested to me that Shanker Chetty's house would suit you best. So I have taken a part of it for your use. Come along with me to the shore. We have first to board a catamaran.

DB 76. ACT IX, SCENE 7

(Shanker Chetty's house. Some months later. Aurobindo in a room on the top floor. Moni and Bijoy.)

MONI You have fasted for the last 23 days. When are you going to stop it?

AUROBINDO *(with a smile)* To-day.

MONI To-day! What shall we prepare for you?

AUROBINDO Nothing special. Normal food.

BIJOY All your ways are strange. How was it possible for you to carry on your eight-hour walk, your literary activity and meditation, every day with no omission of any item during such a long fast? May I know? And now instead of starting with bits of fruit and suchlike things you'll take a full normal meal!

AUROBINDO Do Yoga and you will understand. You are aware that in the Alipore jail I fasted for ten days. I was then in the thick of Yogic practices. No doubt, I began losing weight. But I could easily lift above my head a big pail of water, which I could not do before.

MONI Is it ever possible to prolong life without food?

AUROBINDO Certainly.

MONI But how?

AUROBINDO By drawing energy from the Vital Plane instead of depending on the physical elements and nourishment.

MONI I shall try it. Bijoy, do you want to follow me?

BIJOY Most gladly, and by all means. But first you come out successful. After all, life is very precious.

MONI Not for nothing did Rabindranath sing, *Ekla Chalo Re* [Walk your way alone].

BIJOY   But not for long are you to walk alone. I shall dog you the moment I see a particle of success in your risky adventure.

AUROBINDO   *(with a smile)* Moni, it seems you are putting the cart before the horse.

(Bijoy bursts into a roar of laughter. Moni looks crestfallen.)

DB 77. ACT IX, SCENE 8

(Shanker Chetty's house. K.V. Rangaswamy Iyengar, the zamindar of Kodailam, comes to meet Aurobindo.)

K.V. IYENGAR *(bowing down)* I have come to place myself at your feet.
AUROBINDO How do you mean?
K.V. IYENGAR My Guru while leaving us for his Heavenly abode advised me to take spiritual help from you.
AUROBINDO Me! How could he know of me?
K.V. IYENGAR His words have come literally true.
AUROBINDO How?
K.V. IYENGAR He said to me that a *Purnayogi* from the North would be coming to the South seeking refuge. Now that you are no more in the vortex of the country's politics and have come here for a life of seclusion, I am sure that you are that very Purnayogi.
AUROBINDO *(giving a smile)* Is it so?
K.V. IYENGAR I will come to you again with whatever help I can afford for your service. Pray give me your blessings. *(Bowing down he looks up at Aurobindo's face.)*
AUROBINDO My blessings are already with you.

THE DESCENT OF THE BLUE

DB 78. ACT IX, SCENE 9

(Subramanya Bharati, the greatest poet of Tamil Nad, visibly excited sweeps into Aurobindo's room.)

AUROBINDO   Why so excited?

BHARATI   There is a grave reason for it. The British Government have conspired with the French Administration to have us, the political refugees, moved out of Pondicherry.

AUROBINDO   Well?

BHARATI   We must escape. Immediately or as soon as possible.

AUROBINDO   Where?

BHARATI   To any of the three places — Jibuti, Indo-China or Tripoli.

AUROBINDO   Mr. Bharati, I am not going to budge an inch from Pondicherry. I know nothing will happen to me. As for yourself you can do what you like.

BHARATI   Your stand bewilders me. No, it inspires me. I will follow you, irrespective of what others may do.

AUROBINDO   Rest assured, nothing will happen to us.

BHARATI   I truly feel that not only Pondicherry is hallowed by the touch of your feet, but the whole of South India. No mere sentiment, this.

DB 79. ACT IX, SCENE 10

(Aurobindo's house, 41, Rue François Martin. Time: evening. Aurobindo and his associates. Enter Biren, Aurobindo's cook.)

BIREN *(addressing Aurobindo)* I have been here in your service for six months. Now I long to go home. But before that I must disclose my identity. I was employed by the Bengal Intelligence Department to keep watch over you and send reports on your movements. I mean you and your associates. To my extreme amazement, I have always received the kindest possible treatment at your hands. None of you have felt the least bit of suspicion about me except, I fear, Moni Babu, and that too very recently.

MONI Why do you think so?

BIREN You always dress well and look smart. But you chose to shave your head the very day I shaved mine.

MONI How does that prove I suspect you?

BIREN I have shaved my head of set purpose, to be easily identified by the secret police here, and you have shaved to foil my purpose and puzzle them. Anyway, that is immaterial. I now want to take leave of you. But before I do so, I must make a clean breast of what I was here for.

MONI Can you satisfy us that you are a B.I. spy?

BIREN What more proof can I give than an offering to you, my master, of all my savings from the Government pay?

(He brings out of his pocket a sum of Rs. 50 and places it at the feet of Aurobindo. Tears run down his cheeks.)

BIREN Sir, you have been all kindness to me. Be more kind to me and forgive me my gravest misdeed. *(In a choked voice.)*

If you do not, my life-long remorse will be my life-long death. *(In a trembling voice.)* You, Sir....

AUROBINDO   *(compassionately)* I wish you well. We will forget all this. Love your country. Live a better life.

SRI CHINMOY

DB 80. ACT X, SCENE I

(Aurobindo's residence. 15 August 1913. Birthday celebration. A small gathering. Amrita pays his homage to Aurobindo for the first time. Time: 5:15 p.m. One of the callers garlands Aurobindo amidst cheers. The guests are seated in rows and served with sweets. Aurobindo slowly passes by, facing each of the party for a moment. Amrita's eyes sparkle with delight. After the repast, the guests take leave of Aurobindo one by one. Amrita stays on.)

IYENGAR   *(to Amrita)* You would see Babu privately?
AMRITA   That's what my heart longs for.
IYENGAR   Then you'll have to wait some time more. Three important persons, Bharati, Srinivasachari and V.V.S. Ayer, are expected. Do you want to meet Babu with them or with the inmates?
AMRITA   Preferably with the inmates.
IYENGAR   If so, you must wait.

(As these three leave after paying homage to Aurobindo they glance at Amrita with a shade of curiosity in their eyes as if to know if he wanted to be one of Aurobindo's inmates. Time: 8:15 p.m. Aurobindo at a table. Amrita goes into Aurobindo's Presence with folded hands, walks around him and finally stands in front for a moment, their eyes meeting. Aurobindo signals to an inmate to give Amrita a sweet. Amrita withdraws from the Presence, visibly moved.)

THE DESCENT OF THE BLUE

DB 81. ACT X, SCENE 2

(1914. Calcutta. C.R. Das in his study with a friend. He is absorbed in reading the English version of one of the poems in his Sagar Sangit *[Songs of the Sea] rendered by Sri Aurobindo. He reads aloud.)*

> All day within me only one music rings.
> I have become a lyre of helpless strings,
> And I am but a horn for thee to wind,
> O vast musician! Take me, all thy mind
> In light, in gloom, by day, by night express.
> Into me, minstrel, breathe thy mightiness.
> On solitary shores, in lonely skies,
> In night's huge sieges when the winds blow wild,
> In many a lovely land of mysteries,
> In many a shadowy realm, or where a child,
> Dawn, bright and young, sweet unripe thoughts
>   conceives,
> Or through the indifferent calm desireless eves,
> In magic night and magic light of thee,
> Play on thy instrument, O Soul, O Sea.

C.R. DAS   Could any rendering be more beautiful than this? I, too, have attempted an English translation of the book. But mark the difference here between a born poet and a made poet. It can easily pass for original work, and as a true poet he has taken the liberty to improve upon the original in many places. To read his work is to enter into the splendour of Beauty that is Aurobindo. God has listened to my prayer. He had acted through me as an instrument in the Alipore Bomb Case and it was He who brought about Aurobindo's release. Aurobindo is now His chosen instrument in His

Play to save man from himself, the world from itself and set up His own Empire upon earth. Who knows that, in the great work of His re-creation of Man, Aurobindo will not release into our minds, hearts and souls an Himalayan stream of divine poetry?

FRIEND   Your prevision strikes an echoing note in the depths of my heart. The days are not far off when you may hear a call to participate in his great undertaking.

THE DESCENT OF THE BLUE

DB 82. ACT X, SCENE 3

(Aurobindo's house. Seated two of the inmates. 29 March 1914. Time: evening.)

A   Well, I have seen a new arrival from France meeting Aurobindo to-day. Do you know anything of her?

B   Only this much, that in France she was carrying on sadhana almost on Aurobindo's lines — of course, without knowing it; and, what's more, she had several visions of someone she called Sri Krishna!

A   Interesting! Wonderful, too! Then?

B   And the very moment she saw Aurobindo, she recognised him as the Krishna of her vision.

A   What predestination! This is the way the Divine does His work!

B   And you have marked how simple and affable she is as if she has come home to her own people.

A   That's my feeling too. Over and above that, she inspires regard.

B   Quite natural for her personality, for one who could see Aurobindo inwardly from across the seas and who could tread the path the Master has chalked out for us here.

A   I marvel at the coincidence.

B   We may marvel, without doubt. The coincidence seems a symbol of West joining East in a great synthesis.

A   That is exactly my feeling.

B   Let us put this question to the Master. Let us hear him on the point.

A   Very well. To-morrow itself, if possible.

SRI CHINMOY

DB 83. ACT X, SCENE 4

(The verandah of Aurobindo's room. Time: evening. Date: 30 March 1914. Aurobindo seated in a chair on the verandah. A and B, his associates, seated opposite to his table.)

AUROBINDO   Anything you want to ask?
A   A little about the French lady who visited you yesterday, if you please.
B   The striking thing about her is that she seems to be home here among us, strangers, in a strange land in strange surroundings.
AUROBINDO   Long before her arrival here I had been aware of her. You will know her more and more from day to day. Even then she will be far above what you can know. As regards her being at home here, or in any other place, nothing would make any difference for her. She is in all the world and all the world is in her. In a large sense, she is an Indian soul born in a European body.

   A and B *(almost in one voice):* A similar thought struck us yesterday — as if she would link up East and West in a golden chain.
SRI AUROBINDO   *(smiling)* Yes, and much more.

THE DESCENT OF THE BLUE

DB 84. ACT X, SCENE 5

(A's room. Arrives B. Date: 31 March 1914.)

A   We have our Master's view of the great lady. How to know her view of the Master?
B   I have had it and I am come to show it to you. The same thought was working in my mind, too. And happily I chanced to come across her and I seized the opportunity of sounding her on the point. And true to her simplicity and her kindness, she showed me her recorded view. Here it is. *(He reads out).*

Le 30 Mars 1914

.... Peu importe qu'il y ait des milliers d'êtres plongés dans la plus épaisse ignorance. Celui que nous avons vu hier est sur terre; sa présence suffit à prouver qu'un jour viendra où l'ombre sera transformée en lumière, et où effectivement, Ton règne sera instauré sur la terre ....

[....it matters not if there are hundreds of beings plunged in the densest ignorance. He whom we saw yesterday is on earth: His presence is enough to prove that a day will come when darkness shall be transformed into light, when Thy reign shall be, indeed, established upon earth.]

A   Oh, a revelation! Read it again.
B   To be sure, it's a light to our blind eyes. It is God's Blessings received through her. We are infinitely blessed to have been at his feet. So is India, so is the world,

A And the few words of Aurobindo about her are packed with a far-reaching significance.
B Certainly. We have now come to a radical turn in the course of our life here.

THE DESCENT OF THE BLUE

DB 85. ACT X, SCENE 6

(Pondicherry. Aurobindo's house. The Mother looking up the Arya *accounts, etc. Amrita comes in with a heap of the morning mail. Placing it on Aurobindo's table, he lingers.)*

AUROBINDO   *(looking at Amrita)* Yes, Amrita?

(Amrita had the standing instructions of Aurobindo that he should remind him of the matter for the Arya *a week before the day fixed for going to press.)*

AMRITA   I am reminding you about matter for the *Arya*, please. Just seven days left.
AUROBINDO   Oh yes. Thank you. I shall set about it forthwith.
AMRITA   But once you sit at your desk you will forget everything else and go on till you finish. Why not dispose of the post first?
AUROBINDO   Very well. You are always business-like. That's all to the good.

(Running his eyes through the letters, one by one, he writes marginal notes, and stops short at one.)

AUROBINDO   Here's a reader of the *Arya* asking me how I, a literary man and a politician, could become all of a sudden an out-and-out philosopher! It has struck him rightly. I must write to him that I knew precious little about philosophy before I did the Yoga and came to Pondicherry. How did I manage to do it and why? Because X proposed to me to co-operate in a philosophical review — and my theory was that a Yogi ought to be able to turn his hand to anything....

AMRITA But it has never struck me as strange. Your articles, even your speeches, were at no time unmixed politics or pure literature. They have always been a happy blend of all the three, each at its best — I mean, politics, literature and philosophy, although the fire of love of country and her freedom predominated,

AUROBINDO But hasn't the *Arya* a different complexion altogether?

AMRITA Undoubtedly.

AUROBINDO Then you concede that he is justified in asking me....

AMRITA I do. Oh, that the man in question could see you filling page after page without halting anywhere, as if your very fingers were inspired!

AUROBINDO But that is exactly the truth! Strange to say, a Power comes directly into the fingers, as if it did not have to pass through anything else! Just now I said that a Yogi should be able to turn his hand to anything. Well, the word "hand" can be applied in a very literal sense where the *Arya* articles are concerned.

Now take these letters and make up replies from my marginal notes. Let me now start work.

THE DESCENT OF THE BLUE

DB 86. ACT X, SCENE 7

(Residence of the Tagores, Calcutta. Seated Dwijendranath, the eldest brother of Rabindranath, in his study. He sends for his personal secretary, Anilkumar Mitra. Enter Anil.)

DWIJENDRANATH   Have you received the latest issue of the *Arya?*
ANIL   Yes, Sir. It has just come. I am bringing it. Anything else?
DWIJENDRANATH   Do you read it as regularly as I?
ANIL   No, Sir. I tried for a time but found it brain-racking, too high, too deep for my intellect.
DWIJENDRANATH   Ah, my friend, that's a wrong approach. It's no intellectual pabulum. It's for the soul. From my study of the whole range of philosophy, Eastern and Western, I can freely declare that what Aurobindo Ghosh says in his articles has never been said by anybody else anywhere. *(After a pause.)* Go deeper than your intellect when you read the *Arya* next and you'll find it clearer.

DB 87. ACT X, SCENE 8

(1918. A.B. Purani's first visit to Aurobindo. No. 41, Rue François Martin, the Arya *Office.)*

AUROBINDO   How are you getting on with your Sadhana?
PURANI   It is difficult to concentrate on it so long as India is not free.
AUROBINDO   Perhaps it may not be necessary to resort to revolutionary activity to free India.
PURANI   *(all surprise)* But without that how is the British Government to go from India?
AUROBINDO   That is another question; but if India can be free without revolutionary activity, why should you execute the plan? It is better to concentrate on yoga — the spiritual practice.... Suppose an assurance is given to you that India will be free?
PURANI   *(knowing full well that Aurobindo alone can assure him)* Who can give such an assurance?
AUROBINDO   Suppose I give you the assurance?
PURANI   If you give the assurance, then I can accept it.
AUROBINDO   Then I give you the assurance that India will be free.
PURANI   *(apologetically)* Are you quite sure that India will be free?
AUROBINDO   You can take it from me, it is as certain as the rising of the sun to-morrow. The decree has already gone forth...."

(Being fully convinced of India's freedom Purani bows down to Aurobindo and takes leave of him.)

THE DESCENT OF THE BLUE

DB 88. ACT X, SCENE 9

(Calcutta. Barin receives a letter in Bengali from Aurobindo, dated 7 April 1920, after his release from the Andamans. His joy knows no bounds.)

BARIN   *(reading aloud)* "First about your Yoga. You wish to give me the charge of your Yoga, and I am willing to take it, that is to say, to give it to Him who is moving by his divine Shakti both you and myself, whether secretly or openly. But you must know the necessary result will be that you will have to follow that special way which He has given to me and which I call the integral Yoga."

(Barin looks into the distance....)

BARIN   Rest assured, I will do my utmost to follow your directions.

(He continues reading.)

"After these fifteen years I am only now rising into the lowest of the three levels of the Supermind and trying to draw up into it all the lower activities. But when this Siddhi will be complete then I am absolutely certain that God will through me give Siddhi of the Supermind to others with less difficulty."

(His face lights up.)

BARIN   Your words open a vast world of undreamt-of possibilities for us. Your Supramental Siddhi will be a landmark in the history of human evolution. And you will put India in the centre of the world-map for all future.

(He continues reading.)

"I do not want hundreds of thousands of disciples. It will be enough if I can get a hundred men, empty of petty egoism, who will be instruments of God."

(With a sigh — and then a smile.)

BARIN Ah, here is the snag. Well, Sejda, have you ever moved back even by a single step from any difficulty in life? You, who have already achieved the impossible, will it not be within your power to turn crude matter like us into your "complete" men? So long as we have you as our Head, we have no fear. Your work must triumph.

THE DESCENT OF THE BLUE

DB 89. ACT XI, SCENE I

(1923. Sri Aurobindo and a Gujarati disciple, Punamchand)

PUNAMCHAND   Before I settle down here as a permanent sadhak, may I have your permission to go home and come back with my wife?
SRI AUROBINDO   Yes. What is Champaklal doing there? Bring Champaklal with you also.

(To Champaklal this remembrance of him by Sri Aurobindo and the spontaneous call to him are a most cherished memory. He first came to Sri Aurobindo in 1921 as a boy of 18. Now in 1923 he comes to stay for good. The Mother and Champaklal.)

CHAMPAKLAL   My Mother, I intend to wash my Father's dhoti.
MOTHER   I shall speak to Sri Aurobindo.

(Exit the Mother. Enter Sri Aurobindo)

SRI AUROBINDO   You want to wash my dhoti! People will laugh at you, joke about you, mock you. Are you ready?
CHAMPAKLAL   *(firmly)* I am, Father.

SRI CHINMOY

DB 90. ACT XI, SCENE 2

(5 June 1923. Sri Aurobindo and C.R. Das. Sri Aurobindo's residence, Pondicherry.)

C.R. DAS   A serious problem, Aurobindo.

SRI AUROBINDO   What is it?

C.R. DAS   I wish to take to spirituality.

SRI AUROBINDO   *(smiling)* How can it be a problem at all?

C.R. DAS   It *is*, Aurobindo.

SRI AUROBINDO   How?

C.R. DAS   Politics dogs me night and day.

SRI AUROBINDO   But you know the two cannot normally go together. The aims and ideals of the usual political activity are almost always opposed to those of spirituality, to say nothing of the forces at work in politics....

C.R. DAS   Ah, you have understood my problem. Aurobindo, help me into the spiritual life.

SRI AUROBINDO   I wish I could.

C.R. DAS   What prevents you, dear friend? Aurobindo, you are to me something far more than even a dear friend. And you know that.

SRI AUROBINDO   Chitta, you must be aware that you cannot make satisfactory progress in your inner life if you do not move away altogether from absorption in politics. It influences the consciousness in a very undesirable way.

C.R. DAS   You are perfectly right. But....

SRI AUROBINDO   I understand your difficulty. All right, then; you go on with your political activities, but at the same time do your best to live your inner life. Gradually you may find that your interest in politics is giving way to your interest in a higher life.

C.R. DAS   What a burden you have taken off my shoulders! I see a way of light and breathe in a little fresh air. But one thing more. I need your help also in another matter. Our "Swarajya Party" needs your unstinted support.

SRI AUROBINDO   I feel strongly for it. I give its stand my full inner support. You will always feel my presence in it.

C.R. DAS   I feel doubly relieved. With your presence in me all will go well with me. Do you remember my prophecy about you at the Trial? — "His words will be echoed and re-echoed...."

SRI AUROBINDO   But what would Norton think of you if he were to overhear you?

C.R. DAS   Oh, he is now a different man. He works hand in hand with me. He now appears against the Government in political cases.

SRI AUROBINDO   Good that he is now on the side of the weak and the striving. His chivalry will pay.

DB 91. ACT XI, SCENE 3

(1923. Pondicherry. Sri Aurobindo's residence. Enter T.V. Kapali Sastri, an eminent Sanskrit scholar of South India.)

KAPALI   *(bowing his head to Sri Aurobindo)* Sir, six years back when I first came to you I asked you about India's possibilities and you gave me an inspiring answer, "not possibility but certainty". This time you are giving me another inspiring thing — your golden complexion. It is no longer deep brown as before. In you, Yoga incarnate carries now its true complexion.
   Now I have come, my mind made up once for all, to throw myself at your feet and upon your Grace for ever. Pray, how should I proceed in the first step of your Yoga?

SRI AUROBINDO   My Yoga aims at transformation of the whole being, not excluding the physical.

KAPALI   How and where to begin?

SRI AUROBINDO   One has to bring the Divine Consciousness right down into the very cells.

KAPALI   Too difficult even to think of. But I cannot try the too-hard so soon. I repeat, I throw myself at your feet and upon your Grace, now and for ever. Do with me as you please.

(Sri Aurobindo gives a gracious smile and a nodding assent. With a parting pranam Kapali leaves the Master's presence, profoundly happy.)

THE DESCENT OF THE BLUE

DB 92. ACT XI, SCENE 4

(1925. Pondicherry. Naren Das Gupta visits Sri Aurobindo.)

SRI AUROBINDO   Naren, how are you getting on with your sadhana?

NAREN   My sadhana! That you know better than I.

SRI AUROBINDO   Of late I have received a number of letters about you from the Professor of English, Feni College. Some time ago your indifference to earthly life and austere method of sadhana caused much fear in your friends. Besides the Professor, others too have written to me of your exclusive absorption in sadhana. Do you know what I have replied to them? I have asked them not to disturb you in any way, adding that all will be well.

NAREN   *(shedding tears of delight)* They did all that! And received directions from you! I was all in the dark. Now I have a prayer.

SRI AUROBINDO   What is it?

NAREN   I wish to see the Mother before I leave for Bengal.

SRI AUROBINDO   Ah, that's your prayer!

(Exit Sri Aurobindo.)

NAREN   *(to himself)* Oh my Guru, strange are your ways, more so is your affection for your sons. Pondicherry is a far cry from Feni. Your Grace and Presence nullify Space and Time.

(Enter the Mother.)

NAREN   *(prostrating himself before the Mother)* Mother, I must leave for Bengal.

THE MOTHER   You must?

NAREN   *(apologetically)* Yes, Mother. There is no other way.

THE MOTHER   Why do you want to go?

NAREN   It's the family pull, Mother.

THE MOTHER   How long will it go on?

NAREN   I am now going to pull the family here and leave it at your Feet.

THE MOTHER   *(with a compassionate smile)* That's fine.

THE DESCENT OF THE BLUE

DB 93. ACT XI, SCENE 5

(24 November 1926. Amrita comes down from upstairs and starts informing the disciples of the Mother and Sri Aurobindo to assemble in the upstairs verandah facing the Prosperity room.)

6:30 p.m. Barin, Nolini, Amrita, Purani, Champaklal, Pujalal, Rajani Palit.... Twenty-four all told are seated on mats. 7 p.m. Enter the Mother and Sri Aurobindo.)

NOLINI   *(looking all around)* Satyen has not come. Shall I call him?
THE MOTHER   Yes, all, all.

(Sri Aurobindo takes his seat in a low cushioned chair, while the Mother is on his foot-rest a few inches to the left. He stretches out his left hand over the Mother's head, and with the right begins to bless all the disciples who are bowing to him and the Mother, one after another. A complete silence. Sri Aurobindo looks Omniscience and Omnipotence. The Mother looks Eternal Love and Compassion.)

DATTA   *(inspired)* "The Lord has descended. He has conquered death and sorrow. He has brought down Immortality."
RAJANI   *(in a whisper)* Barin-da, I have a special request. I am in a terrible fix.
BARIN   What is wrong?
RAJANI   I feel I am in Heaven. The pressure is simply unbearable. Please tell the Mother that I must tell her a few words.
BARIN   Rajani, you are not the only case. It is more or less the same with every one of us.

RAJANI   Maybe. But that is no concern of mine. I pray you to plead with the Mother for my sake.

BARIN   I shall try. More than that is beyond me to-day.

RAJANI   Barin-da, how I wish to hear from you what has actually happened to-day.

BARIN   Rajani, *(with a broad smile)* your Barin-da is as blind as you.

THE DESCENT OF THE BLUE

DB 94. ACT XII, SCENE I

(Early 1927. A Parsi youth of twenty-two, seeking out ochre-robed sadhus in various corners of Bombay. His studies, his own literary talents, his ultra-modern frame of mind, the ease and comfort of his home-life, all that is beautiful in the visible and the known have lost their charm for him. A sudden touch from somewhere has cut him off from his moorings. He is drifting about in a quest of the Unknown. Some method of meditation he has gathered and tried. Yet his thirst grows on unappeased. Now he comes across a Theosophist and questions him.)

THE THEOSOPHIST   *(after a little talk)* Excuse me, young man, you are a complex problem.
THE YOUTH   How?
THE THEOSOPHIST   There is a passion for poetry in you and there is also an urge towards philosophy.
THE YOUTH   But now I am swayed by neither. The one thing that is master in me at present is a pull towards the Unknown.
THE THEOSOPHIST   True. But the other things have only got pushed into the background. They are biding their time.
THE YOUTH   I don't think so.
THE THEOSOPHIST   Human nature is not so simple. All the elements in you will come up at their proper moment.
THE YOUTH   What am I to do, then?
THE THEOSOPHIST   Nobody can take you up in all your complexity, except one Master.
THE YOUTH   *(eagerly)* Who, please?
THE THEOSOPHIST   Aurobindo Ghose of Pondicherry. He has the Cosmic Consciousness.

(The very mention of the name acts like another mysterious touch, a saving, answering touch. The Parsi youth stands still a few fateful moments. The Theosophist scans his face. Sometime later, the youth goes to Bombay's Crawford Market for a new pair of shoes. Back home, as he unwraps the shoe-box, right before his eyes falls that part of the newspaper sheet which bears in bold type the headline "The Ashram of Aurobindo Ghose". The third touch? Assuredly the youth takes it as a "sun-burst". He devours the long article written by a visitor and finds in it the needed fact: the prospect of a new existence, not rejecting but transforming common life and its concerns. Also, for the first time he comes across those words: "The Mother.")

K.D. SETHNA *(speaking to himself)* Here's the end of my search. I must write to the Ashram authorities. But will they accept me?

THE DESCENT OF THE BLUE

DB 95. ACT XII, SCENE 2

(Chittagong. Two disciples of Sri Aurobindo and the Mother.)

A   I have time and again told you that the Mother and Sri Aurobindo are one.
B   But have you ever felt it?
A   I have no need to feel it. I know they are one.
B   But how?
A   How? Sri Aurobindo has clearly said that his Consciousness and the Mother's are one and the same.
B   You think I have no faith in Sri Aurobindo?
A   If you have, then why such hesitation?
B   Not actually hesitation, but....
A   You must not call yourself a disciple of Sri Aurobindo if you fail to believe in him. Apart from it, it is you who will be the loser, if you are wanting in faith in him. I can tell you something quite striking. Just yesterday when my mother had a heart attack I called upon Sri Aurobindo to protect her. Whom I actually saw, you know, was the Mother by the side of my mother. And to the surprise of the doctor and others my mother has come round. And to-day when I concentrated on the Mother out of the fulness of my grateful heart I saw Sri Aurobindo before me with his benign smile.
B   *(clasping A)* True! I fully believe you. Now tell me a little more about their oneness of being and action.
A   Sri Aurobindo says: "The Mother's consciousness and mine are the same, the one Divine Consciousness in two, because that is necessary for the play. Nothing can be done without her knowledge and force, without her consciousness — if anybody really feels her consciousness, he should know that

I am there behind it and if he feels me it is the same with hers."

THE DESCENT OF THE BLUE

DB 96. ACT XII, SCENE 3

(Ashram. Sri Aurobindo alone in his room, surveying within himself his ideal and his mission.)

SRI AUROBINDO "It is not for personal greatness that I am seeking to bring down the Supermind. I care nothing for greatness or littleness in the human sense. I am seeking to bring some principle of inner Truth, Light, Harmony, Peace into the earth-consciousness; I see it Above and know what it is — I feel it ever gleaming down on my consciousness from Above and I am seeking to make it possible for it to take up the whole being into its own native power, instead of the nature of man continuing to remain in half-light, half-darkness. I believe the descent of this Truth opening the way to a development of divine consciousness here to be the final sense of the earth evolution. If greater men than myself have not had this vision and this ideal before them that is no reason why I should not follow my Truth-sense and Truth-vision. If human reason regards me as a fool for trying to do what Krishna did not try, I do not in the least care. There is no question of X or Y or anybody else in that. It is a question between the Divine and myself — whether it is the Divine Will or not, whether I am sent to bring that down or open the way for its descent or at least make it more possible or not. Let all men jeer at me if they will or all Hell fall upon me if it will for my presumption, — I go on till I conquer or perish. This is the spirit in which I seek the Supermind, no hunting for greatness for myself or others.

"I have no intention of achieving the Supermind for myself only — I am not doing anything for myself, as I have no personal need of anything, neither of salvation *(moksa)* nor supramentalisation. If I am seeking after supramentalisation, it is because it is a thing that has to be done for the earth-consciousness and if it is not done in myself, it cannot be done in others. My supramentalism is only a key for opening the gates of the Supramental to the earth-consciousness; done for its own sake, it would be perfectly futile."

THE DESCENT OF THE BLUE

DB 97. ACT XII, SCENE 4

(Ashram. A visiting sadhak and Sri Aurobindo.)

SADHAK It seems both you and the Mother are working hard for a new humanity to begin on earth. Is it not only the Orient who will be able to rise to the occasion? To be more precise, those alone who belong to this land of ours, where the Indian race has done Yoga for millenniums, seem capable of realising your Supermind. What about other peoples?

SRI AUROBINDO "We are not working for a race or a people or a continent or for a realisation of which only Indians or only Orientals are capable. Our aim is not either to found a religion or a school or philosophy or a school of Yoga, but to create a ground and a way of spiritual growth and experience and a way which will bring down a great Truth beyond the mind but not inaccessible to the human soul and consciousness. All can pass who are drawn to that Truth, whether they are from India or elsewhere, from the East or from the West."

SRI CHINMOY

DB 98. ACT XII, SCENE 5

(The Mother and an inmate of the Ashram.)

INMATE   Mother, we know that you are always with us. But in what sense? Please throw some light on this query of ours.
MOTHER   "I am with you, that signifies a world of things, because I am with you on all levels, in all planes, from the supreme Consciousness down to the most physical; here, at Pondicherry, you cannot breathe without breathing my consciousness.... There is a special personal tie between you and me, between all who have turned to Sri Aurobindo's and my teaching, — it is well understood, distance does not count here, you may be in France, you may be at the other end of the world or at Pondicherry, the tie is always true and living. And each time there comes a call, each time there is a need for me to know so that I may send out a force, an inspiration, protection or any other thing, a sort of message comes to me all of a sudden and I do the needful.... With those whom I have accepted as disciples, to whom I have said 'yes', there is more than a tie, there is an emanation of me."

THE DESCENT OF THE BLUE

DB 99. ACT XII, SCENE 6

(January 1928. The old Library room in the Ashram. An interview with the Mother. Having turned his back upon his old life, K.D. Sethna, afterwards renamed Amal Kiran by Sri Aurobindo, sits smartly dressed in European style, facing the Mother across a table.)

SETHNA   Mother, I have seen the world thoroughly. No more of it. I am sick of intellectual pursuits as well. Now I want nothing except God.

MOTHER   You have seen the world thoroughly? How old are you?

SETHNA   Twenty-three.

MOTHER   Only twenty-three and....

SETHNA   Yes, Mother. Can I stay here for good?

MOTHER   *(compassionately)* Don't decide in a hurry. Stay here now and see how it suits you. Then....

(The Mother rises.)

SETHNA   Wait a moment, Mother. Let me make my pranam to you. You know, we Indians make a pranam to our Guru.

(The Mother smiles. She does not mention that at least a hundred times each day the Ashramites make pranams to her. Sethna prostrates before her. She blesses him. Later she relates to Sri Aurobindo how a young Parsi "taught" her the Indian way with one's Guru! Sri Aurobindo enjoys the joke.)

(Some weeks later. Sea-side, Pondicherry. Sethna, meditating alone in the morning on the pier. He was worrying in his mind about not having an opening in the heart or any extraordinary spiritual experience. He had been told that he might think of a book in the heart, opening. The mention of a book had put him out a little, for he was sick of the mental pursuits associated with books. In the course of his meditation now, he felt as if the sea were swaying right through his heart in a rhythm of wide delight.)

(Some time after 21 February 1928, when Sethna has his first Darshan of Sri Aurobindo and the Mother. Sethna and the Mother.)

SETHNA   May I ask if Sri Aurobindo has said anything about me?

MOTHER   "He has a good face." That's what Sri Aurobindo has said.

(The remark strikes home. Sethna is all surprise. He at once remembers that he himself had fixedly scanned Sri Aurobindo's own face at the Darshan moments and found it "good"!)

(15 August 1928. Sethna had his second Darshan, and offers to Sri Aurobindo a poem of his. He comes downstairs into Purani's room and sits still, head bent in dejection. He seemed to have lost the inner consciousness that had abided with him for a long time, almost starting from that moment at the sea-side. He had somehow faced Sri Aurobindo now with the outer mind again.)

PURANI   What's the matter?
SETHNA   I don't know.

(Suddenly he feels as if a huge solid mass were pressing from above into his head, causing giddiness, bringing strange tears into the eyes and making the heart beat wildly with joy. In the afternoon he comes to the Mother to receive a Blessing-garland from her. The Mother takes him into her interview-room.)

MOTHER   Do you know what Sri Aurobindo has said this time? There is a great change in you, he has said, and he is very pleased.

(Sethna falls at the Mother's feet and takes her Blessing.)

SRI CHINMOY

DB 100. ACT XII, SCENE 7

(Sri Aurobindo Ashram, Pondicherry. Time: 10 a.m. 29 May 1928. Sri Aurobindo and, at a distance, the Mother. Sri Aurobindo had sent his secretary Nolini Kanta Gupta to receive Rabindranath Tagore on board the steamer when it was berthed at the pier, and escort him upstairs into the Darshan Room. The Poet came up the stairs and, throwing off his cap and shoes, rushed in, hands outstretched, at the sight of Sri Aurobindo standing at the other end of the room. Sri Aurobindo caught his hands and requested him to sit in a chair. At this first look and touch, the Poet appeared overwhelmed and drawn back within himself.)

TAGORE   It is eighteen years since you left Bengal. All this time I have longed, off and on, to see you. My longing is fulfilled to-day. But I know it couldn't have been if you hadn't made a special concession for me. Hence, I am all the more grateful to you. As I have already written to you, I am now on my way to Europe. I ask: if they want to know of you, what shall I tell them?

SRI AUROBINDO   I, too, am glad to meet you. As for Europe, if they want to know of me, they are free to come here. My Ashram is open to sincere seekers from anywhere.

TAGORE   I wonder how you can run your Ashram and do your world-wide work from within your room in a corner of the earth. My wonder increases a hundred-fold when I think of my tremendous struggle and labour, in India and abroad, for the Viswabharati. Now I am out seeking help overseas.

SRI AUROBINDO   I am not troubled about the future. It's the Divine's work which the Divine does.

THE DESCENT OF THE BLUE

(Exit Rabindranath quite a different man. He had come all the way upstairs, talking with Nolini Kanta, complimenting him on his literary abilities, appreciating his originality and terseness of expression of thought and wishing him to turn to short stories: in a word, he was vivacious and "social". After the interview with Sri Aurobindo he came down concentrated and silent. Returning to the steamer he shut himself up in a cabin and spent a long time alone. The Poet's classic reaction to the interview came out in the Modern Review *of Calcutta some time after.)*

DB 101. ACT XIII, SCENE I

(1940. An eminent Indian political leader and a well-known disciple of Sri Aurobindo.)

LEADER   What does your Guru say about the outcome of the War?

DISCIPLE   He says the Allies will win and he is doing his best to see that they win.

LEADER   The Allies despite their series of reverses and their ineptitude? And, even if they win, won't their victory reinforce and perpetuate their imperialism?

DISCIPLE   None knows the Allies, their ins and outs, more than Sri Aurobindo, and none has given the British Empire a greater shake-up than he.

LEADER   And yet he lends them his support? Indeed, it is a puzzle to me.

DISCIPLE   No puzzle. He has given his crystal-clear and far-reaching reasons for his stand.

LEADER   Tell me, please.

DISCIPLE   The Allies will stand for freedom and progress, whereas the axis-powers for world domination. And the axis-powers in the ascendant will throw the world back into serfdom. He has written, speaking for the Mother and himself:

> We feel that not only is this a battle waged in just self-defence and in defence of the nations threatened with the world-domination of Germany and the Nazi system of life, but that it is a defence of civilisation and its highest attained social, cultural

and spiritual values and of the whole future of humanity. To this cause our support and sympathy will be unswerving whatever may happen; we look forward to the victory of Britain and, as the eventual result, an era of peace and union among the nations and a better and more secure world-order.

LEADER   Those who know Sri Aurobindo well may share his view but the multitude....

DISCIPLE   *(interrupting)* The Seer and the multitude.... When did they ever see eye to eye?

SRI CHINMOY

DB 102. ACT XIII, SCENE 2

(On the eve of India's Independence, 15 August 1947. Sri Aurobindo's room. A disciple and Sri Aurobindo.)

DISCIPLE   To-morrow is your birthday and India's — India's rebirth in independence. A divine coincidence. The occasion has attracted an unusually large number of visitors for Darshan.

SRI AUROBINDO   It is no accident, to be sure.

DISCIPLE   It is the victory of the struggle for independence you led under the captaincy of God, the fulfilment of the word He gave you in Alipore Jail. The Mother has had a flag-staff set up on the top of your room. To-morrow she is going to hoist the flag, because it is India's spiritual flag as well.

SRI AUROBINDO   You are right. But a divided India is a mixed blessing. It will entail on the Mother a continuing burden of problems till India has attained her integral solidarity.

DISCIPLE   I am sure, if that is God's Will the Mother will bear it with your help and guidance. No truth can rest divided for long.

SRI AUROBINDO   That's it. All divisions all over the world must go before it becomes one for the ONE. His Will will triumph over human folly.

THE DESCENT OF THE BLUE

DB 103. ACT XIII, SCENE 3

(Sri Aurobindo's room. Sri Aurobindo and his scribe, Nirod.)

SRI AUROBINDO   Take up *Savitri*. I want to finish it soon.

(Puzzled at the words Nirod looks at the Master's face and finds it impassive. He reads out.)

> A day may come when she must stand unhelped
> On a dangerous brink of the world's doom and
>   hers .
> In that tremendous silence lone and lost
> Cry not to Heaven, for she alone can help.
> She only can save herself and save the world.

SRI AUROBINDO   Ah, it is finished? What is left now?
NIROD   The Book of Death and the Epilogue.
SRI AUROBINDO   Ah, that? We shall see about that later on.

SRI CHINMOY

DB 104. ACT XIII, SCENE 4

(4 December 1950. Sri Aurobindo has not been keeping well for some time. But to-day he seems to feel better. He sits in a chair in spite of his attendants' objections.)

AN ATTENDANT   At last, our prayer has been heard! Are you not using your force to get rid of the disease?
SRI AUROBINDO   No.
AN ATTENDANT   *(failing to believe his ears)* Why not? If you don't use the force, how is the disease going to be cured?
SRI AUROBINDO   Can't explain; you won't understand.

THE DESCENT OF THE BLUE

DB 105. ACT XIII, SCENE 5

(Sri Aurobindo's passing. Date: 5 December 1950. Ashram premises. Inmates in tears. A disciple comes down with a message from the Mother and reads.)

To grieve is an insult to Sri Aurobindo, who is here with us conscious and alive.

(A profound stillness falls over all. Into drooping spirits passes the force of the Mother's words. An air of assurance reigns. Tears give way to confidence.)

SRI CHINMOY

DB 106. ACT XIII, SCENE 6

(Outside the Ashram. A and B, two disciples of Sri Aurobindo and the Mother, in a reminiscent mood.)

B Mother's words have put heart into me. Oh, what a folly had overtaken me! Sri Aurobindo is above Life and Death — the one cannot bind Him, the other cannot touch Him.
A That's what the Master Yogi is. And even more. His physical presence in the Ashram was never its confinement. With the whole earth for his sphere of action, he was wherever his presence was called for. Space and Time are for us humans, not for the Master of Supramental Yoga. Let us never forget what the Mother has said:

9 DECEMBER 1950

TO THEE WHO HAST BEEN THE MATERIAL ENVELOPE OF OUR MASTER, TO THEE OUR INFINITE GRATITUDE. BEFORE THEE WHO HAST DONE SO MUCH FOR US, WHO HAST WORKED, STRUGGLED, SUFFERED, HOPED, ENDURED SO MUCH, BEFORE THEE WHO HAST WILLED ALL, ATTEMPTED ALL, PREPARED, ACHIEVED ALL FOR US, BEFORE THEE WE BOW DOWN AND IMPLORE THAT WE MAY NEVER FORGET EVEN FOR A MOMENT, ALL WE OWE TO THEE.

(The plates bearing these words of the Mother in English translation and in the French original are fixed on the two sides of the Samadhi, north and south. They attract an assembly of sadhaks, coming up, reading it and pausing beside it, file after file, in a meditative silence.)

THE DESCENT OF THE BLUE

NOTES TO THE DESCENT OF THE BLUE

DB 2,2. *(p.445)* Sri Aurobindo's translation.

DB 2,3. *(p.445)* Sri Aurobindo's translation.

DB 9,12. *(p.459)* Sri Aurobindo's translation.

DB 19,2. *(p.474)* Sri Aurobindo's translation.

DB 22,4. *(p.478)* From here to the end of the scene the speeches are quotations from K.M. Munshi's memoirs.

DB 24,9. *(p.480)* From here on some of the sentences spoken by Lilavati and Charu are from Charu Dutta's memoirs.

DB 37,2. *(p.502)* Sri Aurobindo's words in this scene are from an actual speech of his.

DB 51,2. *(p.522)* B.C. Chatterjee, *Alipore Bomb Trial*.

DB 64,4. *(p.544)* National College: Now Jadavpur University.

DB 75,2. *(p.557) Pousse-pousse*, "Push-push": a three-wheeled vehicle pushed from behind by the *rickshawalla* and directed by the passenger himself with the help of a rod attached to the small front wheel.

DB 84,5. *(p.569)* La Mère, *Prières et Méditations*.

DB 87,3-12. *(p.574)* Lines until the end of Act X, Scene 8 are taken from A. B. Purani's *Evening Talks*.

DB 89. *(p.577)* Adapted from Narayan Prasad's *Life in Sri Aurobindo Ashram*.

DB 103. *(p.601)* Based on Nirodbaran's booklet *I am Here! I am Here!*

PART VIII

MATSYENDRANATH AND GORAKSHANATH: TWO SPIRITUAL LIONS

MATSYENDRANATH AND GORAKSHANATH: TWO SPIRITUAL LIONS

SRI CHINMOY

MG I. DRAMATIS PERSONÆ

MATSYENDRANATH
GORAKSHANATH
LORD SHIVA
PARVATI
ASURA
YOGI
FIRST DISCIPLE
SECOND DISCIPLE
THIRD DISCIPLE
FOURTH DISCIPLE
FIFTH DISCIPLE
OTHER DISCIPLES
FIRST CITIZEN (A JEWELLER)
SECOND CITIZEN
CUSTOMER (A THIEF)
OTHER CUSTOMERS (FROM OTHER SHOPS)
KING HARABHANGA
QUEEN (CONSORT OF KING HARABHANGA)
MINISTER OF KING HARABHANGA
KING'S ATTENDANTS
PALACE GUARDS
POLICEMEN
STRONG MEN
CROWD
GATEKEEPER OF MAYAPURI, THE ILLUSION-CITY
DANCING GIRLS
KING
QUEEN
PRINCESS
FIRST PEASANT
SECOND PEASANT

MATSYENDRANATH AND GORAKSHANATH: TWO SPIRITUAL LIONS

MG 2. ACT I, SCENE I

(Matsyendranath's ashram. Matsyendranath is seated in very high meditation, surrounded by five of his disciples.)

FIRST DISCIPLE   Our teacher is such a great spiritual Master. Although he has tremendous spiritual and occult powers, he never misuses them. He always uses his power for God, only to fulfil God in humanity in accordance with God's express Will.

SECOND DISCIPLE   See how he is diving deep within! Let us meditate with him.

(All meditate for a while.)

MATSYENDRANATH   *(coming out of trance)* My dear spiritual children, you are my most intimate disciples. Did you hear any conversation just now?

THIRD DISCIPLE   No Master, we didn't hear anything. There was nobody here, so how could we hear anything? We were all meditating with you in deep silence.

MATSYENDRANATH   Did you see a glow around my face or an aura behind my head?

FOURTH DISCIPLE   I did, I did!

FIFTH DISCIPLE   I saw something like a glow around your face, Master.

FIRST DISCIPLE   And behind your head, an aura! I know that you have many auras, but I must have been seeing your most beautiful aura!

SECOND DISCIPLE   What delight to have this kind of experience!

MATSYENDRANATH It was all due to the presence of Lord Shiva. Shiva appeared before my inner vision to give me a special message. He told me that my best disciple, my absolutely best disciple, will be coming to me today for initiation.

(The disciples are inwardly shocked and displeased, but outwardly each one gives the Master a broad smile.)

MATSYENDRANATH Hypocrisy and spirituality don't go together. Be sincere. I know you are all sad that my best disciple is going to come to me today, and you will definitely be jealous of him. Now tell me why you are sad inwardly, although outwardly you are showing me happy faces? Why are you already jealous of him?

THIRD DISCIPLE Master, you know it is not easy to conquer jealousy. We have been trying very hard for many years, but still it is extremely difficult for us to conquer jealousy.

MATSYENDRANATH Just try to remember that we are all in a battlefield. You are my soldiers; I am your commander. But we are not strong enough to fight against our enemies, the brooding forces of night, alone. We need someone really strong to come and take our side. Naturally, if he also adds to our strength, we are bound to win.

FOURTH DISCIPLE O Master, now we are extremely happy! The happiness in our hearts shows in our happy faces.

MATSYENDRANATH You are lying to me! Inwardly you are not happy at all. You are extremely jealous. You are jealous of him because you feel that it is his power that will enable us to win the victory, not yours. When he appears on the scene, when he takes our side, only then will it be possible for us to win. If he does not come, we cannot win. So you are jealous because while you do not have the inner power to bring about the victory, he does. It is useless for you to tell me lies, because I can easily read your thoughts. If anybody wishes to challenge my inner vision, that person should stand up.

(Nobody stands.)

FIFTH DISCIPLE   Master, it is useless to try to deceive you, but we know that our deception is no match for your compassion. Your compassion is infinitely more powerful than our deception. That is why we stay with you.

MATSYENDRANATH   You are jealous that my most devoted disciple is going to come because he will be my favourite. You are jealous that he will be the one who can win the victory for us. But instead of being jealous, why don't you consider the arrival of this brother of yours as the result of your many years of prayer and meditation with me? You have prayed for peace, light, bliss and power in boundless measure. Now why can't you take his arrival as the answer to your prayers? Do not think of him as an individual with personality. Think of him as the bringer of peace, light and bliss. This peace, light and bliss is coming to you because of your sincere prayers. Your meditation for divine victory has borne fruit. You prayed to God in me for the fulfilment and transformation of your nature. Now God is granting you this boon by sending you this unparalleled brother who will be my best disciple. Take him as the fruit of your aspiration, not as a rival who is endowed with much more capacity than you have. If you can do this, then you can cherish no jealousy towards him.

(Enter Gorakshanath with the traditional gifts of fruit for the Master.)

GORAKSHANATH Master, last night I had a vision. In the vision Lord Shiva appeared before me and told me that you are my Guru. So today I have come to you. Please initiate me.

FIRST DISCIPLE This time, in all sincerity, I feel that all of us are inspired by our Master's advice.

THIRD DISCIPLE We are actually feeling in this new brother our own living presence.

FOURTH DISCIPLE We see and feel that his arrival is the result of our own aspiration.

FIFTH DISCIPLE Master, we are most sincerely happy, delighted and proud to see this youth. We see in him our own achievement.

MATSYENDRANATH My dearest and best disciple, if I have ever had divine pride in my life, then all my divine pride I offer to you. I know who you are and what you are. You are of me and you are for me. You have come to help me shoulder my responsibilities, and for that I shall be eternally grateful to you.

GORAKSHANATH You will be grateful to me? It is I who have to be grateful to you! You will initiate me and give me light in abundant measure. From you I will receive my realisation and liberation.

MATSYENDRANATH You are grateful to me because I will give you my realisation, but I am grateful to you because you will be able to receive my realisation. I have been here now for many years, but I have not found anybody really receptive to whom I can offer my entire realisation. You are able to receive and I am able to give. It will take you a very short time to realise me. It is a matter of a few months. In these few months I shall be working most powerfully inside you to give you realisation and liberation. Once you receive my realisation, you will be able to manifest the Supreme in me. Now let me bless you and initiate you in the traditional way.

(Matsyendranath blesses Gorakshanath and gives him a string of beads.)

MATSYENDRANATH   I am giving you these japa beads. I have sanctified them, and they are only for you to use. This is a very special mala. Let me tell you a story about it.

MG 3. ACT I, SCENE 2

(A forest. Matsyendranath's voice is heard; then characters enter and take over the story.)

MATSYENDRANATH Once Lord Shiva and his consort, Parvati, were roaming in the forest of Manapuri. When they wanted to go back home, they discovered that they had lost their way. Lord Shiva was extremely hungry, so he asked his consort to make him some food.

SHIVA Parvati, you prepare a meal for me, and in the meantime let me go and look for a road so that we can come out of this forest. I will try to find a road that leads to the city. I am sure there is one.

(Lord Shiva begins to leave. Suddenly he has a vision.)

SHIVA Parvati, I have just had a vision. I saw that as soon as I leave you a hostile force will come to attack you.

PARVATI Please, please, if you have seen this then don't leave me here alone!

SHIVA Don't worry. You can stay here in perfect safety. I am drawing a circle on the ground. You stay inside it. Do not go out of the circle. Now, I am leaving my trident with you. As soon as this asura comes, you just throw it at him, and he will be killed. I must go now.

(Parvati begins to prepare the meal. Enter a giant asura.)

PARVATI O God! This asura is a giant! What a ferocious looking creature! I shall throw the weapon of Lord Shiva at him and pierce his heart.

(She throws and hits him. He falls.)

PARVATI   Oh! This awful asura is bleeding profusely. Look! His blood has fallen on my meal. The impure blood of the giant has poisoned Shiva's food!

(Enter Shiva.)

SHIVA   Parvati, are you all right? What a tremendous asura! A giant!

ASURA   Shiva, your consort has struck me with your weapon. Since my life has been brought to an end by you two, I am all gratitude. All my life I have done undivine things. I have become the champion devotee of ignorance. Now your divine weapon and your consort, who is the divine Mother, have taken my life away. Please grant me one boon, only one boon: that I may not recover. Do not use your power to revive me. Just let me die here. But first, please allow me to touch your feet and be blessed by you.

(He touches Shiva's feet.)

SHIVA   O giant, you will now be liberated. On the physical plane you will die, but on the inner plane you will be immortal because of your most sincere prayer for liberation.

PARVATI   My Lord, the impure blood of this hostile force has fallen on your food and polluted it.

SHIVA   I am concentrating on it, and with my compassion-power I am purifying it.

(He concentrates.)

SHIVA   Now that I have conquered this undivine force with my spiritual power, I shall taste a portion of this food. The world is full of ignorance. When ignorance is transformed it is a divine miracle. I am offering this portion of food to the giant, and I am using my spiritual power to transform the food that is left into mala beads. Whoever uses these beads for japa will get realisation without fail.

MG 4. ACT I, SCENE 3

(Exactly the same as Scene 1.)

MATSYENDRANATH   My child, you are destined to get realisation very soon in this incarnation; therefore, I am offering you these beads. My children, let me look at you to see whether you have again become jealous. No, you are not jealous at all. I see you have the firm conviction that it is the result of your aspiration that has been manifested in the arrival of your new spiritual brother.

GORAKSHANATH   Master, Master, here I am seeing five faces just like my own! Five bodies, five hearts, five souls just like my own! Am I right, Master, or is this just a hallucination?

MATSYENDRANATH   You are absolutely right, my son. These are not your mere spiritual brothers and sisters, but they are part and parcel of your very existence. In you they have found their divine pride, and in them you have found your divine duty. It is you who will help them to realise the Highest, and it is they who have brought you here with their most sincere aspiration.

MG 5. ACT II, SCENE I

(Two citizens meet in the kingdom of King Harabhanga.)

FIRST CITIZEN   Unbearable, unbearable! The King is unbearable.

SECOND CITIZEN   Unpardonable, unpardonable! The King is unpardonable.

FIRST CITIZEN   He has gone crazy!

SECOND CITIZEN   He has become insane!

FIRST CITIZEN   Look at that fool! He wants his kingdom to surpass Heaven in prosperity, beauty and divinity.

SECOND CITIZEN   Look at his audacity! You say stupidity; I say stupidity plus audacity! How can his kingdom surpass Heaven?

FIRST CITIZEN   Impossible!

SECOND CITIZEN   Impossible!

FIRST CITIZEN   He has created absolute chaos in the whole kingdom. He says that everybody has to be equal, and he feels that the only way to bring this about is for everything in the market to be sold at the same price!

SECOND CITIZEN   Unthinkable! Unthinkable! How can gold and rice be sold at the same price? A seer of gold and a seer of rice! Ha! Ha! What a stupid king we have! There are things on earth which are extremely rare and there are things on earth which are extremely common. How can they be given the same price? Look at the stupidity of this king! He feels that this will make his kingdom most prosperous, and that all will become friends. Ha! Just wait and see what unimaginable things will soon happen.

FIRST CITIZEN   Well, when one loses one's brains, one does all sorts of things. The King thinks we will lead a perfectly happy life if the price of everything is equal. He is a fool, a real fool. What is worse, he is adamant in his command and we are helpless.

SECOND CITIZEN   We are helpless, true, but I abominate him — his utterance, his decree, everything he does.

FIRST CITIZEN   My friend, you hate him, and I wish to say that his very name has become anathema to me. He is despised and he will ever be despised by his entire kingdom. I am a jeweller. From now on I have to sell all my most expensive jewellery at the price of eggplants, potatoes and tomatoes.

SECOND CITIZEN   No matter, friend, how many aspersions you cast on him, you cannot change his mind. This is our fate.

FIRST CITIZEN   Fate? I don't believe in fate. I shall abrogate my fate! You will see. A day will come when Harabhanga will realise his folly and this kingdom of ours, this beautiful country, will again have real life — a life of love, a life of harmony. Once more only the right will deserve the fair. A man of knowledge will have prestige; a man of ignorance will have to work for knowledge and only then will he get prestige. People will work hard in order to achieve something and only those who deserve it will get appreciation. Two different things cannot be of the same value. A man of ignorance and a man of knowledge cannot be put on the same footing. A man of sincerity and a man of insincerity, a thief and a saint, cannot be considered equal. Just by having all eat the same food, just by selling everything at the same price, this stupid Harabhanga cannot equalise all his subjects. Impossible! His brain has reached the zenith of stupidity.

SECOND CITIZEN   And I tell you, the lion in me will not eat grass like the sheep who are the King's ministers. The King's ministers have no voice of their own. It is they who have agreed to the King's proposal. I am a lion; I shall devour the King and his sheep!

MATSYENDRANATH AND GORAKSHANATH: TWO SPIRITUAL LIONS

MG 6. ACT II, SCENE 2

(Gorakshanath is meditating in his room. Enter Matsyendranath.)

MATSYENDRANATH   My son, are you still here? Don't you know what King Harabhanga is doing to his subjects? He has said that everything has to be sold at the same price. Gold and eggplants will be sold at the same price.

GORAKSHANATH   I know, Master. I have heard and I have read the newspaper. But I am a little amused. I am curious to see what will happen.

MATSYENDRANATH   Curious, my son! Curiosity even at this stage? You have realised God. Now why do you allow curiosity to enter into you? I know your curiosity is innocent. You are pure; your heart is all purity, all luminosity, my son. But curiosity is still a dangerous thing. Very soon this whole kingdom will be ruined. A catastrophe will take place, and I am afraid something will happen to you. I am concerned for you, and not for this kingdom. I cannot help the innocent subjects. I can only sympathise with them.

GORAKSHANATH   Master, do you know what the King said? He says his kingdom has to surpass Heaven in beauty, prosperity and divinity.

MATSYENDRANATH   *(laughing)* You know how he will make his kingdom superior to Heaven! He is an old man now. He has become senile.

GORAKSHANATH   Master, forgive me, I wish to see the end of this fun. If you allow me to stay here and see the end, I will be so grateful to you.

MATSYENDRANATH   I shall allow you to stay, but I tell you that your suffering is my suffering. If something serious happens to you, it is I who will have to help you or save you.

GORAKSHANATH   O Master, then I shall go away. I don't want you to suffer because of me.

MATSYENDRANATH   No, no, stay here, Gorakshanath. I want you to enjoy this. I want to feed your innocent curiosity. Don't worry about me. I will be able to protect myself and I will be able to help you out, too.

GORAKSHANATH   Then with your permission, Master, I shall stay.

MATSYENDRANATH   Yes, you stay, with my permission. Let us see what happens.

(Exit Matsyendranath.)

MG 7. ACT II, SCENE 3

(First citizen in his jewellery shop. Enter a customer. The customer begins looking at a beautiful ring.)

CUSTOMER   How much does this ring cost?
FIRST CITIZEN   One hundred rupees.
CUSTOMER   One hundred rupees? Why, this could not weigh much more than a few cloves of garlic! Let me go next door to the grocery store and see the price of garlic.

(Exit customer. First citizen is beside himself with rage and despair. Customer returns.)

CUSTOMER   The price of garlic is one anna. Your ring certainly does not weigh as much as a whole bulb of garlic, but I will give you one anna for it. And I won't make a report to the King against you for telling me the price was one hundred rupees. Here is one anna. Good bye.

(Customer snatches the ring and starts to leave. Jeweller begins shouting.)

CUSTOMER   If you shout I will stab you. You know it is the King's order that everything be sold at the same price.
JEWELLER   I know it is the King's order, but I refuse to sell a gold ring for one anna. It's extremely valuable!

(Customer stabs the jeweller and runs. Jeweller starts shouting.)

JEWELLER   Help, help! Somebody save me! Thief! Thief! Arrest that man!

(Immediately from other shops people come in. The customer is caught and brought back in by the police.)

JEWELLER   That's the man. He has stabbed me.

MG 8. ACT II, SCENE 4

(The King's palace. The King is on his throne. Enter minister.)

MINISTER Your Majesty, the man who stabbed the jeweller was put in jail yesterday, but today he has escaped.
KING How?
MINISTER He was a strong man. It seems he was able to break some of the bars of the prison window, and somehow he escaped.
KING What is to be done?
MINISTER That is up to you. Please tell me, I am at your command.
KING Well, if you can't find him, look for any strong young man of his size, and bring him to me.
MINISTER Only one person?
KING No, bring everyone. Bring all the men of his size, and I will make a selection. I will have the strongest person hanged. It is an insult to me that a prisoner can break out of my prison and escape. So the strongest man will be put to death.

MG 9. ACT II, SCENE 5

(Gorakshanath is meditating in his room. Enter Matsyendranath.)

MATSYENDRANATH My son, now see, the worst calamity is about to take place. Has your curiosity been fed? Are you satisfied now? I am sure you have heard that all the strong young men in the kingdom are to be brought before the King. The King will select the strongest and have him hanged. He feels that the man who has escaped from his prison has insulted him, and he cannot brook that kind of insult. You are a very strong man. I do not know what may happen to you. Let us try to escape.
GORAKSHANATH Master, I am at your feet. You are also strong. They may catch you as well. Although you are mature you are not yet old. I am afraid you are also in danger. Since I made the mistake, if the King sentences me to death, I am prepared. But if something happens to you, Master, I shall never forgive myself.

(Enter four guards and arrest Matsyendranath and Gorakshanath.)

MATSYENDRANATH AND GORAKSHANATH: TWO SPIRITUAL LIONS

MG 10. ACT II, SCENE 6

(The King's palace. The King and Queen are sitting on their thrones. Many strong men have been brought in, including Gorakshanath and Matsyendranath, and the King is about to make a selection. The guards begin pushing the men before the King one by one.)

FIRST MAN   No, your Majesty, I didn't do it. I wasn't even there.

SECOND MAN   I was out of town.

(In this way many men are brought before the King.)

KING   Now all of you stand in a line. Instead of having you come up to me, I will go down the line. Let me see who is the strongest.

(The King goes down the line. He picks out Matsyendranath and Gorakshanath.)

KING   Undoubtedly one of you will be hanged today, but it may take me a few minutes to decide who is actually the stronger.

MATSYENDRANATH   O King, look at my health, examine my physique. I tell you, if you want to kill the stronger of us two, then it is undoubtedly I who should be killed. Look at me. Look at my arms, look at my chest, look at my feet, look at my forehead, look at any part of my body. I am far stronger than this man.

GORAKSHANATH   Do not believe him, your Majesty. Look at me, look at my body. I am obviously stronger than this man. And besides, I am younger. You wanted to have a young man, and I have young blood. He is an old man. It is clear to see. Why, he was my teacher. He may be stronger than me in some things — in knowledge or wisdom — but if you want physical strength, I am the man for you.

KING   Yes, I want someone who is physically strong and not strong mentally or otherwise.

GORAKSHANATH   So, King, it is I who should be killed.

MATSYENDRANATH   King, believe me, I am stronger than this young man. Since you want a really strong man, it is I who should be hanged. You are such a great, compassionate king. I have never seen such a compassionate king on earth. You want to make everything in your kingdom equal to surpass Heaven in every way. I wish to say that, since I am older than he, I will not be of use to you much longer. Let the young man stay here in your kingdom to serve you. He is much younger than I, and he can serve you for many more years. Let me go to Heaven.

GORAKSHANATH   King, compassion is one thing and justice is another. This man is showing his compassion. I was his student. We are like father and son. When there is danger, the father wants to embrace the danger and let his son remain safe. But there is something called a promise. King, you are most honest. Now what did you say? You said the strongest man in your kingdom would be hanged. Your Majesty, how did you become great? You became great by keeping your promises. You should continue to keep your promises, so it is I who should be killed.

KING   I really can't understand it. For the first time I am seeing two men simply dying to please me. Here all are shedding bitter tears because they may have to die. If I selected them, they would be the most miserable people on earth. But here I am seeing two men fighting over the opportunity to embrace death. I have never seen anything like it.

MATSYENDRANATH AND GORAKSHANATH: TWO SPIRITUAL LIONS

What is the matter with you two? I want to know why you are eager to die. Is there some special reason?

MATSYENDRANATH *(pretending to be hesitant)* Well, there *is* a special cause. You think that we are very kind, nice and generous. But, O King, we are not so kind, we are not so nice, we are not so generous; our hearts are not so big. Both of us are very clever.

KING Clever? What kind of plot do you have?

MATSYENDRANATH No plot. It is only that both of us know a little bit of astrology. I am an astrologer and I taught him how to cast a horoscope. That is why he was telling you that I was his teacher.

We also meditate a little. This morning we had a vision and heard an inner voice. But King, perhaps you do not believe in visions.

KING Visions? Certainly I believe in visions. I believe in God. God has created Heaven so beautiful. It is my prayer to God that my kingdom should surpass Heaven. Now tell me, what kind of vision did you have? What did the voice tell you?

MATSYENDRANATH Both of us had the vision at the same time, and we heard the voice say that whoever dies today at four p.m. will go to the highest Heaven. That is why we are fighting for death. Otherwise, do you think that we would be so foolish?

GORAKSHANATH So, King Harabhanga, now the secret is out. It is for that purpose that I wanted to die. I wanted to go to the highest Heaven. It was not actually that I have such love for my Master. I wanted to die so that I could go to the highest Heaven.

MATSYENDRANATH It is the same with me. It was not my affection and love for my student that made me fight for the opportunity to die. I knew that I could go to the highest

Heaven immediately if I could manage to die at four p.m. in some way.

KING You think I am a fool. All the time I have been crying for Heaven, for the highest joy. Here I have pleasure, but I am not satisfied. I want something more. I know that Heaven is full of Joy and Delight. Do you think I am such a fool that I will allow one of you to go to Heaven while I remain here on this corrupt and imperfect earth? In my kingdom everybody is quarrelling and fighting all the time. That is why I wanted my kingdom to be like Heaven — even to surpass Heaven. I am so grateful that you two astrologers have told me this secret. *(Addressing has minister.)* Get ready. Invite all my subjects and all the royal family. This is my order. I am going to be hanged. I want to go immediately to Heaven. This world is corrupt. I don't see any hope for it. I wanted to bring happiness to my kingdom, but I see this will never be. It is only when I have something myself that I can give it to others. Now I am distressed, but in Heaven I shall be most happy. And from there, I will be able to send happiness down to my kingdom.

(Exit Minister.)

MATSYENDRANATH Your Majesty, I wish to say that your happiness is our happiness. If you feel that by going to Heaven immediately you will be the happiest man, then go. We shall miss you, the kingdom will miss you, but we want to be happy in your happiness.

GORAKSHANATH It is you who wanted to have the Kingdom of Heaven on earth. Now you will enter into the Kingdom of Heaven. And once you enter there, I am sure you will be able to bring down the Kingdom of Heaven into this world. In your happiness is our happiness. We wanted to go to Heaven at four p.m., but we would rather make you happy.

(The Queen starts crying bitterly.)

KING   *(to Queen)* I thought that you loved me. Now that I am going to be happy, why do you weep?

QUEEN   I *want* you to be happy, but how can I live here alone without you?

KING   Don't worry. Once I am in Heaven I will bring you there to join me. It is only a matter of time. Perhaps tomorrow I will be able to get you. When I am in the highest Heaven I will have everything, and from there I will be able to send a messenger to take you.

(The Queen smiles.)

(All the subjects and the royal family are outside the palace. Suddenly four bells chime.)

CROWD   The King is dead.

        (Wild shouts and cheers.)

MATSYENDRANATH AND GORAKSHANATH: TWO SPIRITUAL LIONS

MG 12. ACT II, SCENE 8

(Gorakshanath and Matsyendranath are in Gorakshanath's room.)

GORAKSHANATH   O Master, I went along with you, but please tell me, why have you done this? Have we done the right thing? Oh, I know whatever you do is right, but please explain to me what we did. I want to know more from you.

MATSYENDRANATH   My son, do you feel sorry for it?

GORAKSHANATH   I do feel sorry....

MATSYENDRANATH   Why? Why do you feel sorry? You should be wise. This king was ruining the whole kingdom with his stupid laws. How can everything be of the same value? How can everybody have the same status? Is it possible? God has given some men more capacity than others. God has made some things more valuable than others. On this hand two fingers cannot be the same. They are all different. If one person prays and meditates, and another does not, naturally the former will realise God sooner than the latter. You have prayed, you have meditated and you have realised God. Equality does not come without equal merit. King Harabhanga thought that just by making the price of everything the same, all people would become equal. But that is impossible. Everything has its own value. You cannot put a lion and a sheep together, feed them the same food and expect them to become the same. The sheep will remain a sheep, and the lion will remain a lion. Spiritual people will be spiritual, and ordinary people will be ordinary. God's Kingdom is vast and everybody has his own place. One cannot mix with those who are of a different standard and expect them to become equal. Now once again this kingdom will have a sane life. A new king will take Harabhanga's place — perhaps his own son — and you will see that, like other kingdoms, this kingdom will have prosperity. It will have judgement, peace and divine glory, for everything will have its proper value according to its capacity and according to its merit. My son, you and I have done a great service for the Supreme.

GORAKSHANATH   Master, I have understood your philosophy. I am always at your feet and at your command. To please you, to be unconditionally yours, is the sole object of my life.

(Gorakshanath sings.)

*Taba sri charan mama aradhan
taba darashan mama harashan
taba parashan mama naba man
taba alodhan mama niketan*

(My supreme adoration is Your Feet.
Your very sight is my delight.
Your very touch is my new mind, and Your Light
    of infinite Wealth is my true home.)

MATSYENDRANATH AND GORAKSHANATH: TWO SPIRITUAL LIONS

MG 13. ACT III, SCENE I

(Matsyendranath's ashram. Gorakshanath is meditating. Enter an itinerant Yogi.)

YOGI   What an ugly, undivine, unbearable place! I have never been to an ashram that was so unspiritual. What kind of cow-dung Master you must have!

GORAKSHANATH   Don't you dare speak about my Master that way! I have tremendous occult power.

YOGI   Show me your occult power!

GORAKSHANATH   *(grabbing a knife)* Here is a knife. If you strike me anywhere on my body you will not be able to injure me at all. That is my power!

(Yogi begins stabbing Gorakshanath.)

YOGI   All right. When I struck you, you were not hurt, but my blows always created a sound. But if you strike me with the same knife, not only will you not be able to injure me, but also you will not be able to produce any sound.

(Gorakshanath stabs the Yogi several times.)

GORAKSHANATH   You are right! Not a sound! How is it possible?

YOGI   If one identifies with the Infinite, then no sound will be produced by a blow. This proves that I am superior to you in occult power.

(Exit Yogi.)

GORAKSHANATH *(to himself)* O Master, where are you now? I must speak to you about this. I will concentrate on you and see where you are and what you are doing.

(Gorakshanath sits down and begins to concentrate.)

MATSYENDRANATH AND GORAKSHANATH: TWO SPIRITUAL LIONS

MG 14. ACT III, SCENE 2

(Matsyendranath is seated amidst great luxury, surrounded by beautiful girls. Some of the girls are dancing.)

GORAKSHANATH How can this be? My Master is of the highest order. Perhaps my vision is wrong. Let me concentrate again.

(Gorakshanath concentrates.)

GORAKSHANATH My Master has fallen! He is surrounded by so many beautiful girls, all singing and dancing. He is enjoying all kinds of vital life. I must save him! I will transport myself to this spot occultly.

(Gorakshanath approaches the group but is stopped by the gatekeeper.)

GORAKSHANATH I wish to speak with that man. He is my Guru. He is Matsyendranath of Kaul. I must see him.
GATEKEEPER Matsyendranath, Your Guru? Is that the renowned Matsyendranath of Kaul? He has fallen! What he was and what he has become now! He has fallen to such an extent that I cannot believe my ears when you tell me that this is Matsyendranath.
GORAKSHANATH I must rescue him immediately!
GATEKEEPER If you can rescue him from this place, you will be extremely lucky. This is Mayapuri, the Illusion-City. Once a person enters here it is most difficult for him to leave again.

(Gorakshanath tries to approach Matsyendranath, but the dancing girls will not let him near.)

GORAKSHANATH   It seems I shall have to use my occult power to make myself into a beautiful girl, or I will never get near my Master.

(Exit Gorakshanath and re-enter as a beautiful girl. Matsyendranath does not recognise him.)

GORAKSHANATH   Master, what are you doing here? What kind of life are you leading? You are a God-realised soul. What are you doing here enjoying vital life?

MATSYENDRANATH   Oh! I am fallen, I am fallen! I am fallen to such an extent! Now save me!

GORAKSHANATH   I shall use my occult power and take you away from here.

MATSYENDRANATH AND GORAKSHANATH: TWO SPIRITUAL LIONS

MG 15. ACT III, SCENE 3

(Matsyendranath's ashram. Matsyendranath is seated in meditation, surrounded by his disciples. Enter Gorakshanath with another Matsyendranath, who goes to the meditating Matsyendranath and enters into him.)

GORAKSHANATH   *(addressing one of the disciples in amazement)* Has Master been away for a few weeks?
DISCIPLE   No. For the last few weeks Master has been here, and we have all been with him.
GORAKSHANATH   How can this be? Master, please explain this experience I have just gone through. I cannot fathom the mystery of what has actually happened.
MATSYENDRANATH   I had to do all this just for you, for your perfection. You have all kinds of occult power, but your pride was too great. I sent that Yogi to smash your pride, to prove to you that you are not the world's greatest occultist. There are many with far more occult power than you have. Also, you were very austere and rigid in your spiritual life. You looked down on women. I told you repeatedly that by looking down on women you would not be able to transform and perfect your life, but you did not care for women's liberation from ignorance. You are my best disciple. I gave you all kinds of occult power, but you were defeated by that Yogi only because of your pride. Now that you have been humiliated, now that your pride has been smashed, I wish to tell you something. Although you are my student, and although you lost to that Yogi, before long you will surpass both him and me. Because today you conquered your pride and saw the Truth in a divine way, and because by becoming a woman in order to approach me you learnt not to shun or

despise women, your tremendous potentiality will now be able to come to the fore. You are bound to surpass us. There is nothing else that I can teach you. All that I have, I have given to you.

MATSYENDRANATH AND GORAKSHANATH: TWO SPIRITUAL LIONS

MG 16. ACT IV, SCENE I

(Matsyendranath's ashram. Enter Matsyendranath and Gorakshanath.)

MATSYENDRANATH   My son, you have now equalled me in spirituality. You have inner peace, light and bliss in boundless measure. I want you to leave my ashram and open one of your own.

GORAKSHANATH   *(bursting into tears)* Master, Master, this can never be! I can never leave you, and I shall never leave you. You are my life.

MATSYENDRANATH   Son, two lions cannot live in the same den. We should not stay together now. You should now roam somewhere else. You have the capacity to guide world-souls as I am guiding them. Now you must use it. You are not getting the opportunity to flourish here.

GORAKSHANATH   Master, who wants to flourish? Not me! Not in the least! I came into the world to serve you, not to equal you. It was your mistake that enabled me to equal you.

MATSYENDRANATH   Whether it was my mistake or your tremendous capacity that has enabled you to equal me is not the question. You *have* equalled me, and now it is God's Will that you should serve Him by inspiring and guiding other souls. The world badly needs a Master of your calibre. Now go, my son. This is my soulful demand and command. If you really love me then you will obey my command. After six years you may come back and pay me a visit.

GORAKSHANATH   Master, I shall obey you although my heart is crying and bleeding within me. Please bless me once more before I depart.

(Matsyendranath blesses Gorakshanath.)

GORAKSHANATH   Although I shall not see you outwardly, please do not forget me. I shall come back in six years.

(Exit Gorakshanath.)

MATSYENDRANATH AND GORAKSHANATH: TWO SPIRITUAL LIONS

MG 17. ACT IV, SCENE 2

(Matsyendranath's ashram, six years later. Several disciples are seated in meditation. Enter Gorakshanath.)

GORAKSHANATH   Where is my Master? Where is Matsyendranath? I wish to see him.

FIRST DISCIPLE   We can't tell you where Master is.

GORAKSHANATH   Please tell me. I have not seen him for six years. I was his dearest disciple.

SECOND DISCIPLE   You were his dearest disciple? Then how is it that you have not been near him for six years? When a disciple leaves his Master for such a long period of time he loses all his position and all his prestige. You are no longer the Master's dearest disciple, if you ever were, which I doubt.

THIRD DISCIPLE   You are just trying to make yourself important, but if you were really the Master's dearest disciple then you would immediately listen to his command. He told us that nobody should be allowed to know where he is.

GORAKSHANATH   What! Will nobody tell me where my Master is, when I have waited six years to see him and travelled from one end of India to the other?

FIRST DISCIPLE   An order is an order. Master said nobody was to know where he is.

GORAKSHANATH   *(furious)* I shall curse you if you don't tell me instantly where my Master is! For twelve years you will have no rain at all in this land. That means no crops, no food, no drinking water. All of you will die of starvation if you stay here. Only on condition that you bring my Master back here will this curse be lifted before the end of twelve years.

SRI CHINMOY

MG 18. ACT IV, SCENE 3

(Matsyendranath's ashram, two and a half years later. The Scene is the same as before, but everything is dry and parched. Gorakshanath is sitting in meditation. Enter two starved-looking peasants.)

FIRST PEASANT O great Yogi, will you not lift this curse from our countryside? We are starving; our children are starving; all around us everything has become a barren desert where once before there was beauty and plenty.

SECOND PEASANT Why do you punish an entire country for the fault of your Guru or of his disciples? Is it fair? Is it right? Do lift your curse, O great Yogi, and free us from this terrible scourge.

(No response from Gorakshanath. Exeunt peasants, dejected. Sound of trumpets and noise approaching. Enter attendants, followed by King.)

KING *(taking the dust of Gorakshanath's feet):* Gorakshanath, do lift this curse from our unfortunate country. What have we done to deserve such a fate? You are ruining us, destroying us, and because of your great occult powers we cannot prevent you. Gorakshanath, have pity. All my subjects are either dying or leaving the country, and my treasures are being exhausted only to buy food and water.

(The King pauses. No response from Gorakshanath.)

KING Gorakshanath! *(Pause.)* Gorakshanath, you rogue, you are destroying my kingdom! How I wish I could destroy you in return!

MATSYENDRANATH AND GORAKSHANATH: TWO SPIRITUAL LIONS

(Exit King, followed by his attendants. Gorakshanath continues meditating. Enter Matsyendranath.)

MATSYENDRANATH My son, I am so happy to see you again.

GORAKSHANATH *(prostrating at Matsyendranath's feet)* Forgive me, Master. I am ashamed of what I have done to these people, to this entire country.

MATSYENDRANATH You have not done anything wrong. These people were all corrupt. They deserved this kind of punishment. It will help them to lead a better life.

GORAKSHANATH But I did not know that. I did not do it to help them. I was angry, and I merely wanted to punish them. My action was bad because my motive was bad.

MATSYENDRANATH My son, you are wrong. Your soul knew that they deserved punishment, otherwise it would not have allowed you to become unreasonably angry. What you have done is right.

SRI CHINMOY

MG 19. ACT V, SCENE I

(A palace. The King, Queen and Princess are together.)

KING The great spiritual Master Gorakshanath is all love and compassion. Everybody is full of appreciation, admiration and adoration for him. Not only his own disciples, but also those of other Masters have tremendous devotion for him. Even people who care nothing for the spiritual life have tremendous admiration for him. You know that I, too, have become a very great admirer of his.

QUEEN Had you been an ordinary king, you would have been extremely jealous of Gorakshanath, and perhaps would have banished him from your kingdom. But instead, you are not at all jealous of his name and fame or of his great influence. For a long time I have also been his admirer, but how can we ourselves go to this spiritual man? Perhaps it is my pride, but after all, we are the King and Queen.

KING Yes, and at the same time, I feel it is not right to send a messenger to such a great spiritual man asking him to come to me. This predicament has been bothering me for a long time, but now I have come to realise that since we are hungry for peace, light and bliss, we should go to this Master. Although I have wealth and worldly power, although my subjects appreciate me, admire me and flatter me, I have no peace of mind. I am always worrying about my enemies who may attack my kingdom. And no matter how much material wealth I amass, I do not get any satisfaction from it. I have no inner joy and no inner peace. My beloved Queen, I think we must go to Gorakshanath. He will be the answer.

QUEEN If you think so, my dearest King, I shall go with you. Daughter, sweet daughter, would you like to come with us?

PRINCESS No, Mother. I think this Gorakshanath must be a crazy man. I don't want to go to a crazy man. You can go; I won't go with you.

QUEEN No, he is not crazy; he is very great. He has many, many spiritual disciples, and he is extremely good and kind. He has realised God, and he can take others to God.

PRINCESS I don't believe in God. I don't need God. If you and Father believe in God and realise God, that will be more than enough for me. You share with me everything that you have. Now you are supplying me with material wealth, with love, with whatever I want. You give me everything I need. So if you gain spiritual wealth, I know you will be kind enough to share that with me too, as you are now sharing your other wealth. If you get anything, I know you will give me all I want and need.

QUEEN All right, dearest child. We will not force you to come with us. You may stay here.

KING Come, let us prepare to leave now. Her mind is made up.

PRINCESS Wait! I want to come with you after all.

KING Why this sudden change of mind, my daughter? Well, whatever the reason, you have made both of us very happy.

(Exeunt omnes.)

(Gorakshanath's ashram. Enter King, Queen and Princess and bow down to Gorakshanath.)

PRINCESS   *(aside)* My parents are bowing down and touching the feet of the Master with utmost devotion, but I am doing it with utmost fear. I am sure this spiritual Master has read my mind and knows what I said at the palace. Now I will be exposed and perhaps insulted by the Master.

(Gorakshanath gives the Princess a compassionate smile.)

KING   Master, we have come here for initiation. Please accept us as your disciples. Although I am the King of this country, I know you are the real King. He who has peace, light and bliss in abundant measure is the King of many worlds, whereas I am a constant victim to worries and anxieties, not to speak of temptation and other undivine things.

GORAKSHANATH   I am very sorry that I shall not be able to initiate you right now, O King. Nor shall I be able to initiate your Queen. You two are not quite ready to accept the spiritual life whole-heartedly. You may feel that you are extremely spiritual and that you can be very devoted, but I see clearly that your hour has not yet struck. You should be happy and proud, though, that the hour of your daughter has struck. I shall initiate her today, and in a few years she will realise God.

KING   We can't believe our ears!

QUEEN   Master, just before we came here, she said that you were a crazy man and that she did not believe in God. She wanted just to share our spiritual wealth if we got any, as she now shares our material wealth. This is the consciousness she has; this is her spiritual development, and you say that she is very spiritual, she will be very devoted and she is the one who can be initiated. Master, please explain this to us. We don't understand.

GORAKSHANATH   This is not your first or last life. What did you do in your previous incarnation? You wanted to be a queen. And you, O King, wanted to be a king. But this girl wanted to realise God in her last incarnation. God is now listening to all your prayers. You two have become King and Queen. And God is fulfilling your daughter's prayers for realisation through me in this incarnation.

QUEEN   Master, if she is going to realise God in this incarnation, why is it that just a few hours ago she didn't even want to come here? She said she had no need for God. And we have never seen anything spiritual in her. She is nice, she is obedient, but nothing striking. She has never even prayed. She is sixteen years old, but she has never, never prayed even once. She has never even gone to the temple. Obviously she does not care for God. So how can we believe you when you say that she is ready to accept the spiritual life wholeheartedly?

GORAKSHANATH   You do not understand world-ignorance. World-ignorance is such that it can obscure everything. No matter how spiritual, how devoted, how divine you are, world-ignorance can cover everything. Your daughter is not yet sixteen years old. What you have seen in her so far is only a cover. I know what is inside. There is a choice hour for everyone — God's Hour — and I know that for your daughter, God's Hour has struck. I am just removing the veil, and you will see what she becomes in a few years. She was preparing herself in her previous incarnation for God-realisation, but God-realisation did not take place. In this incarnation she is bound to realise God; that is what God has decided. Each time we take human incarnation, in most cases ignorance comes right from the beginning and envelops our inner wisdom and inner light earned in our previous incarnations. But spiritual Masters help those aspirants who are striving to become Masters and who are destined to be their successors. Here on earth I, too, lived in ignorance for many years, but I was initiated by my own Master when the time came, and I realised God because God's Hour had struck for me. My Master claimed me as his most devoted and dearest disciple, and I am claiming your daughter as my most devoted, my dearest and my most favourite disciple. As I am working for my Master now that I am realised, even so your daughter will work for me. And it is from her that you will get realisation, O Queen. I shall initiate you both in a few months, but I shall not live on earth to grant you realisation. Your realisation will take place in some other incarnation, and in that incarnation your daughter will be the one to grant you realisation. Of course, at that time you will not know her as your daughter; you will know her as your own spiritual Mother.

QUEEN   What you have said has deeply moved me. If you say this will happen, we shall believe you.

GORAKSHANATH   Whether you believe me or not, this is the reality.

QUEEN   Until now we thought that she was just a silly girl who did not care for God. Now she is going to be a God-realised soul.

GORAKSHANATH   She said I was a crazy man, so a crazy man will give the Princess realisation, and a silly girl will give the Queen realisation.

KING   I have not said a word against my daughter. I am all fondness for her. Now what will be my fate? Who will liberate me? Your Guru has liberated you, Master; you are liberating my daughter, and my daughter is going to liberate my wife. Who is going to liberate me?

GORAKSHANATH   The one who is going to liberate you will soon bless you. Let us meditate for a few minutes.

(While everyone is meditating, Matsyendranath appears in a divine effulgence behind Gorakshanath and blesses him.)

MATSYENDRANATH   I am here to bless my disciple. I am all love for him; I am all admiration for him; I am all adoration for him. He has surpassed me.

GORAKSHANATH   *(blessing the Princess)* I am blessing you with all my love, with all my appreciation, and with all my divine pride. Dearest child, you will be my best disciple. You will definitely realise me.

PRINCESS   *(blessing the Queen)* I am so happy, so proud and so delighted that once upon a time I was able to be your daughter on the physical plane. Now I am his daughter, but one day I shall be your spiritual Mother. At that time I will liberate you.

(Matsyendranath signals the Queen to bless the King.)

QUEEN   My dearest husband, it seems that I am the one who is going to liberate you. Now I am blessing you with all my love and joy. I am truly happy — not out of human pride, but out of divine joy — that I have been chosen as an instrument of God to liberate you. You have done everything to make me happy on the earthly plane. Someday I shall do everything to make you happy on the spiritual plane. One day I shall liberate you from all suffering; therefore, I am truly happy.

MATSYENDRANATH   Only a disciple who has constant, unconditional love, devotion and surrender for the Supreme in his Master can be liberated. All of us should be proud that we will have that kind of disciple, and all of us should be proud that we once were or someday will be that kind of disciple. My dearest son, I am eternally and unconditionally proud of you.

GORAKSHANATH   Master, it is you and you alone who have made me all that I am. Your grace and compassion have lifted me to the highest, and for that my eternal gratitude is at your divine feet.

APPENDIX

NOTES TO THE PRESENT EDITION

Notes to the present edition

Obeying the Author's wish, the present edition follows the typographical style for typesetting drama plays, either in verse or prose, defined by the Imprimerie nationale.

That includes the introduction of characters' lines, rendering of stage directions, division of plays into acts and scenes, *dramatis personæ*, etc.

Sequence of titles

The sequence of titles in Volume I follows the criteria established by the Author.

Plays in both volumes

Some of these plays were published in more than one book. The exact content and sequence has been preserved, so it will be possible to find a play in both volume I and II of the *Plays*.

Individual plays and collections of plays

My Rama is my all, The Singer of the eternal Beyond, Siddhartha becomes the Buddha, Lord Gauranga: Love incarnate, Drink, drink, my Mother's Nectar were published as collection of one-act plays, all with their own dramatis personæ.

The Son, The Descent of the Blue and *Matsyendranath and Gorakshanath: two spiritual lions* were published as individual plays, although the latter was also published as a collection of one-act plays. The first edition of *The Descent of the Blue* presented no dramatis personæ.

PREFACE TO FIRST EDITIONS

Editor's preface to the first edition of The Descent of the Blue

Printed from 1958 to 1962 in *Mother India*, Sri Aurobindo Ashram Monthly Review of Culture.

BIBLIOGRAPHY

SRI CHINMOY:

–*My Rama is my all*, New York, Sky Publishers, 1973, [RA].
–*The Singer of the Eternal Beyond*, New York, Sky Publishers, 1973, [SI].
–*Siddhartha becomes the Buddha*, New York, Sky Publishers, 1973, [SB].
–*The Son*, New York, Sky Publishers, 1973, [TS].
–*Lord Gauranga: Love incarnate*, New York, Sky Publishers, 1973, [LG].
–*Drink, drink my Mother's Nectar*, New York, Sky Publishers, 1973, [DD].
–*The Descent of the Blue*, New York, Sri Chinmoy Lighthouse, 1972, [DB].
–*Matsyendranath and Gorakshanath: two spiritual lions*, New York, Agni Press, 1974, [MG].

Note: suggested citation-key in square brackets.

POSTFACE

Publishing principles

This edition of *The works of Sri Chinmoy* aims to obey the Author's wish: scrupulous fidelity to his original words, use of typographical style by him selected, specific spelling choices, end placement of any editorial content (i.e. not written by Sri Chinmoy himself), particular treatment of some personal nouns in special cases, etc.

Textual accuracy

This edition has been checked to ensure faithful accuracy to the originals. Although much effort has been put in proofreading and comparing different versions of the text, this print may still present lingering errors. The Publisher would be grateful to be apprised of any mistypes via postal mail or facsimile, possibly with scan of the original page where the text is different. Please use original books only, specifying the year of publication, as no online version can be considered authoritative.

Ongoing reprints will include any revised text from these errata.

Acknowledgements

The Publisher is very grateful to the late Professor Lambert and his équipe for his invaluable advice. For many decades Prof. Lambert conducted a small publishing house specialising in hand-made prints of philological edition of the classics. The standard of this edition would not have been the same without his scholarly advice.

The Publisher is also grateful to the international team of collaborators that spent countless hours proofreading and checking the current text against the originals.

Our deepest gratitude to Sri Chinmoy. His living presence can be felt breathing throughout his writings. It is a privilege to be involved with his works, in any form.

Citation keys

Citation keys are used throughout *The works of Sri Chinmoy* to allow accurate cross-reference of texts across titles and editions. Examples: EA 13, ST 50000, UPA 7.

Sri Chinmoy Canon

We could not use better words than Professor Lambert's, who kindly offered the name *Sri Chinmoy Canon*:

> «By defining Sri Chinmoy's first editions as *editio princeps* we chose to follow classical scholarship criteria, not because we consider Sri Chinmoy's work antique, but because we believe it is among the few post ‹classical antiquity› works to rightly deserve to be considered a *classicus*, designating by that term *superiority, authority* and *perfection*.
> «The monumental work Sri Chinmoy is offering to mankind is awe-inspiring and supremely pre-eminent in proportions and quality. It is manifest that Sri Chinmoy's work — which we feel right to call *The Sri Chinmoy Canon* — will be of profound help and source of enlightenment to anyone seeking a higher wisdom, truth and reality supreme.»

[Translated from French by M. G.S.]

TABLE OF CONTENTS

PART I:

MY RAMA IS MY ALL	3
WHY SHOULD I BE RESPONSIBLE?	3
DASHARATHA PROMISES AND RAMA EXECUTES	13
THE GOLDEN DEER	29
DASHARATHA'S DREAM IS AT LAST FULFILLED	41
MY RAMA IS MY ALL	47
FIRE SURRENDERS TO SITA	53
NO FAITH, NO SAFETY	59
RAMA FAILS	65
BROTHER LAKSHMANA, I SHALL FOLLOW YOU	73

PART II:

THE SINGER OF THE ETERNAL BEYOND	83
THE BABY KRISHNA AND HIS FOSTER MOTHER, JASHODA	83
DON'T WORSHIP INDRA BUT WORSHIP GIRI GOVARDHAN	87
RADHA AND KRISHNA ARE PURE	91
O KRISHNA, KEEP ME IN CONSTANT SUFFERING!	99
KRISHNA, I NEED YOU ONLY	105
KRISHNA AND ARJUNA	111
KRISHNA, I SEE DEATH-FORCES ALL AROUND ME	115
THE UNIVERSAL FORM	119
KRISHNA, MY EXISTENCE IS AT YOUR DISPOSAL	123
ASK VISHMA, O ARJUNA	127
UTANKA	133
NOT HOW MANY HOURS YOU MEDITATE, BUT HOW YOU MEDITATE	141

THESE ARE MY PSYCHIC TEARS	147
TWO DIVINE LIARS: ARE THEY REALLY SO?	151
HER COW MUST DIE TOMORROW	161
THINK OF GOD: HE WILL NOT ONLY THINK OF YOU, BUT HE WILL THINK OF YOUR DEAR ONES AS WELL	169
HE EATS GRASS BUT CARRIES A NAKED SWORD	179
KALI AND KRISHNA ARE ONE	189
PART III: SIDDHARTHA BECOMES THE BUDDHA	199
WHO IS THE OWNER: THE LIFE-SAVER OR THE LIFE-TAKER?	199
PRINCE SIDDHARTHA LEAVES THE PALACE	205
SIDDHARTHA BECOMES THE BUDDHA	215
FATHER, GIVE ME MY SHARE, PLEASE	225
THE BUDDHA NEEDS A FEW MUSTARD SEEDS	229
THE MEETING PLACE OF EXISTENCE AND NON-EXISTENCE	237
HERE AND NOWHERE ELSE	241
BUDDHAM SARANAM GACCHAMI	251
SARIPUTRA, YOU ARE A FOOL	261
THE BUDDHA AND ANANDA	265
PART IV: THE SON	273
THE SON	273
PART V: LORD GAURANGA: LOVE INCARNATE	319
FRIENDSHIP KNOWS NO EQUAL	319
O WORLD-RENOUNCER, BE CAREFUL!	325
DAMODAR, I AM FAR ABOVE MORALITY	331
KRISHNA, I SHALL DIE IN YOUR ABSENCE	337
SRIBAS	341
MOTHER TOUCHES THE SON'S FEET	347

O CHAITANYA, I NEED YOUR LOVE	353
MY LAST DESIRE IS TO PLACE YOUR FEET ON MY HEART	357
LORD GAURANGA: LOVE INCARNATE	363
PART VI: DRINK, DRINK MY MOTHER'S NECTAR	371
THERE IS NO GOD	371
MY NAREN CAN NEVER BE AN ATHEIST	377
MOTHER, GIVE ME THE LIGHT OF KNOWLEDGE, THE LIGHT OF DISCRIMINATION AND THE LIGHT OF RENUNCIATION	381
ASK HIM IF HE SERVES ME OR CONTROLS ME	387
THE SYNTHESIS OF ALL RELIGIONS	395
DRINK, DRINK MY MOTHER'S NECTAR	403
THIS BODY WILL NOT LAST VERY LONG	407
SRI RAMAKRISHNA'S PASSING	411
VIVEKANANDA WAITS FOR THE INNER MESSAGE	417
NAREN, YOU ARE THAKUR'S PROMISE	425
NAREN, YOU ARE MY JOY; YOU ARE MY PRIDE	429
TWO MOTHERS AND A SON	435
PART VII: THE DESCENT OF THE BLUE	443
PART VIII: MATSYENDRANATH AND GORAKSHANATH: TWO SPIRITUAL LIONS	609
APPENDIX	655
NOTES TO THE PRESENT EDITION	657
PREFACE TO FIRST EDITIONS	661
BIBLIOGRAPHY	665
POSTFACE	669

*Composition typographique par imprimerie
Ab Academia Aoidon, Paris & Lyon.*

*Un grand merci à Prof Knuth pour
l'utilisation avancée de T_EX.*

A LYON, LE 13 FÉVRIER LXXXVIII Æ.G.

www.ingramcontent.com/pod-product-compliance
Lightning Source LLC
Chambersburg PA
CBHW030110240426
43661CB00031B/1355/J